How to Make Your Child a Winner

How to Make Your Child a Winner

Victor B. Cline

Walker and Company ☼ New York

NOTE:

I will be using *he* when I'm referring to a child of either sex unless I specifically indicate otherwise. This usage is not meant to imply sexist bias in this book but rather reflects the lack of an English pronoun that covers both genders.

Excerpts from "Pornography: A Feminist Perspective" by Diana E.M. Russell, an address to Westminster College, Salt Lake City, 1977.

Excerpts from *Against Our Will* by Susan Brownmiller, © 1975 by Susan Brownmiller. Published by Simon & Schuster. Reprinted with permission of the publisher.

Excerpts reprinted with permission from *Preparing for Parenthood* by Dr. Lee Salk, Copyright 1974 by the author. Published by David McKay Co., Inc.

First published in the United States of America in 1980 by the Walker Publishing Company, Inc.

Trade ISBN: 0-8027-0658-4

Paper ISBN: 0-8027-7165-3

Library of Congress Catalog Card Number: 80-51336

Printed in the United States of America

20 19 18 17

Contents

Acknowledgments

THIS BOOK is the culmination of many years living and the impact and inspiration of many people. The germ idea of the book came from the work of a small team of behavioral scientists at the Human Research Unit No. 2 on the California Monterey Peninsula, who worked on the Task Fighter Project: Robert Egbert, Tor Meeland, Robert Katter, Edward Forgy, Charles Brown, and Martin Spickler, who risked their lives as noncombatants to collect our data in the front lines of an American war in Asia.

I am grateful to Joan and Dennis Ashton, Corry Hammond, Tom Halverson, Courtney Black, and Russell Cline for reading portions of the manuscript and giving their very valuable responses and helpful feedback.

The help of many typists is acknowledged with appreciation, especially Pauline Whitehead, Jean Hansen, Kate Freeman, Kathy Asay, Roxanne Cowley, Chris Macie, and Bonnie Grandy.

I would also like to express gratitude to those other individuals who each contributed in their own unique way to this book: Lowell Durham Jr., Sig and Faye Schreyer; and also to Richard K. Winslow, editorial director of Walker Publishing Co., who believed in the book and its values and saw it through to publication.

A very special acknowledgment must be made to Orson Scott Card who in many remarkable ways helped give this book an extra dimension including the first draft editing. The value of his wise counsel and support cannot be overestimated.

To those special couples who have served as an inspiration to Lois and me—in the special quality of their family life—who represent the values and ideals I've put into this book, mention must also be made: Lee and Lorna Franke, Don and Liz Muller, Cardell and Liz Smith, Allen and Helen Lowe, Merritt and Marsha Egan, Mike and Bonnie Cervino, and Hank and Daryle Hoole—all winners with regards to the things that really count!

And also the family of my origins a tribute must be made for all their love and sustenance through many decades—for their never-ending support: George and Betty Cline, my "winner" parents.

And finally, to the love of my life—Lois: supportive, loving, gutty and courageous; and the nine treasures she helped bring into this life with me: Russell, Janice, Robyn, Christopher, Richard, Constance, Paul, Julie, and Rebecca . . . an acknowledgment is due of her many sacrifices and unending commitment to her husband and family.

Thanks is also due to all those who have given me permission to reprint or adapt material.

Foreword

The Beginning of the Journey

FOR TWENTY-EIGHT YEARS my wife, Lois, and I have been together, sharing the sweat, pain, and great joy of raising nine children. I have also, for twenty-six years, been a practicing clinical psychologist, working with conflicted individuals, couples, and families, and for ten years I have directed a five-county traveling community mental health clinic. I have additionally worked many years as a behavioral scientist and university teacher.

I know children. I have seen them in my own family, in the troubled families that have come to me for help, and in the families of my friends and acquaintances over the years. This book is the culmination of all my training and experience over three decades.

Each child is unique. Each child has an identity, in part because of a remarkably individual set of genes. And I have found that loving, wise parents do have the power to help each youngster make the best of the potential he or she brings into the world. The climate and opportunities we parents provide our children as they grow up in our homes will have a critical bearing on their current adjustment and personal happiness, but they will have an even more profound effect on their later adult adjustment and happiness, especially as they live with and love their own spouses and raise their own children.

It seems unfair when the Book of Exodus (34:7) says that the sins of the fathers are visited upon their children for three generations. However unfair it is, I have discovered in my clinical experience that it is painfully true and applies as well to psychopathology and mental health. In our guidance clinics I have occasionally worked with three generations of the same family. The neurotic illnesses of the grandparents can clearly be seen to reach across the generations, infecting not only their own children but also the grandchildren and even some great grandchildren.

The opposite is also true, however. Mental health and good parenting are just as contagious. Healthy families tend to produce children who grow up to have healthy families of their own.

Unfortunately, there are no easy treatments for sick families, no inoculations a couple can take to immunize them against problems with each other and with their children; but there are things parents can do to increase their chances of having a warm, loving, happy family. If there is already pathology in the family, there are ways to break the vicious chain of sickness in *this* generation so it will not be passed on to future generations.

That's what this book is about—ways to solve the problems your family might already be struggling with and strategies for helping children grow up to be happy, healthy, successful adults. Winners.

All children have problems. Some more than others, but no one is exempt. Because we live in an imperfect world: your child will occasionally be placed with the wrong teacher; your children may have to put up with you when you are struggling with a disabling emotional problem or personal crisis; your children may be rejected by their peers, creating a lot of pain for them. Then there are the inevitable health problems, accidents, family moves, acne, funny-shaped nose, difficult menstrual cycles, straight (or curly) hair, or being too tall or too short. And occasionally there is an unavoidable divorce, or the death of one parent. Such problems are spread randomly through every neighborhood, and the child who avoids one is bound to run into another.

Life in any family, great or humble, is a mix of joy, frustration, fun, tears. The ideal family does not shelter its children from that mix. Rather, good parents will train their children to be able to cope with life's problems sensibly and well, enduring the pain and overcoming it instead of falling apart when things go wrong. We must teach our children grace under pressure, teach them to retain their balance and somehow endure, survive, and mature. We must equip them to be able to face their own problems and find their own solutions long after they are on their own.

I am continually impressed by how tough and hardy children are. I am amazed at how many mistakes parents can make and still find that their children have grown up to be fine people. But there is still a limit to how much and how long a child can endure.

The child's capacity can be increased if the child knows that somewhere there are committed adults who really care if he lives or dies.

John Steinbeck created an unforgettable mother in one of his early novels. She had a very sick child whom she was greatly worried about. She called in not only the family doctor but also the chiropractor, the Christian Science practitioner, and several ministers of various faiths. She didn't want to miss a bet with God or the doctors. Then, just in case the prayers and medicine didn't work, she reached back into her knowledge of folk medicine and used a few herbs and natural remedies.

I see quite a few mothers like that. They care. They don't want to take any chances with their kids' well-being.

Kids know whether their parents care; and having someone really care about you, really love you—that's indispensable in growing up. It creates and strengthens in the child a sense of identity, a sense of worth, a feeling that he has a right to take up space on this planet, that he is *worthy* of being loved.

I know a mother who is a "shouter," and maybe emotionally a little flaky.

When the kids do wrong or self-destructive things, when they don't treat each other right, she shouts at them. And sometimes there are tears. These can be pretty powerful emotional confrontations, but the kids still get the real message. She cares. She really loves them. And I know they'll turn out all right even with a few bumps along the way.

That's the key to raising children. As a therapist who has survived many years of wars and battles for children's hearts and minds, I know that it's possible for miracles, great and small, to occur. People can change. Families can get stronger, healthier. But always, without exception, *always* there is a price to be paid.

Somewhere, someone has to make a sacrifice of commitment, time, and love. At some point, to solve the problem, at least one person has to decide that his love for his family is more important than anything else, and then that person can make changes in his behavior that heal, that strengthen, that nurture. As a therapist I can take you to Mount Everest. But you still have to walk every difficult and painful step of the way.

I have spent many years working with angry, disturbed, inadequate, frightened and low self-image children. I have also seen many that have been more hardy, resilient and tough. And through these experiences I have discovered that the most powerful treatment technique we have involves teaching the parents to be their children's own therapist.

If I should just see the child alone once or twice a week, I am almost always successful in developing good communication and rapport. I am able to communicate many beneficial insights to him. This is great for us and our relationship, but when the child returns home for the other 166 hours of that week, usually very little has changed. He is still frustrated living there. His parents remain baffled, disappointed and often angry. Their disturbed cycle of interaction continues on unchanged. For real change to occur in the child's environment and psyche, the parents have to be involved as therapeutic agents—sometimes at a considerable cost in time and effort for them. And the parents need enlightened, powerful, focused strategies, something they can *do* that will *work*. Not just vague platitudes and head nodding from the therapist.

What I present in this book is a combination: the best strategies for helping children grow up well—taken from the experience and research of many inspired clinicians, taken from my own repeated findings in my private work with children, and taken from the even more private experience with my own family.

And that includes my mistakes. I didn't spring from college with all the wisdom of the world safely enfolded in my brain. Lois and I often wish we knew back then what we know now. There are many things we would do differently the second time around, if there were a second time with children. Of course, there are also things we are glad we did and wouldn't change. Each generation should stand on the shoulders of the one before, learning from

their mistakes in order to avoid repeating them. I will share with you what
we did right and what we did wrong, what we have found that really works,
and when you should throw the book away!

I have also learned from the way my parents raised me. And my colleagues have taught me a great deal—not so much in their formal presenta-
tions and writings as in the private conversations at cocktail parties, after
student oral examinations, or between sessions at professional meetings. This
is where I often found out what really works and what doesn't. This is the
kind of knowledge that psychologists can't publish in scientific journals
because you can't do an analysis of variance or a chi square on it; but it is
often closer to the ultimate truth than the limited and sometimes sterile
studies that can be published within the profession.

In my many years of involvement with families, schools, community
agencies, and private counseling I have seen a good many people being misled
by a lot of hokum and bunk in the area of child-rearing practices. I see unmarried, childless professors teaching classes on child development, family
life, and courtship; they are well-intentioned, but they have no practical experience that helps them sort the wheat from the chaff in the vast amount of
psychological theory they draw upon. I see a clinical psychologist who has
never "made it" in a sustained relationship with a woman write an ava-
lanche of books and articles on sex and marital therapy, some of it nonsense
as far as real life is concerned. I have seen psychologists whose personal
values force them into beliefs and practices that just don't work; I have even
seen whole university social science departments become politicized, hiring
only those faculty whose values and research support a certain bias or narrow point of view. Professionals who are militantly committed to gay rights,
alternate life styles, children's rights, or other such polarized causes
sometimes write, teach, or practice clinically in ways that serve their biases
to the detriment of the needs of families that want to produce healthy, happy
children.

I see a confusion of tongues among some experts on child rearing. This involves a mixture of sense and nonsense, fantasy and reality. This could
mislead anybody trying to determine what the "right thing to do" is in making critical child-care decisions.

In fairness, I would recommend that you regard the many suggestions
that are presented in this book as only suggestions. These reflect my biases
and what works for me. The ideas and theoretical concepts should be regarded as only possible hypotheses. They should be tested and tried, where you
wish, against the crucible of your own judgment and experiences. If
something doesn't work for you, don't force it. It may not be right for you.
Don't be afraid to try out new things. Innovate! If they are wrong for your
children you will quickly find this out. By adapting this book to your own
family you will serve their needs far better than if you rigidly follow my suggestions as if they appeared in an instruction manual that came along with

your children. There *was* no instruction manual with *my* kids, and this isn't the last word on yours. But here is a good and fairly reliable first word. There isn't a tactic in this book that hasn't worked well for someone, and usually for many families.

When is your child a winner? Do you measure their success in wealth; in titles, honors, power, achievements? I doubt it. When I talk about making your children into winners, I'm not talking about just making them competitors against other people, rising *above* everyone. I'm talking about making them winners in the far more important game of life, helping them achieve victory over the problems and challenges that inevitably face everyone.

The winner is a child who gains a deep inner sense of himself, a special kind of confidence, an easy assurance, a quiet courage. A winner is someone who has the capacity to give freely and take graciously. Wherever winners go, good things happen to them; adversity they cope with and leave behind. Like cream they rise to the top.

Other people sense in them a special quality of purpose and confidence. This is not a neurotic striving or exhibitionistic vanity—these only mask self-doubt and insecurity. Rather it is a shine and glow that comes from the deepest recesses of their psyches. It's not just talent, but a style, a way of using their talent that goes beyond art or craft. They are pointed a particular direction, and they chose that direction themselves. They have a vision of themselves, and in that vision they always see themselves *doing* something successfully; they see themselves in control of their destinies. They have the capacity to organize their energies and, when they choose, to work hard on their enthusiasms. Work is often a form of recreation and play for them, providing the most profound inner satisfactions.

One thing Lois and I know for a certainty. It's possible to produce children who are winners, or at least to raise their "winner quotient" significantly. But each child will be a winner in his own way. He or she will choose a standard of success to pursue—and it won't necessarily be the parents' standard. We had to learn this as we went along. We experimented, succeeding often but sometimes failing. But we never gave up.

Inside every kid there's a winner, waiting to get out. No one is better equipped to help than his or her parents. You!

PART I

SUCCESSFUL FAMILY LIFE

1

The Roots of Success:
Early Family Life

IT WAS AT THE HEIGHT of the Korean War. Two observers of frontline combat, S.L.A. Marshall and Col. Anthony Standish, astonished their colleagues by reporting that only about fifteen percent of American frontline soldiers were actually using their personal weapons—even when under direct attack by the enemy. In a few, rare, "gung-ho" Marine outfits this figure rose to about twenty-five percent, but this was exceptional.

At first the Army refused to believe the figures, but further observation proved them right. They called it the "fighter factor" problem, and research began to try to find the difference between the fighters and the non-fighters.

With my brand-new Ph.D., I joined a group of George Washington University researchers who formed Human Research Unit #2 at Fort Ord, California. Dr. Robert Egbert and his associate Dr. Tor Meeland, both psychologists, headed a team that prepared a grand research design. Then one group from our team left for Korea to select subjects from the 2nd, 7th, and 45th infantry divisions in front-line attack positions in the Kumhwa Valley, Pork Chop, and Christmas Hill areas.

Soldiers were selected for testing on the basis of authenticated eyewitness accounts of their performance in front-line combat. From interviews with 647 soldiers, we obtained information on a few more than 1,000 men, of whom 345 were tagged by the selection team to be studied and evaluated. Wartime attrition—either casualties or evacuation—pulled the final sample down to 309 men, of whom 168 were clearly identified as fighters and 141 as non-fighters.

Dividing them into those two groups, on the basis of careful front-line observation at the risk of Dr. Egbert's and Dr. Meeland's lives, was the most important step in the research. If the division was not accurate, then no matter how much any of the other information was analyzed it would have meant little.

How were non-fighters identified? They were the men who, according to their comrades' cross-checked evaluations, "bugged out." They physically withdrew, or cried, or trembled, or even became unable to hold their weapons. The non-fighter might stay in his bunker or down in the trenches

3

when he should be out assisting his buddies under fire. He might refuse a direct order to fire at the enemy or a direct order to rescue or evacuate the wounded or move to another position. He might run away, or else throw away or lose parts of his weapon so that it became inoperable. He might malinger in general or become hysterically incapacitated, seeing nonexistent things and overreacting to these supposed threats.

Fighters, on the other hand, showed a great amount of personal responsibility. They remained calm, rational, and cool under much stress. Even when wounded, they continued to fight; often they were the last men to leave a position that had to be abandoned. They took initiative in caring for and evacuating the wounded. When other men were afraid, they calmed them and gave them strength and confidence. They used their weapons effectively for long periods of time. They often provided natural leadership when the officer in charge was killed or wounded. They were able to take effective aggressive action when the situation demanded it. In sum, they had consistent, continuing grace under pressure.

After the two groups were clearly identified they were brought back to a rear area behind the front lines in small groups, to be given a vast battery of psychological tests, physical measurements, life history interviews, and situational group tests. The whole process took each group six days, and a total of 955 different measures was obtained on each man.

Several years of analysis of the facts collected in these tests yielded a vast treasure of information which, unfortunately, never entered the general pool of scientific knowledge. The results were for the eyes of the military only and were never published. When the group of scientists broke up to pursue their several careers, they were unable to take the data with them.

The reason the study turned out to be so vitally important was that midway through the analysis, we discovered we weren't really finding the difference between fighters and non-fighters at all, except as a by-product. What we were really finding was the difference between stress-prone and stress-resistant individuals.

The fighters were not delinquent, hostile psychopaths or blood-thirsty killers—they were a kind of super-competent man who functioned superbly in any situation, including civilian life. The non-fighters, however, were almost all ineffectual human beings—losers and incompetents, though they were by no means mentally defective or mentally ill.

What we were really studying was winners and losers, competents and incompetents, men who could cope with stress and men who couldn't, the resilient and the inadequate. And we had more data on these men than I have seen in any other study of this type before or since.

So it was with a heady excitement that we plunged into the analysis of the facts to see what our "supermen" were like and how they got to be that way—how the losers came by their inadequacy, incompetence, and psychological impotence. And while some of the findings were specifically limited to males, I realized over those years of being totally immersed in the project that many of our findings could be reasonably applied to females as well.

The Fighters

When we compared the two groups, we found that the fighters scored higher on intelligence tests and showed signs of being more emotionally stable across a broad range of variables. They had greater ego strength.

The fighters were physically healthier. They were more masculine. They were more independent, and tended to come from higher socio-economic levels with a more stable home life and closer ties of affection with both parents, especially their fathers. They had more social skill and poise and tended to have a higher social class status.

The fighters were happier and more tolerant. They were more fluent verbally and showed greater leadership qualities. They were less hypochondriachal, less hypertense, more extroverted, and had a much greater belief in themselves. The fighters tended to be better educated and they were taller and heavier.

Their buddies named them as "most preferred" in all kinds of situations—for example, to have as a companion in combat or to go on a pass with. They were described with such words as *mature, foresighted, practical, adventurous, conscientious, energetic, stable, capable,* and *courageous.* (In contrast, the non-fighters were called *weak, dependent, confused, fearful,* and *distrustful.*)

As we peered and probed into the life histories of the fighters and compared them with those of the non-fighters, we found some very striking differences in how they were raised, differences in the general quality of their early life experiences. We also discovered other areas where there was no meaningful difference between the upbringing of the two groups—for instance, the size of the family they were raised in made no difference at all, and it wasn't important whether the soldier was the first, second, third, or tenth child in the family.

Where we did find major differences was in the quality and nature of family life.

Super-comps and Non-comps

The *fighter* and *non-fighter* labels are now meaningless. From now on I'll call the super-competent group "super-comps" and the ineffectual men "non-comps." Our study took place a generation ago, and the grandchildren of the men who fought in the Korean War are now being born, but what we found then still applies today. While culture evolves and changes, with cycles and styles and fads, our basic neurophysiology and the structure of our psyche are much more stable. The differences between family relationships in 1950 and family relationships in 1980 are much less important than the similarities.

The way we raise our children has a profound effect on the way they live the rest of their lives. Our study of the upbringing of the super-comps and the non-comps shows that. It shows that we do have some choice; we do have the power to make changes in our children's lives. We can give them experiences that will strengthen them. I'll go further—we can work miracles if we know what to do. I and other therapists have seen proof of this many times.

But parents have to be willing to pay the price. There is no such thing as a free lunch; what seems on the surface to be a miracle turns out to have been the result of many painstaking steps. There is a cost. Yet when the price is paid, the results in our children's happiness and achievement in their adult lives make it well worthwhile.

The Way the Family Works

What kind of family did the super-comps come from? Both the father and mother were present, and the father was seen by his children to be a strong person, very actively involved in leading the family. Often he was clearly the head of the home, working with the family with a firm, clear authority, and often he was actively involved with discipline, though in super-comps' families the discipline tended to be verbal rather than physical. There were strong ties of affection between father and son—in other words, he was a person the son could identify with. He represented strength.

The sons saw their mothers as warm, though occasionally they were anxious and concerned; and in their sons' eyes, the mothers handled discipline "just about perfectly." Yet despite the sense of discipline in the home, these young men described their home climate as permissive *and* upward-striving. There was a much greater strength of family kinship ties, much more interaction outside the immediate family with grandparents, uncles, aunts, nieces, and nephews.

In forty percent of the non-comp homes the father was missing due to death or divorce, and even when he was there he tended to be absent a lot or disinterested in his son when he was home. The son lacked an image of competence, someone he could use as a model and identify with. There was a great deal of tension and friction at home for the non-comps, and discipline was erratic, inconsistent, and more likely to be physical. The mother was more often perceived as domineering or over-protective.

The Doer Syndrome

The most frequent and striking difference between super-comps and non-comps was that the super-comps had learned to succeed in a wide number of different activities. Not that they were inherently talented in all these areas; rather they had experimented with many different activities, and stuck with them long enough to get better at them than the non-comps. The non-comps exceeded the super-comps in only four activities—movie-going, painting, cooking, and writing, all of them rather passive or aesthetic.

All their lives, the super-comps had been doers. They may not each have tried everything, but every super-comp had a surprisingly broad range. Their parents had encouraged them to try doing new things; they began each new activity with the belief that they would probably do well at it.

This is not to say that the super-comps never failed at anything, but over the years they learned that they would, with persistence, succeed far more often than they failed. Even in fields they weren't successful at from the start, they could eventually learn to do it well enough to get along. The super-comps took part in every conceivable sport, hobby, or job: they had learned carpentry; they had tended a back yard garden; they had bought their own clothes; they had borrowed large sums of money; they wrote their own checks; they had gone on overnight trips alone to a new city before they were eighteen. They had learned to trust themselves—no matter how hard it was, no matter how strange or unpleasant or frightening, they would get through. They would, in fact, do rather well. And because of the long experience with success, they approached new ventures with confidence, not afraid of failure because they knew that, given time, they would make it through.

What does that mean to parents? Simply this—you don't have to wait nervously, hoping your child will turn out to be a doer. You can encourage your children from the start to enjoy experiencing new things. You can train them to expect to succeed and to keep trying until they do. Obviously, you aren't going to make much headway by trying to force a reluctant child to do something new against his or her will, but a careful parent can lead children into *any* new activity that the child wants to take part in and give the child a reasonable expectation of success.

It's not enough to tell a child that you love him, that he's a great kid. We have to teach him skills so he can actually *be* great at something and *know* it. He has to know he is worthy of his own approval and the praise of others.

Of course, some activities are more important to the children themselves than others. Success in sports is more important to boys than many other activities, because in junior high school the children tend to decide how acceptable a boy is in the social group on the basis of how well he does in sports. This is not an "inborn" trait, but since it is important in the culture of your pre-teens and teenagers, it is important for boys to feel competent at sports.

For girls, sports success is not the foremost concern—girls in junior high school need also to be competent socially, fluent verbally, and attractive physically to be well-accepted by their friends.

This means that concerned parents will encourage their young children in these areas. That doesn't mean a boy should be pushed into being a football star by age eleven, or that a girl should be taught to look like a beauty queen before puberty. Remember, the super-comps were not necessarily specialists, not necessarily *best* at everything they did. Rather they were *good* at *many* things. They had learned that they could do well enough where it counted most.

And where it counts most to young teenagers is in acceptance by their friends. A boy should be encouraged to strive for competence in many different sports activities. A girl should be encouraged in sports, too, but also should learn to converse well, to take care of her physical appearance, and if she has a tooth, nose, or skin problem it should be corrected as soon as possible. Whenever a child ventures into one of the crucial activities in those teen years, he should know from his own experience that he will not be humiliated by failure in front of his friends. He won't miss the baseball every time it's thrown to him. She won't have a ghastly case of acne. He won't always be one of the last few to finish the race. She won't always find herself at a loss for words when she's talking to a boy or girl she wants to impress.

Success in these crucial areas transfers to other activities. If a girl has the acceptance of her peers, she is better able to succeed in her schoolwork, her first few jobs, and other new or difficult activities. If a boy has the acceptance of his peers, it is a foundation for reaching out to other activities. But even careful parents can suddenly find that their child has come upon an area where he feels he cannot succeed no matter what he does.

Thus a fine young basketball player with many friends can still have terrible problems with reading that make him petrified to enter any new academic situation, and this failure can shatter his self-confidence.

Can you do anything for your child if that happens? That's what this book is about, of course.

Learning to Read Early and Well

We live in a verbal society. Despite the advent of television, success usually means education, and education usually requires good reading ability.

Dr. Ethna Reid, for many years head of the Exemplary Reading Center in Salt Lake City, has repeatedly taught so-called poor readers or even nonreaders to read. She first does a very searching, careful diagnostic evaluation to find out the cause of the problem, which is often a mild form of dyslexia. Then she programs remedial training to fit the problem. But she is usually faced with an even bigger problem: the child's low motivation. After years of failure in the classroom the child usually comes to think, "If I don't try then I can't fail."

To help such children, she first assembled a library of books with large type, exciting illustrations, and an even more exciting story line with plenty of action and adventure. She has classified these according to reading grade level, though she uses a code so the child won't know. Then, if she has a fifth-grader who is barely reading at the third-grade level, she will take him to the second-grade level shelf and have him read to himself.

He quickly finds that he can read a whole book successfully in ten or fifteen minutes or less. These books have few pages, lots of pictures, and not too many words in them. He doesn't know it's a book for "little kids." All he knows is that he just read, in a few minutes, a whole book—maybe for the first time in his life, and the story and pictures were exciting. He *liked* it. Then, as if the books were peanuts or *M & M*'s, he goes back for more. Soon he is hooked on books.

When he has exhausted that grade level, he moves to another shelf of slightly more difficult books. But now he's not afraid to stretch a little and try to build his vocabulary. He is experiencing success. He's reading. He's no dummy. A new world of ideas and adventures has opened up to him, and it's a heady, wonderful feeling.

Of course, each child's unique reading problems are carefully treated by Dr. Reid and her staff. What the graded library does is teach the children—or even non-reading adults who have had long histories of school failure and defeat—that they can be good enough at reading to enjoy themselves.

Parents also can program success in their children's experiences in life. They can bend the twig to determine the pattern of the child's later mature growth. Parents must be flexible, of course, with concern for their child's unique talents and weaknesses. We must encourage and suggest, give direction, persuade, lead, but only rarely can we "pull rank" on a youngster. We want him to assume some responsibility in the development of his talents. But we provide the opportunities and support him until he has the confidence to try many things on his own.

Building Self-Sufficiency

We have a rule at our house: "Don't do for the child what he can do for himself." When our oldest son, Russ, was fourteen, we noticed he had a tendency toward shyness, a reluctance to express his inner feelings, a certain apartness from the family. He was very smart and doing well in school, but he was struggling to find his identity and selfhood. He tended to be his own man and didn't accept suggestions from others, even his parents, with any great eagerness or enthusiasm.

We happened to learn that a college instructor by the name of Larry Olsen was beginning to run survival training experiences for college students and teenagers in a summer university program. In this thirty-day program he planned to take small groups of students into remote wilderness areas and teach them how to survive and live without any modern food or conveniences, how to make fire in the rain without matches, how to survive on edible wild plants and animals.They would also learn how to keep warm and sleep on a freezing night without a blanket, how to catch a deer bare-handed, how to climb impossible mountains, and how to cross unfordable rivers.

Above all, though we didn't know this at the time, Larry had an almost magical impact on young people. He was a super-comp who became a great model for those who lived with him for those thirty days.

At first Russ didn't want to go. Neither he nor we really knew what would actually occur on the survival experience. But in the end he went, shuffling and reluctant, but he went.

Those thirty days passed quickly. We went to pick him up where the trucks brought their charges in from the wilderness area, and there I witnessed a sight that can never be erased from my mind. As Russ got off the truck I saw my son covered with dust, his clothes shredded and torn, but in his eyes and on his face I saw a look of supreme triumph. He seemed to be walking six feet off the ground. He had found himself.

He poured out a tale of exciting adventure in mountains and desert, of carrying a sixty-pound backpack nearly 300 miles in the most torturous terrain, of eating creatures and plants whose names we never heard of, and finally of living through a five-day wilderness solo, alone day and night, sustaining himself by his own wits and knowledge of survival techniques. He knew, as few men know, that if a nuclear attack destroyed all civilization and he somehow managed to live through it all he would and could survive indefinitely. Russ has never been quite the same since. We did the right thing at the right time with the right son. Luck? I don't know. But would that we could repeat it with each of our children. We keep trying. And so must all caring parents. Help your children be doers. Never stop helping them learn new skills and competencies.

Stress-proofing Your Child

In our study the super-comps could cope with stress, the non-comps couldn't. The preparation to handle the kind of stress found in battle does not happen overnight. It takes years and starts at a very early age.

Personality responds much as the body does. When you run or engage in some sport that puts demands on your body, your muscles develop to meet the challenge. Likewise, when a child grows up taking part fully in the normal stresses of problems in his own life, without being shielded from them, his personality develops resources to cope with stress, and later challenges are taken in stride.

To carry the analogy one step further: there are also stresses too great for the body to handle. For instance, falling off a forty-story building is obviously too much of a shock and happens too fast for the body to learn to cope with it. There are similar shocks to the psyche, and parents *do* need to protect their children from really terrible experiences that they could not possibly cope with. But the normal give-and-take of childhood is good for children, and they should not learn to think of their parents as a wall protecting them from everything outside the family. Eventually they begin to see the wall, not as a protection, but as a confinement, yet they are utterly unable to cope with the world when they finally break free and try to face it alone. They simply haven't developed the resources.

Marvin is about twenty-five, unmarried, living at home with his parents. I occasionally see him, and others like him, both men and women, on a professional basis. He is dependent, somewhat fearful and apprehensive. He can't seem to hold a job for long—he doesn't even want to. He loves his parents, but he also hates them. He is mentally and physically sound, but he is afraid to try anything on his own. He manipulates his parents through guilt—they are afraid to push him out of the nest because he has led them to believe that he just couldn't make it or take it out there on his own. His parents have awful visions of him starving to death, not being able to find a place to sleep on a cold wintry night. They even vaguely fear that he might take his own life if he were away from their loving ministrations.

So their guilt and their need to "be good parents" and "give the children everything they need" cripples them, and they can't help him make it on his own—they know that if they pushed him out and anything happened to him, it would be entirely their fault. Often in such cases one or both of the parents has impaired health or works unusually long hours in order to sacrifice for Marvin—Marvin, who is much stronger and healthier than his parents, but takes them for all their worth by convincing them, with his pained look and his brilliant performance in the role of the tortured, inadequate soul, that if they didn't keep sacrificing for him he would die. In fact he is usually lazy, pampered, and cozily dependent.

His parents aren't completely blind. They know Marvin is backward; they hate his put-downs, his tantrums, his sarcastic remarks and cruel words. They just don't know how to break free of his manipulation and their own guilt and fear for him.

In wartime, this is the type of young man who ends up as a non-comp. In civilian life he's the one who tries to get others to carry his load. He's the goof-off. He plays sick. He pretends to be helpless. He constantly needs others to do him favors because he "just can't" do it himself. Eventually nearly everyone catches on and withdraws. And then, overcome with self-pity and depression, he moves on to the next mark and begins the same game all over again.

As far as stress is concerned, punishment sometimes hurts the parents at least as much as it hurts the children—punishing someone we love is painful, and we often long to avoid doing it. A loving parent does not easily take away privileges from a child, or exact penalties, or show concern or even anger on occasion. But this stress, to both parents and children, may save and strengthen the child, not destroy or harm him, if it's handled right.

And the child does learn (though he might deny it at the time) that punishment arises out of the parents' love for him—a real love and desire for his future happiness, not a pathetic need for his approval now. The message received is: "I care so much about you that I am willing to risk your immediate displeasure by punishing you, because what you have done, if you persisted in it, could seriously harm yourself or someone else."

After the first flash of anger or resentment, the child knows intuitively that the parent was right. The punishment was deserved, the child performed the forbidden act knowing it was wrong, and with a child's innate sense of justice, he would not feel right if the punishment had been avoided.

I remember reading killer Gary Gilmore's many letters to his girlfriend Nicole. I was doing a psychological assessment of him prior to his execution at the Utah State Prison, for publication in the Salt Lake *Deseret News*. He had a long history of participating in extreme types of antisocial behavior, and it wouldn't be wrong to call him a recidivist psychopath. Yet in committing many dark deeds he explained that he always had a faint inner sense that what he was doing was wrong. He knew it, but he squelched those feelings and proceeded to do what whim and fancy dictated. He did what he wanted to do—but he still knew right from wrong.

So it is with most children—despite their tearful denials, they know what they did was wrong. Although it costs us and them stress, disciplining them for wrongdoing reinforces their inner instincts of decency, truthfulness, responsibility, and honor. We are helping, not hurting them, when we insist on responsible behavior—by pushing overage children out of the nest, by denying the use of the car to a child who has repeatedly abused his car privileges, by cutting off the allowance when it's being spent on drugs, by making them return shoplifted items to the store manager in person. It means we love them, we care about them. We should never allow neurotic guilt to cripple us in our parenting role. Being a parent isn't a popularity contest.

Upgrading Your Child's Peer Culture

You should choose the neighborhood you live in at least as carefully as you choose the particular house, for the neighborhood will provide the peer culture for your children as they grow up, and that can make a critically important difference in their lives. A house can be repainted or remodeled, but you can't singlehandedly change the character of the neighborhood. And the relative affluence of the homes in a neighborhood isn't necessarily a good guide to whether the neighborhood is healthy for children. You have to make discreet inquiries to find out.

Imagine three concentric circles around your house. The innermost circle includes the neighbors up and down your street ten doors away on either side of your house and on both sides of your street. The second includes an area of five or six blocks either way from where you live—easy walking or bicycling distance—and if your children aren't being bused, the second circle also includes the houses along the route to the local junior high school. The outermost circle includes the entire community you live in.

Generally speaking, your preschool and elementary-school-age children will choose as companions and playmates those children living in the innermost circle. If there is a lot of pathology in the neighborhood—wife- and child-beating, acute alcoholism, extremes in marital discord, sexual perversions—your younger children will sooner or later be affected through their interaction with the disturbed children living in these homes or through direct contact with the adults who have these problems. Avoid such neighborhoods as if they were quarantined with the bubonic plague.

Do your homework before buying. I've seen an instance where every family on one side of a block is getting a divorce. The women talked to each other and fed each others' neuroses, paranoia, and hostility towards their husbands. This is infectious; it can spread.

The second circle affects the junior high school youngsters. They look beyond the immediate neighborhood for friends. Their territory usually includes that second circle of six to eight blocks and the area on the way to the junior high school. (Obviously the situation is different for families in rural areas or where busing occurs, but the general principle holds.) The older the child, the larger the surrounding territory where he will find his friends.

This means that the part of town you live in and the schools the children go to should be chosen with as much care as you use in choosing food for your family. There are sick schools in every community. Private and religious schools are not immune. In the sick school you often have an ineffectual principal or one with acute personal problems in his life; an increasing number of poor teachers gravitate to this dumping ground because they know not much will be expected of them. The good teachers that remain usually have morale problems and try to get out as soon as possible, regarding the school as a sinking ship. Because they are unhappy there, they may develop an attitude of despair, resignation, or indifference.

Children quickly tune into this climate and take advantage of it with high rates of sluffing, doing just enough to get by, and getting into assorted mischief.

Sometimes a sick school is a super-disciplined school with locked doors, police and security guards stalking the hallways. The public and private schools within any system can vary greatly in quality, and when you move into a new area or to another town, this should be checked into.

The third circle includes what might be regarded as the governed community. It includes the area that feeds into your high school and beyond. This will be the turf your high school teenagers will be operating in and on. If this area is rampant with prostitution, hard-core porn, and easy access to booze and drugs; if stable families are fleeing the community because of a high crime rate and a lax police force, then you should have some concern about moving your growing family there even if you have an excellent job opportunity.

There is indeed a "quality of life," a tempo, a heartbeat, a spirit of a community which reflects in difficult-to-measure but very real ways a community's conscience—its values, its work ethic, and its moral climate. Living in this milieu or in this third circle will especially affect your older teenage children for better or worse.

I know a West Coast physician who lived in what might be termed a sick community. While his home was located in a safe neighborhood with affluent and mostly responsible neighbors, fine for his pre-teenage children, the larger community and its schools were filled with pathology, and it was beginning to have an impact on his teenage children, despite a strong and healthy family situation. If you live in a sewer, it's hard to come out smelling like a rose. The physician moved inland at a considerable reduction of income to a community where there was much less pathology. The general tone was constructive and the citizens had a high degree of interest in the quality of life. There was vigorous citizen participation in community activities, schools, and civic organizations.

In a word, the people cared. Not surprisingly, this has made a significant difference with his children. And while it may be true that every community has drugs and some social pathology, it's still not necessary to live in a place where these are the social norm.

A Strong Marriage and Happy Children Go Together

The super-comps came from stable homes, with both parents present. If you lavish huge amounts of time and attention on your children or devote that time to your job in order to earn more money, you still aren't doing your children a favor *if* you let your marriage deteriorate in the process.

A fact I've learned from twenty-five years of clinical practice is that every wife has grounds for divorce. I've heard the speech so often I've memorized it:

"I don't like my husband very much. He turns me off. My job and my children are my only real sources of satisfaction. In fact, to hell with him. And I'm sure he feels the same about me. Of course, he's here so little it's hard to tell."

And the wives aren't alone—every husband has grounds, too. So what else is new? Every wife is at least a little neurotic and "impossible" at times, and every husband is often insensitive, difficult to communicate with, and sometimes a little sociopathic. So when the husband tells his mistress, "My wife doesn't understand me," it's always true to some degree—but it's also true in the best and happiest of marriages. In every marriage there are misunderstandings and insensitivities and unreasonable demands.

I frequently see somewhat mismatched couples with good, or even *very* good marriages. What they all have in common is commitment to each other in the marriage. They *make* it work. Sometimes this takes skill-building, counseling, and learning more effective communication techniques. But whatever is required, they do it. Love is a daily decision for them. They consciously choose to love each other, to be patient with each other, again and again. Sure, there's pain, there's discomfort, discouragement, or distance at times. But, like raising good children, having a good marriage requires the couple to pay a price.

The "unholy trinity" of sex, in-law, and money problems is blamed for most marriage break-ups. But I have discovered that underlying all three is usually significant selfishness on the part of at least one of the partners, leading to lack of commitment, disturbed communication, or an inability to deal with anger appropriately. This doesn't mean, of course, that there isn't occasionally the profoundly mismatched couple who should get divorced as quickly as they can and try again with somebody else more on their wavelength, with similar shared values. But sacrifices and commitment are still essential ingredients in any good relationship.

While on a business trip to Houston, Texas, I found myself eating delicious two-and-a-half-inch steaks at the home of a divorced psychiatrist. As we talked about how even competent therapists, including marriage counselors, could fail in their marriages, he said, "You know, my great Jewish mother told me two things were necessary to have a successful marriage. The first was that you marry the right person. I did that.

"The second admonition I didn't pay much attention to," he went on to say, "and it was that, once married, you have to invest a significant amount of energy, commitment, and care to make it work. And that I didn't do. My career and personal convenience came first. I had assumed that since I managed to marry the right person the marriage would just somehow take care of itself." It didn't.

In a major study I have been conducting for the last five years in marriage and marriage counseling (funded by the National Institutes of Mental Health), I found in the literature some 127 crucial variables related to success in marriage. It is very clear that no matter how well one chooses a spouse, it's never possible that you will be compatible on all 127 variables. This means, in essence, that every marriage will have some areas of pain, abrasiveness, conflict, and difficult adjustments. There are no exceptions to this.

For most of us, having to make these often painful adjustments with a spouse is still better than being permanently alone or shifting partners so frequently that in some cases it approaches short-order harlotry. Constant switching is a brutal way to live, profoundly damaging to our capacity to trust, commit, and love. To some males, a sexual smorgasbord looks great, but in time it becomes a disaster for them. They live in a world of lies, deceptions, acting, and faking-out. And eventually they die inwardly as they have lived outwardly, by the proverbial sword—phallic, in this instance.

A gentleman came into my office recently because he was three months into his seventh marriage and found that it was a total disaster. It just wasn't working. He was very depressed and, as he ruefully put it, "I would have been much better off if I had stayed with my first wife. Our differences weren't that great, but this is terrible, a calamity—it's worse than all the rest before."

In carefully reviewing his history I soon discovered that he was arrogant, impatient, and demanding, insistent on always having things on his terms. He skillfully manipulated, badgered, and bullied to always get his way. Whenever one of his spouses attempted to have an identity, show strength in negotiation, or participate in decision making, he chucked them out or they got rid of him. He could take, but he couldn't give much. Yet that not-giving, that refusal to negotiate, was a conscious choice based on personal vanity, ego, and selfishness. The price he paid was great—as much in psychological as in economic terms—and he was paying alimony and child support all over the country.

What does all of this mean? If you want your children to have a chance at being winners, you have to provide them with a stable, secure family experience. Fifty years of behavioral science research, including the "fighter factor" study, have led to this conclusion with monotonous regularity. And at the core of the stable family are a father and mother who love each other and unselfishly try to meet each other's needs.

The single most important thing a father can do to strengthen his children is to love their mother. When she feels secure in her husband's love and support, then she can more easily love their children and make them feel secure—even if she has some hang-ups and a few nagging neuroses. Her energies can focus on the children, not having to battle for her life in a marriage where she is under constant attack or wondering why she is not able to hold her husband's love and attention.

No matter how you put it, if the marriage is mucked up, the children always pay a price. And this rule is just as true for psychologists, psychiatrists, and social workers and their children as for schoolteachers, bricklayers, members of the Mafia, university presidents, and army chaplains.

"Doctor, it's been hell living with Sharon. She's been impossible. I don't know why I stay. I guess it's because of the children." I've heard it often, and it's always followed by a litany of her unloving attitude, her constant barrage of criticism, her angry, vinegar nature; then he finally tells me about his series of affairs as a justified escape for the abuse he gets at home.

But shortly thereafter Sharon is in my office giving me a grim recital of her husband's inadequacies, errors, and outrageous behavior, and her feeling that she has reached the end of the rope.

"Well, why don't you just divorce him? Who would want to live with somebody that awful?" I sometimes ask.

"I don't know. I thought about it a lot. I guess, maybe, I stay with him because I love him."

"But how could you love someone who has done all of those things to you?"

"Well, doctor, it hasn't been all that bad. There have been good years. And he's a good father."

And as I explore further with Jack, her husband, I find that despite all, he still loves his wife, that he would never actually marry any of the women he is involved with. So despite all of the pain that both feel, I find a lot of couples hoping that somehow lightning will strike, a miracle will occur, and they will break out of their destructive pattern.

Usually they tell me they tried marriage counseling, but it didn't work. "We saw this male counselor, but he seemed to favor my husband. I didn't ever feel he was really hearing what I had to say." Or, "We went to one counselor once or twice, but my husband objected because of the money, and he felt irritated at having someone tell him how to behave and run his home. So my husband stopped coming even though I continued for about three months. I think it really helped me understand myself, but it didn't change the marriage that much."

What are some realistic solutions if you are caught up in such a situation? Divorce the beast and go it alone? Or hang tight and attempt to work through the many areas of your conflicts? And is it worth all that effort?

It is not doing the children a favor to stay in a sick marriage that has no hope of change. In my experience a divorce is usually a better alternative when the spouses are unable to make a good marriage. It is better for children to have one stable parent than live in the continuing hell of acute marital stress that devastates both parents and the children as well. This doesn't mean that the other parent will be lost to the children. In some cases they invest more time in their children after the divorce than before.

But let me suggest a checklist you might review before making such a decision:

1. If your spouse has a mental or neurotic illness, the longer he or she has had it and the more serious it is, the less the chance for change. This includes sexual deviation, alcoholism, psychosis, or serious neurotic hang-ups. The key issues are: How is it affecting the children? And to what extent can you tolerate and live with it?

2. If your spouse has had an affair the key issues are: Is this a life-long pattern or an isolated event? Does it involve a major emotional involvement or is it more a transient sexual experience? Can you forgive him or her (if the spouse wishes to return to you) without constantly throwing it in his or her face for the next ten years? Can you wait till the involvement ends? Is it still possible to improve the relationship, negotiate solutions, and renew trust?

3. If you have major communication problems, would your spouse be willing to participate in special workshops or get professional help that would improve your skills in this area?

4. Would your spouse (and you) be willing to see a marriage counselor? And if the first didn't work out for you, would you try another one or two until one is found who is right for your situation?

5. Are there interfering in-laws? If so, would your spouse be willing to leave the area or otherwise remove their destructive influence?

6. In the case of "spouse abuse" (physical or verbal), is this a life-long pattern of violence or just rare outbursts under extreme provocation? Would your spouse or you be willing to get professional help to gain control?

7. Sexual incompatibility in nearly all cases can be treated and helped by competent therapists. Would your spouse be willing to get counseling from a therapist he or she could relate to and be comfortable with?

8. In the case of a conflict of values, including the choice of friends, the big issue is whether you can live with a spouse who may be of a different religion or who rejects your set of beliefs or your personal life philosophy. This is not likely to change much. Can you accept your spouse for what he or she is? And can your spouse accept *you*?

9. Are money problems a temporary issue in your marriage, or is your spouse unable, as a life pattern or because of chronic poor judgment, to contribute significant economic support to the family? Can you live with this if it doesn't change much from the pattern of the last three years? Remember, the past is the best predictor of the future.

10. Does your spouse have the *capacity* to change? (Look at your history together to determine this.) Does your spouse have the *desire and commitment* to change? (Deeds, not words, count here.) If not, can you live with him or her? What will it be like ten years from now for you and the children?

11. How destructive or inadequate are your spouse's parenting skills? How damaging is his or her impact on your offspring? Is your spouse willing to change, to get help? Can your spouse change even if given help? Has your spouse changed for the better at any time in the past? What positive contributions does your spouse make to the children now?

Are Marriage Counselors Worth It?

Some are disasters. They can create problems instead of solving them. But there are some who are extraordinarily skillful in helping couples resolve conflicts. In my experience this has nothing to do with what profession they belong to, their sex, age, or whether they have a university affiliation. Also, a particular therapist may have an outstanding reputation but for a particular couple may prove unsuitable. So what do you do? Check around with friends, family physicians, and people in the mental health area to find several names of therapists who have repeatedly been found to be helpful. Then remember that while a particular therapist may be talented, able, ethical, and helpful to most people, he still may not be the one for you.

I would suggest going at least two or three times to the best therapist on your list. If your chemistry somehow doesn't work out and you are unsatisfied, tactfully cancel your next appointment and see another therapist. You should feel no chagrin or guilt over doing this. It's your life that will be affected. In some rare cases you may have to visit up to a third or fourth therapist before you find the one that's right for you.

In my experience it's better that husband and wife work with the same therapist for marital or family problems. It's a high risk to see separate therapists because, to put it bluntly, neither therapist will know the whole truth about the relationship and will be unable, no matter how skillful he or she is, to correct for the distortions and biased information you or your spouse will inadvertently provide.

I have repeatedly had the experience, after hearing a wife tell a tale of woe about having to live with a man who abused her for many years, of wiping a tear or two away with my handkerchief, wondering how she ever put up with the bum. But after listening to her husband's story (which I always insist on hearing if I am to help the couple), I have my handkerchief out again, wondering how he ever endured all those years of misery living with her. Sometimes it's so bad I use two handkerchiefs.

The striking differences between their stories are almost universal, even when both are being truthful. Good counseling is impossible unless the counselor has a chance of finding the truth by hearing both spouses' versions of it.

In addition to help from a really good therapist, I highly recommend that couples struggling to overcome communication blocks take part in such experiences as the Minnesota Couples Communication Workshop, available in most communities in the U.S., and conducted regularly by family counselors, social workers, and psychologists with special training. To find out details on how to attend and participate, you might contact a community social services agency or the college that includes social work at your local university.

Another highly recommended experience is the Marriage Encounter weekend, conducted by Catholics, Lutherans, Episcopalians, Presbyterians, Jews, and other religious groups, which adds a powerful spiritual dimension (without a lot of dogma) to an extremely potent experience in improving couple communication. A non-spiritual version of this is the Marriage Enrichment experience pioneered by marriage counselors Dr. David and Vera Mace through their national program ACME (Association of Couples for Marriage Enrichment). You can get information on times and places where these are run by contacting or writing ACME (P.O. Box 10596, Winston-Salem, North Carolina 27108). Those sponsored by various religious groups welcome non-members. Contact the local church or Parish for information. These are all very safe experiences and given at a very reasonable cost. Couples are treated lovingly with no possibility of embarrassment or abrasive confrontations with other couples. The dignity and privacy of the couples are respected.

Adding Up: The Ground Rules

Rule 1 Put together a great marriage; strengthen the family by meeting your spouse's needs. If the two of you are making it, this will profoundly help your children's sense of security. There are a lot of powerful strategies that can strengthen your relationship even if one or both of you have damaged pasts, are neurotic, or can't communicate effectively. Or, if your marriage has a "terminal cancer," get out as early as possible. Minimize the damage. There is no need to be masochistic and suffer for another ten years with divorce still the inevitable conclusion.

Rule 2 Teach your children all kinds of skills and competencies in work, recreation, music, and sports. Give them every possible experience, adventure, and growth-promoting advantage you can. Make "doing" fun. Model it yourself. Subscribe to three newspapers and ten magazines. Get TV viewing under control—even if you have to lock up the set. Do things as a family. Do things with the children individually, giving them special private time with you. Help them to experience success. Stimulate their minds every way you can.

Rule 3 Pick a great neighborhood and community to live in. In fact, do this with even greater care than you take in selecting the particular house you live in. In doing this you are choosing the quality of their peer culture and schools. You may have to drive twenty minutes longer to get to work, but during your children's crucial growing-up years this may be worth it to you and them.

Rule 4 Cultivate in your children an ethical, moral sense, a regard for the worth and value of every individual, a capacity to be generous and have concern for others. You may seek help here from your religion, besides exposing your children to some great friends who model the values you would like to see them have. If you are turned off by organized religion there are groups like the Quakers and Unitarians who, with little or no dogma, have concern for their fellow man, teaching a general reverence for life and highly principled ethical conduct.

Rule 5 Cultivate in your children the capacity to endure stress, to show grace under pressure, to have flexible, resilient psyche s. You do this by giving them responsibility when young, by expecting them to do well in their home chores and schoolwork, by training them in decision making, and by letting them suffer reasonable penalties when they break family rules.

2

How to Build Your Child's Self-Image and Self-Esteem

THE VITAL CORE of every human being is his self-image, the picture of himself that he carries around in his mind. It is the product of many different things, built up over the years piece by piece, like a mosaic.

"You're nothing but a rotten little thief," the store clerk tells the child when he is caught shoplifting at age five, before he really has a clear idea of property rights.

"You have such a sweet way about you," his mother tells him. "You make people feel better just by being around."

"Let's face it," her father says brutally, "you're going to have to make it on brains, because good looks you're never going to have."

"Would you be willing to babysit my children?" the neighbor asks. "I'm sorry to keep asking you, but you're the only really responsible girl around, and I know I can trust you completely."

This composite picture contains many contradictory pieces of information, both good and bad, both true and false. No one really understands why or how the information is put together into the picture that the person really believes. Some people shrug off the negative information and believe only the positive, gaining a great deal of confidence in themselves. Others are somehow able to verify a great many true pictures and throw out most of the false ones, so that they understand themselves pretty well. While others, for unknown and perhaps unknowable reasons, believe only—or mostly—the negative images.

Actually, the healthiest situation is to have the self-image come quite close to the truth. The more congruent the self-image and the truth about a person, the better job he'll do in dealing with the world. He won't expect himself to be able to do everything well; he won't remain blind to his faults and so unable to improve; he won't be so timid that he never reaches his full potential.

Patricia was eighteen, a high school senior with a wholesome, natural beauty and a warm, affectionate personality. She came to my office—but only reluctantly, at the urgent request of her two best friends. They preceded her into my office, telling me privately that she was steadily dating an ex-convict, ten years her senior. They were extremely concerned because he had a long history of anti-social behavior, including physically assaulting and abusing some of his former girlfriends. They knew of at least two girls he had got pregnant and then abandoned. They had strongly urged her to break off the relationship, but their entreaties were to no avail.

When Pat came in, I decided on a direct approach. My first question was simple: "Do you love him?"

She shook her head. "No," she said, almost inaudibly.

"Do you like him?"

Again a shake of the head and looks that said, "No."

Puzzled, I asked, "But, Pat, why do you go with him?"

There was a long silence. Tears briefly welled up in her eyes. Then, hopelessly shrugging her shoulders, she said, "But who else would have me?"

As I looked at this beautiful, decent girl it took a few seconds for me to get my composure. Then I began to explore her background. I quickly learned that her parents had a long history of marital warfare. The husband, a brutal, rough man, found that direct verbal attacks on his wife bothered her very little, but he had discovered that if he verbally attacked their daughter Patricia his wife invariably got upset.

So at opportune moments, usually at the evening meal, he would make cutting remarks to his daughter.

"Pass the butter, stupid!"

"Nobody will ever marry an ugly thing like you."

The father took great delight in watching his wife's discomfort and attempts to hush him up, but he either didn't notice or didn't care that Pat believed his cruel remarks. These destroyed most positive feelings she might have had about herself. She felt like a nothing. And when a young woman feels like a nothing, guess what kind of a man she dates and marries! A nothing!

Psychologist Stanley Coopersmith found through careful research that four major factors contribute to a person's self-image: acceptance, competence, virtue, and power.

Acceptance   People notice from earliest childhood whether they are respected, enjoyed, and loved by the important people in their lives. Acceptance is a gift. It's unconditional. As Rabindranath Tagore put it in "The Judge" (from *Collected Poems and Plays*), "Say of him what you please, but I know my child's failings. I do not love him because he is good, but because he is my little child."

The child can get this message the first day of life. He feels it: "I am wanted. This is a good world to live in."

It can also be felt when parents discipline the child for the right reasons. The message he receives is: "They care about me. It makes a difference to them whether I am a decent, responsible person." Though discipline may cause some tears and temporary tension, most children unconsciously understand whether their parents really care about them.

Competence The child tests and evaluates his own worth by how well he performs, how well he develops the skills and abilities that are important to him. His achievements in schoolwork, sports, social interaction, debate, rappelling, drama, music, housework—all of them contribute to his view of himself.

You can tell a child he's a smart kid all you want, but if he can't catch on to math and regularly fails, he won't believe you. It takes more than just telling a child he is loved to give him a good self-image. *His sense of personal worth has to be validated by some tangible successes.* He must do some things that are important to him well enough to bring genuinely earned praise and recognition. Every child has to slay a few dragons.

In particular, some success in school is important because of the many years he spends there. No child can stand to have his school experience be a total disaster. He may not be good in math, but he had better be good in something else—shop, reading, English, or the school band—in order to compensate.

Virtue Dr. Coopersmith found that children need to have a sense that they are basically good and decent people. They need to know that they are living up to some acceptable level of ethical and moral behavior. To satisfy this need, they must be taught a system of ethics that is achievable, and then actually live up to it. This is easiest when they are raised with a clear knowledge of the family's basic religious commitment of chosen ethical standards and sense of social responsibility.

Power The child needs to feel that he can influence his own life and the lives of others. If a child can't make any changes or have any effect on his environment, he may eventually give up. This is referred to as "learned helplessness," the major symptoms being depression and despair.

This in no way is to suggest that it is healthy for a child to "rule the roost" or tyrannize his parents or family. But he needs a healthy balance of give and take within reasonable limits.

Creating a Good Self-Image

Dr. Coopersmith's research suggested that high self-esteem children are most likely to come from homes where the parents run a tight ship: the parents are fairly strict, expect high but attainable standards of achievement, and clearly define and enforce reasonable limits of behavior.

Low self-esteem children more frequently come from permissive, loose homes where they have relatively little guidance in making decisions. Such children feel uncertain and anxious about doing the right thing.

Structure, standards, and discipline tend to give children a safer, more predictable world to live in. Creating such an environment requires that parents have clear goals and values. Their children sense that they are part of a more orderly universe, and this seems to help in the development of a child's self-esteem. Or the improved self-image may occur in such homes because the children sense that their parents care more or are willing to invest more energy and commitment in caring for them.

Boys with higher self-esteem also tend to have had closer positive relationships with their fathers. They not only had a model of the masculine role to identify with but also formed a significant emotional and psychological bond with their fathers. And it is not just coincidental that these are the very fathers who invested high-quality energy in their children, both sons and daughters. This helped make them feel more worthwhile.

We parents are mirrors to our children. From us they obtain a notion of what their true self is like. Positive reflections produce positive self-esteem and self-images, but only if they are anchored in reality. Flattering our children with insincere praise accomplishes worse than nothing. If your child has been behaving obnoxiously in social situations, he needs to know it. There may be some pain as he learns from you—his mirror—that some of his behavior is offensive, but without that feedback from people he knows love him he cannot improve. If you excuse or overlook his abusive treatment of an adult or the neighbor's child you set him up to be more cruelly hurt by social rejection later.

If you are kind in honest criticism and warm in honest praise your child will learn that he can trust your feedback, both positive and negative, and this will contribute to his general feeling of security. He will know his parents care, that they level with him.

Just as a thoughtful mother warns her daughter just before a date that she needs to brush her teeth or apply more deodorant, so you need to be honest in warning your children about obnoxious or inappropriate behavior that will make it harder to live well among other people.

But be careful not to criticize your children in ways that convey a message of rejection or ridicule or worthlessness. It isn't helpful to say, "Good heavens, Mary, you're not wearing that dirty dress again, are you? Look at that stain. Stop being such a slob! Do I have to dress you before every date so you don't make an idiot of yourself?"

It's much more helpful to be matter-of-fact, to keep the criticism focused on the obnoxious thing that must be eliminated, to avoid labeling the child negatively: "Uh-oh—you've got a stain on the back of your dress. Let me get some cleaner. It'll just take a minute. You look too nice tonight to have anything spoil it."

And it is especially important not to ignore real achievements while constantly criticizing minor failures. It seems absurd, but many very bright children are made to feel quite stupid by their parents because of such comments as: "Look at this—an A-minus. You're perfectly capable of getting straight A's all the time, but you just can't seem to get it together, can you!" Or, in another field, "Sure, your team won the game, but no thanks to you. Fifteen yards on that pass reception and then you tripped and fell—you could have run it for a touchdown. Talk about clumsy. I don't know why they leave you on the team."

I've seen some children who neurotically and compulsively push themselves to excel in a particular field, but no matter how well they do it's never good enough. They are constantly miserable and self-critical, plagued by feelings of failure even though everyone around them quite correctly regards them as successful people. Perhaps that neurotic compulsion to be absolutely perfect helps them achieve more than they might have otherwise, but I doubt it. People aren't at their best when they are neurotically afraid of failure. And grown-up children who are still trying to prove their worthiness to over-critical parents are missing out on a lot of happiness and, quite possibly, on the even greater success that might come to them if they were able to relax a bit. Even after their parents are dead, these children still seem to hear their voices saying, "Look at that! Elected President of the United States, but only by half a million votes! When are you going to do something right?"

This doesn't mean that you shouldn't ever push your children. I doubt that there would be many piano players in the world if there were no parents pushing their kids into lessons, yet it's hard to find many pianists who aren't grateful for that initial push. There is a difference—a huge difference—between the neurotic, never-satisfied parent and the parent who pushes his children to try new things and achieve competence, and then is satisfied when they achieve it. The neurotic parent produces a neurotic, self-hating child; the parent who insists on broad experience and competence produces a confident, competent child—a winner who knows when he's won!

The Child with the Inflated Ego

That sounds like the title of a monster movie—and sometimes it can seem like that to those who have to live with one. You know the type. He never seems to tire of reciting his own exploits. To hear him tell it, every success of any group he belongs to was the direct result of his own great talent. There's nothing he can't do better than anyone else, and he loves to show off. And if you don't happen to agree with his opinion that he is God's greatest gift to the world, he'll shun you as if you had a highly contagious strain of leprosy.

"Conceited," you call him. "Arrogant." "Vain." And it's a fairly accurate description, as far as it goes. Unfortunately those words only label the obnoxious symptoms—and those symptoms can mean two very opposite diseases.

The first type of "inflated ego" is a phony. The show-off really doesn't believe any of that stuff he says. He's like the Wizard of Oz, putting up giant illusions in order to hide how weak and powerless he really is. Inside, the show-off really feels worthless, wonders if he's any good at anything, and is so afraid of people discovering how incompetent he is that he blusters. He puts on a thorough—and sometimes obnoxious—display of the very talents he's sure he doesn't have.

The second type of "inflated ego" is a spoiled, over-indulged child. A doting parent—usually his mother—has taught him that he can do no wrong. She applauds his miserable recitations and piano pieces as if they were brilliant; she constantly brags about him where he can hear; if he has a disagreement with anyone she automatically takes his part; she doesn't insist that he actually succeed in everything, she merely acts as if he already has! She's the opposite of the neurotically critical parent—she's blindly uncritical. The child, worshipped all his life, reaches the perfectly natural conclusion that he deserves the worship.

The spoiled child is very difficult to help because he doesn't clearly perceive that he has a problem, and even if he does, he has invested his entire self-image in that misperception of himself. The more evidence he acquires that he really isn't all that great, the more he rejects the facts and clings to his mother's glowing image of him.

When other people reject them, his mother tells him, "Don't worry—they're just not good enough for you. They're just jealous. They're not up to your level." When he fails in one job after another, she insists, "Those menial tasks just can't occupy someone like you, dear. They're boring for a mind that can be doing so much more important work."

Children who are raised with this impossibly good image of themselves are difficult to live with in marriage because they are takers, not givers. No one has ever expected them to give anything to anyone. They demand tremendous amounts of service and respect from others—and are oblivious to other people's real needs.

The first kind of "inflated ego" can be helped with genuine praise for genuine achievement. If you are the parents of a child who tends to brag about things he hasn't done or who tends to inflate the importance of his successes, you need to give him more opportunities to do things he can really succeed at, praising him in a low-key way while virtually ignoring the overblown self-praise. When he stretches things in saying, "The teacher said my report was the best in class today, and five other kids told me after school they wish they could give reports like that," you merely answer, "That's nice, dear. I'm glad you're back from school." But then, when he really does something well, you praise him warmly. "Thanks for fixing the broken light switch. You did a good job, and it sure is great to have some of the problems at home fixed without my having to do them. I really appreciate it." Gradually, the child will unconsciously respond to the fact that his dishonest self-praise doesn't get any payoff while his genuine achivements get genuine, believable praise.

As for the spoiled child—and the spoiled adult—if you are his parent, stop spoiling him! Don't immediately become critical but do start praising his successes in proportion to their real value, mentioning a few places where he might improve. At first, he'll probably respond with fury or tears, accusing you of hating and rejecting him. After all, he's been taking your praise like an addict takes heroin, and withdrawal is painful. Eventually, if you're lucky and your doting hasn't gone too far, he will begin to come into contact with the real world again.

It's harder if you are the parent who *hasn't* been spoiling him, and you can't stop your spouse from destroying the child. I urge you to seek professional help to cure that sickness in your family; your spouse is probably using the children to satisfy some unmet need in his or her life.

Building Your Child's Self-Image: Eleven Rules

Here are some rules that every parent should use as a guide in order to help his children have good, accurate, healthy self-images. In fact, they aren't a bad guide to how to treat almost anybody you ever meet!

1. Teach your child to be competent (See Chapter 1) If your child is to have confidence, to think of himself as a competent person, he has to have some objective proof that he is competent. And the only way he'll get that is if you introduce him to experiences that he can succeed in and then insist that he become competent. He may be reluctant or afraid or easily discouraged, but if you give in to his fears, you'll only strengthen his inner conviction that he's not the kind of person who does well in new things. If he has failed at something that was simply beyond his abilities, make sure he is also involved in other activities that he *can* succeed at. And if he is failing at a task that he *has* to succeed at, like reading or math in school, then get him special help and make sure he gets sincere praise for every small achievement he does make in that area. Success begets success.

2. Like your child, and make sure he knows you do Parents don't live on Mt. Olympus, dispensing judgments with all the wisdom of Zeus—but children sometimes get that feeling. Sure you're busy, but make sure you take the time to be your child's friend. Sometimes you have to play sergeant—assigning chores, making sure work gets done, disciplining, settling quarrels with brothers and sisters. But you need to make sure he knows that you also like him as a person. Have fun together: play games, share athletic activities, go to the movies, hike through the woods, go shopping together. Let there be times when your guard is down, when you talk about your own dreams and your own feelings about things, where he gets a sense of you as a person. By treating him this way, you are telling him that he's the kind of good, interesting person that you would choose for a friend.

3. Give him many sources of praise Make sure that your child has enough competence to win praise from people who aren't related to him. Your praise means more than anybody else's, but if you're the only one who ever praises him he'll eventually conclude that you're the only one who thinks he's worth anything, and he may become too dependent on you. That doesn't mean you should call up all of his teachers and say, "Please be extra nice to my kid." It does mean that he should have plenty of chances to show competence to others—eventually they'll notice and let him know that they respect him for it. That means that when he gets a real job, it would be better not to work for you. He should work for someone else so that the praise and criticism come from other people. It's fine if you help him learn to swim, but why not give him lessons at some point along the way? Then it's the teacher who's telling him that his backstroke is great, but he needs to work on the butterfly. After all, every new person he meets is a new experience, and he needs to gain confidence in meeting people by having experience in doing it successfully.

4. Help him fight his personal dragons I know quite a few very competent people who have almost absurd bugaboos. There are businessmen who are excellent at influencing people, who are extremely well-liked, but they panic at the thought of speaking in front of a group of people. There are adults who would rather let their teeth rot in their mouths than visit a dentist. There are people who used to be overweight, but finally licked the problem and are in good shape—yet they still think of themselves as if they were fat and refuse to buy and wear fashionable, good-looking clothing. Most of these "dragons" are symptoms of failures or fears in childhood that were never defeated then and are much, much harder to defeat now.

If your child has an irrational fear of something, don't conspire with him to help him avoid facing it. At the same time, don't keep throwing him back into a frightening situation unprepared to succeed. Is he afraid of giving oral reports in front of his class? Role-play with him. Be the "teacher" and let him give his reports to you, over and over again. Bring in your spouse when he gains a little more confidence; have him give the report to friends or relatives that he knows well and is relaxed with. Make sure that you help him overcome some of the worst problems, but don't insist on perfection either. Just help him be competent so that he'll have a good shot at doing well in front of the class. *Then*, when he's well-armed, you can send him back to fight the dragon, confident that this time he'll win—on his own!

Is your daughter convinced that she's too ugly to wear the latest fashions? Then help her. If she really is overweight, help her lose the pounds. *Then*, when her real problems are solved, buy her those styles she doesn't dare to wear, and insist that she wear them around the house. At first she'll feel silly and shy, but after a while those clothes will begin to feel natural and comfortable, and a glance in the mirror will tell her she really does look great. It won't be long before she goes out in public dressed well—even if it takes a few more prods from you to get her to do it.

In other words, practice may not make perfect, but it certainly makes them more *competent*.

5. *Give him chances to make decisions, to be responsible* (See Chapter 7) You wouldn't put your child in a cage with a bear to teach him to wrestle, and so you shouldn't put him in situations where he simply isn't competent to act alone. At the same time, he'll never learn anything if he's always holding your hand. As he gets to a reasonable level of maturity, insist on his doing things on his own. Give him duties at home that only he is responsible for—mowing the lawn, planting the new hedge of roses, reorganizing the spice cabinet in the kitchen, vacuuming the stairs. Give him experiences that will build his confidence. Teach him the city bus system, and send him on errands alone. Send him alone into the barber shop to get his hair cut before age ten, and when he's older, get him a checking account to handle his own finances. Each successfully completed task or challenge will build his self-image. He'll see himself as more adult, more competent, more powerful in altering his own life and changing the world around him.

In short, never do for him what he can and should do for himself.

6. *Don't criticize his honest mistakes* Anybody can make mistakes. The child who spills a glass of water isn't a clumsy oaf—but if you call him that, he may become one. The kid who accidentally forgot to pick up the milk on the way home from the football game isn't a thoughtless idiot—but calling him one won't help him become more thoughtful, either. If he spills, hand him a towel so he can clean up. If he forgot the milk, send him back out to get it. He knows he made a mistake; you don't have to abuse him for it. The best teacher is the natural consequence. Enough messes cleaned up, and he'll be more careful to stop making them. Enough extra trips to the store, and he'll start finding ways to remind himself to do all his errands on one trip. And instead of a negative self-image, he'll think of himself as a person who can be depended on to make up for his honest mistakes, rarely making the same mistake twice.

The only time you need to take special note of mistakes is if they follow a habitual pattern. If your daughter always manages to forget something so that she has to come back home from school, completely missing first period, then you have every reason to suspect that she is having some kind of problem at school that she wants to avoid. If your son habitually sleeps late and claims he "forgot" to set his alarm, you may have to start some strategies to make his alarm into an attractive alternative—like waking him up with a clash of cymbals, or checking his alarm after he has gone to sleep and waking him up to set it. But in these cases, again, recriminations and criticism are only appropriate when his mistakes are voluntary or habitual. A genuinely accidental error is never grounds for abuse from you.

7. Don't make impossible demands While you shouldn't make life a bed of roses for the child, you also shouldn't make it a bed of nails. While you're making sure he has a lot of experiences that challenge him and make him grow, you should also make sure that he doesn't have too many experiences that inevitably lead to failure so that he begins to believe he can't do anything right. Your four-year-old may be capable of learning to count, but you shouldn't also demand that he learn to read, play the piano, ride a bike, and do long-column addition all in the same week. Your sixteen-year-old may be perfectly competent to do chores around the house, but it isn't fair to set up so many things for him to do that he doesn't have enough time to complete all his work at home *and* succeed in school *and* do well in all his extra-curricular work. Better to achieve a little less—and get used to success.

8. Don't lean too heavily on your children for your own support Often after a divorce—or even before it—one parent will find a child who is particularly helpful or sympathetic and use the child as confidante, helper, crutch, and security blanket. The child may be perfectly willing to fulfill your needs, but too much dependence on the child takes from him things that he shouldn't have to give so early in life. Find adult or even professional help to meet your personal needs and help you through crises; let your children be children.

9. Have regular times alone with each child Of course you try not to play favorites with your children, but even if it were possible to measure out exactly equal amounts of your love and time for each child, there would still be some who felt they were not getting enough of your love and attention. The best way to help meet their need is to make sure they have some time alone with you that they can count on. Even the most well-meaning parents can get so involved in the interesting projects and problems of their older kids that the youngest begins to feel like he amounts to nothing in the family. Or, quite the reverse, new babies or younger children can take so much of mother's time that an older child can feel he just doesn't matter anymore. So, to make sure you don't accidentally hurt tender feelings and make good children feel worthless, set aside special time for each of them—and never miss it.

10. Create a climate of encouragement in your home It isn't enough for your children to receive praise; they need to learn to give it to each other. Make sure the whole family knows about their achievements. Every week in our Monday evening family conferences each child has a turn in the spotlight—one each week. We go around the family circle and all of us say something nice about the person in the spotlight—something good he did that week or something about his personality that is important to us. That kind of positive experience is as important for the kids giving the praise as it is for the one receiving it.

11. Give him plenty of reason to think of himself as a good person Often parents encourage their kids to be good in sports or develop their talents, but forget to teach them skills in moral, altruistic behavior. There is pleasure in doing good for other people, and they should learn to experience that pleasure so that they will want to feel it again and again. You might plot a pleasant surprise for another family member and conspire with one of the other children to make him some cookies or leave him a note one day, telling him how much he is loved. Or you might take a child with you to visit a sick friend. Bring your kids along to help a neighbor whose basement is flooded, or when you get a midnight call to help pull a friend's car out of a ditch, wake up one of your older children and ask him along for muscle power. Your kids will share your sense of pleasure and excitement in helping other people, and they'll come to think of themselves as the kind of people who go out of their way to help others and make them feel good. Then, when they're adults and someone asks for help, your kids won't think of not helping—after all, their image of themselves requires them to do it.

The best way to raise kids who really are responsible, competent, confident, good adults with a good self-image is to *prove* to them that they're responsible, competent, and good when they're young.

3

How To Teach Your Child Effective Social Skills

EVERY PARENT WANTS HIS CHILDREN to grow up to be productive, happy adults. But what makes people happy? More than any other single factor, I have found, happiness comes from an ability to get along with other people. Unhappy people are usually those who cannot get along well with spouse, children, parents, friends, associates, or strangers. And those who are happy are those who have close, warm relationships with a significant number of people—especially those most important to them—like spouse, children, siblings, and parents. Even when disasters strike, people who are able to form close relationships with others are better able to remain happy despite grief or loss. And those who are unable to maintain affectionate, open relationships are the least able to cope with such problems.

So one of the most important things you, as a parent, have to do for your children is to help them develop social skills. You need to prepare them to establish good relationships with others.

Social success comes on several levels. The socially successful person makes a good impression on strangers, causing them to want to become friends with him; he is attractive personally. Also, the socially successful person is able to meet other people's emotional needs; friendship with him is rewarding. Finally, the socially successful person does not have irrational or impossible expectations of others; he is secure enough in himself that he can cope with rejection.

Personal Attractiveness

It is important that you recognize—and teach your children from an early age—that personal attractiveness is much more than native good looks. Inborn beauty is not a deciding factor in whether you want to be with another person. Some people seem to have been cruelly treated by nature—their teeth are uneven, their facial features unpleasant, their bodies unproportioned, their movements ungainly, and their smiles more like grimaces. Yet I have known many such people who are marvelously attractive, always surrounded by friends, extremely successful in establishing close, lasting, productive relationships. And there are many sad cases of people with a great deal of outward beauty who are quite unattractive—cold, austere, intimidating. They draw no one to them and fail repeatedly in establishing good relationships.

What *is* important in being personally attractive to strangers, in making a good first impression? One vital thing is a good self-image and personal security, but I'll deal with those later. Here we'll just discuss the superficial things that you can help your children do to be personally attractive.

Cleanliness Even the ugliest, most deformed people can minimize their problems and increase their attractiveness simply by keeping themselves clean, grooming themselves carefully, and making sure they have no offensive breath or body odors. From the time your children are little, they should be accustomed to bathing regularly, dressing neatly and tastefully, and being sensitive to whether others are offended by smells or dirt.

Looking Like their Peers Don't do anything to make your child look funny to his friends. If his friends all wear jeans to school, don't make him dress in a suit—he'll be "weird". Don't put your daughter in those cute and frilly short dresses when her friends will all be wearing jeans. In short, don't make your child stand out; it will alienate others and interfere with his ability to make friends. And as your child gets into the fashion-conscious teenage years, do everything you can to help keep him in style. Your child's self-image in high school and junior high school is shaped in large part by what his peers think of him, and if they think he's weird, there are two strikes against him from the start.

Manners These are taught more by modeling than by instruction—and it goes far beyond which fork to use at the dinner table. The manners you need to teach your children, beginning at home, are the simple rules of courtesy that help smooth social relationships. Most parents try to teach their children to say "please" and "thank you". Basic rules like not hitting and refraining from taking toys from other children are also guides to good manners later. But there are other, subtler things your children ought to learn.

They need to develop basic respect for other people's desires, thoughts, opinions, and needs. And they will only learn that if you treat *them* with such respect. If you greet their thoughts and opinions with derision—"That's dumb"—they will learn to treat their friends that way, which will soon lose them friends. If you are constantly interrupting them, refusing to listen to what they say, they will do the same to others—and others will soon avoid talking to your children.

For the sake of your children's personal attractiveness, it is important, then, that you listen to what they have to say, and when you disagree, disagree politely, respecting their right to hold a different opinion. When they have an objection, try to avoid ending the discussion by saying, "It's going to be this way because I say so!" If they are going to be thwarted, they have a right to understand your reasons. Go out of your way to help them accomplish the things they want to accomplish, when you can, even if it means inconveniencing yourself. They will get the message and learn to inconvenience themselves for others' sake. Treat the mistakes of others with tolerance and understanding. They will soon learn that this is how good and mature people treat each other.

Competence This is covered thoroughly in several other chapters, but it is important to remember here that to be attractive, your child should be interesting and valuable to others. Nothing accomplishes this like helping your child achieve competence in many areas. He should be welcome on the baseball team in fourth grade, so teach him to be competent at sports. Help him to find interesting things to do that he can be good at, so that he can talk with authority and experience about his sculpturing or his mountain climbing or his piano playing or his gardening. If he is competent at nothing, he will have little to offer others.

Verbal Skills The overwhelming majority of our social interactions, even in such intimate relationships as marriage, take place on a verbal level. Make sure your family life is highly verbal. Talk frequently with your children. While you will often talk to them about things that interest them, also talk to them about things that interest *you*. If they have frequent practice in expressing themselves and are able to converse about a broad variety of subjects, they will be able to enter into conversations with strangers with confidence. Don't avoid talking about "adult" subjects like politics or car repairs or the current best-seller; you'd be surprised how much they understand and how much their world will be broadened by getting a perspective on such things. Once they have learned the basic courtesies of listening there is no reason to exclude them from your conversations with your friends. The more intelligent conversation they overhear, the better able to converse they will be.

Verbal skills go much deeper than mere small talk or conversation, however. In order to sustain a healthy relationship with their future spouses and associates and friends, your children need to learn to communicate about their feelings. Don't be afraid to verbalize your own feelings, so that they learn the vocabulary of self-expression. In fact, the more you are able to deal with emotions on a spoken level, the better able your children will be to cope with their own emotions. "Right now I feel so much love for you I just can't hold it in," you will say sometimes; other times you'll say, "When you don't come home at the time you say you will, it makes me feel very concerned, and I wonder if I can trust you to do what you promise. It really means a lot to me to be able to trust you." Let such expressions of emotion be common enough in your home that your children will be able to create a communicative atmosphere in their own homes later.

Eliminate Unpleasant Features If you possibly can, you should help your child overcome any negative traits that will cause others to avoid him. Braces should only be put on your children if necessary, but if your child does have crooked teeth, by all means get them straightened as soon as practicable. Acne can ruin a teenager's life and color his personal relationships for years, and in almost every case it's completely unnecessary. Consult a dermatologist as soon as your child starts developing pimples, so that the pocking and cratering of his face can be avoided. It's a rare case of acne that is completely beyond control. Also help your children avoid obesity, even in their preschool years. Once they learn to think of themselves as fat, the battle to become physically fit is so much harder.

The same is true of obnoxious personal traits. If your child is a grabber or a screamer or a pouter, help him overcome those problems early by careful discipline and positive reinforcement of the opposite traits. Anything that will make his life harder should be got under control early.

This is not to say that you should try to make your child "perfect". If you are constantly badgering him and trying to make him over physically, he will soon get the idea that he is really an unacceptable person that you are trying to save. It is only the most obnoxious features that you should try to help him eliminate.

Give Him Plenty of Practice One of the most important parts of developing all your child's interpersonal skills is giving him plenty of practice. The world is sometimes pretty frightening, and there are parents who want to spare their children the dangers and shocks and hurts of the world. But keeping your child tightly within the family and never giving him outside experiences will only guarantee his incompetence in later life.

Too often parents think that school provides their child with ample opportunities to learn social skills. For many children it does, but school is also a social situation that can sometimes aggravate a problem. If a child already has social skills he will prosper; if he lacks important skills he will often fall further and further behind as other children ignore him and no one helps bail him out.

Obviously, you should do all you can do to give your child plenty of practice with other children before he enters school. The importance of a strong preschool experience for your child cannot be underestimated. In a good preschool your child will be involved with other children in many activities, low on stress and high on interest. Good preschool teachers are able to bring out shy or timid children and give them confidence before they enter the more intellectually stressful school situation. The very brevity of the preschool day—usually only a few hours—helps your child get used to school-type situations gradually.

Another thing you can do to help, both before and after your child enters school, is to keep your home and yard open to other children. Not that you should try to be surrogate parents to all the children on the block. Rather you should keep an "open-door" policy and encourage your child to bring his friends over, though when he is very young you should do the inviting. When your child deals with people at home, he has your support. He is on his home ground. He knows his way around and becomes the natural leader, at least for a short time. The more practice he gets in dealing with his friends in his own home, the better he'll be able to deal with them on neutral or even hostile ground at school.

Above all, never do anything to embarrass your child. It is as bad to brag about him to his friends ("See the pretty painting my Junior drew?") as it is to criticize him in front of them ("It's nice of you to come play with Junior; he's so shy.") Let him meet them on equal terms, with the confidence that his secure home environment provides.

Older children will be helped in their social development if they get involved in extracurricular activities. Dancing can be quite important in teen years—see to it that your kids learn to dance so that they can go to dances with confidence that they'll look good on the floor. Make sure they learn the dances that *they* will need. If they will be going to disco-type dances, the fox trot may be useless. Also encourage them to get involved in the drama club, the school newspaper, the pep club, the chorus—wherever their interests or skills lie. It is often outside the class, where kids are working together to achieve a common goal, that real friendships are made. Structured groups like Boy Scouts, Girl Scouts, the YMCA or YWCA, and church groups can provide that kind of experience. The more your child gets involved, the more ease and skill he will acquire in his social relationships.

Helping Your Child be a Good Friend

First impressions aren't everything. Your child will have a pretty miserable life if he attracts a lot of people but still can't create and maintain any long-term, close, rewarding relationships. And to do that he needs to be the kind of person who gives love and affection to others, the kind of person who can be depended on, the kind of person who is sensitive to others' needs. In other words, your child needs to be *affectionate, trustworthy,* and *helpful.* It sounds like the *Boy Scout Manual* or the key teachings of almost every major religion, and that's no accident. Almost every philosophy or group calls on individuals to be that kind of person, for the simple and compelling reason that no society will survive very long if such behavior is not encouraged and rewarded.

In fact, almost every chapter of this book is designed to help you raise your children to be that kind of person. But let's go over these virtues, briefly.

Affectionate If your child is unloving or undemonstrative, others will not get emotional support from him and they will turn elsewhere for their close friendships. Every living person needs to feel loved, and they will go to almost any source that provides that feeling. How can you help your child be loving? You yourself need to make sure you love your children and tell them in everything you say and everything you do that you care about them, that you want them to be happy, that they matter to you. If you are openly supportive, they will learn from you the ways that love is shown. They will also learn what love feels like.

Teaching your children to obey rules is important, but it is completely useless if you do not work even harder to create an atmosphere of love in your home. Your children should also see your warm feelings toward others outside your family. When Grandma has just left after a visit, it's a good idea to tell your kids, "Wasn't it great having Grandma here? She's so much fun to talk to, and I love her so much." When some of your friends have just left or when you're about to invite them to your home, tell your children, "They're such kind people and they care so much about us, I love to have them here." When your children are constantly exposed to open expressions of love and learn to associate feeling good with giving love, they will tend to become loving people.

Trustworthy In the chapter on responsibility I go into this in detail. Your child needs to have practice in sustaining relationships by being dependable. Again, you need to model correct behavior. If your child hears you frequently criticizing your friends or ridiculing them to others, they will also do that sort of thing. Encourage them to speak loyally of their friends, to look for good things in them. If your child comes home from school angry because of some rotten thing one of his friends did, it's a good idea, along with sympathizing with his pain, to remind him of the good things about his friend.

You should also encourage your child to be forgiving. He should not reject people because of mistakes or flaws. You can help him a lot by forgiving him for *his* mistakes, too. "I'm really sad because you broke my camera, and I'm going to have to require you to help me earn the money to replace it, Sandy. But I know you didn't mean to break it, and so I don't like you or love you any less because of it." If they see that you are able to respond negatively to some things they *do* without rejecting them as people you love, they will learn to behave in the same way toward others.

Trustworthiness can be learned, but it can also be an "inborn" trait. Some children seem to be naturally more dependable, more stable in their feelings toward people, than other children. You should not expect your children to be uniformly trustworthy. Rather, recognize where each child is and help him develop from there. Don't make his development of dependability a point that he is going to feel undue stress over, but when he does prove to be dependable praise him sincerely for it. "You could have got mad at your sister over that, Lizzy, but you didn't. I really respect you for that. It takes a good person to forgive people's mistakes and still like them anyway."

Helpful There are many kinds of help your children need to learn to give. One of the earliest is actual physical help in accomplishing a task. When you teach your three-year-old to take the silverware out of the dishwasher and load it in the silverware tray so that Mommy doesn't have to do the work alone, you are setting the stage for your child's future happiness. Years later, he will take it as a matter of course to pitch in and help a friend who has to trim a hedge or run some errands. He will know that part of being a friend is to work together.

Just as important as physical help, however, is emotional help. Your children need to learn to be good at giving comfort, as well as receiving it. When they are very little, they can learn to help each other that way. "Look, Darrell, Amy fell down and hurt her knee. See? We need to help her feel better. Let's give her a love." Years later you can still keep the same thing growing in your family by bringing appropriate problems into the open. "You need to be especially nice to Don tonight, Ben. He's been through a bad day—Sarah broke up with him. Maybe you could help him take his mind off it by getting him out to shoot a few baskets." Your children should feel all their lives that they have a responsibility toward the people they love; they should know that they can actually help other people feel better and that it's important that they try.

Of course, this doesn't mean that you should raise your children to be patsies all the time, allowing themselves to be manipulated by the Tom Sawyers of the world who are forever getting others to whitewash their fences for them. If one of your children gets his brother to "cover for him" by doing one of his chores, that's perfectly acceptable—as long as it doesn't always go one way. "Terry, I'm sorry, but I can't allow Sally to do the dishes for you again tonight. This is the third time in three weeks that she's taken your turn for you."

Sally may even say, "But I don't mind, Mom."

"*I* mind," you answer. "Terry is beginning to get the idea that because you love her and want to help, she can do anything she wants and you'll clean up after her. So I'll tell you what I'll do. Since you're doing Terry's work in the kitchen, you will also get Terry's time with the car." The point must be brought home that good relationships are balanced relationships. High demand is good, because every satisfied need between friends increases the bonds between them. But the high demand must work both ways, or it soon degenerates into a master-slave relationship.

One of the best ways to teach this lesson is in the parents' relationship with each other. Parents should often be seen helping each other, not just

Mom always helping Dad or vice versa. When children grow up knowing that their father is willing to come change a diaper so Mom can get dinner ready and that their mother is willing to come hold a flashlight so Dad can do the rewiring on the storage-room light, they will get the idea that friendship and love mean helping each other—equally.

Teaching your child to be affectionate, trustworthy, and helpful doesn't mean that you should insist he perform perfectly in every friendship. For your child to form a friendship that will last any length of time, he and his friend must first be attracted to each other. Telling your child to go "make friends" with a child who isn't the least bit interesting or attractive to him just won't work very often. Beyond the initial attraction, however, there must be a common liking and common interests to bind them together. The friend your child spent every free minute with during baseball season might not be the friend he sees much of when the mitts are put away. This doesn't mean your child isn't trustworthy—it just means that by silent agreement the friends are spending their time and investing their emotions elsewhere.

Another important facet of friendship is *being perceptive*. Unfortunately, there's no way to teach your child *how* to understand people—even the best-trained psychologists often don't fully understand a particular person. But at least you can train your child to *try*.

"Why do you think Arnie got so angry at you?" you ask your daughter.

"I don't know," she says.

"Well, what are some things that *might* have caused it?"

And so she thinks, and together you come up with a list of possibilities. The actual answers you come up with aren't half so important as the fact that you are teaching your child to look for answers. And the more he looks for the reasons others do things, for the desires and frustrations behind their actions, the better he will get at really understanding what other people are all about and the better friend he can be.

Personal Security

Perhaps the most important element of all is your child's personal security. A person who does not believe he is desirable or interesting is unlikely to put himself willingly into social situations, so it is important to help your child develop a good *self-image*. (See Chapter 2.) A person who has never been in a demanding social situation before, who has no concept of how to behave or even how to carry on a conversation is going to be afraid and timid. He is far more likely to fail, and each failure will add to his certainty that he just can't cope. It is important, as I pointed out above, for your child to have plenty of experiences at which he succeeds in order to build his *confidence*.

Friendship requires a certain amount of self-disclosure—letting someone else see you as you really are, warts and all. How can you let another person know your fears and your dreams, the things that hurt you and the things that make you feel good, unless you have a great deal of inner faith that even if that person then rejects you, you will still be able to try again? Those first steps of self-disclosure are incredibly difficult; it takes courage to risk rejection.

And let's face it. Rejection by another person is one of the most painful things that happens in life. Even total strangers can ruin your day by saying critical things about you—ask any actor who gets a bad review in the morning paper! And when someone you love dearly, someone you have trusted, turns away from you and rejects your friendship, it can be harder to cope with than if that person had died. Death of a person you love is painful because you no longer have him with you, but at least you are sustained by the knowledge of what you had. However, when the person you love turns on you and rejects you, it destroys not only your future but also your past. You look back and find that every good experience you had together is poisoned, and you can easily start hating yourself for having trusted him in the first place. Why else are divorces so terribly painful, leaving scars that widowhood is not half so likely to cause?

One thing is certain—you don't toughen up your kids against rejection by rejecting them repeatedly to get them used to it! What you do is help them build up a good, accurate self-image; help them gain competence in a wide variety of activities so that failure in one thing does not make them think they are total failures. Make sure they know your love for them is irrevocable and complete, that regardless of who else loves them they know you always will. No one is so lonely as the adult whose parents never loved him—that initial rejection is the only one that is almost impossible to get over.

Inevitably, as your children grow up, they will have experiences in rejection. Other children may ridicule them or exclude them from a group. How do you handle it? "They're not good enough for you anyway," is one strategy many parents use, but that really doesn't help. It just teaches the child that when he is rejected, he should reject back, and double! Getting even isn't a particularly good strategy to teach your child.

Instead, you should begin by comforting the child, reassuring him subtly or openly of his worth as a person so that he does not feel utterly lost. "I know you a lot better than they do, and I like you a lot," you say. Your child may pretend that that doesn't help at all: "Yeah, but you're my mother," he says—but he's only pretending. It does help a lot.

Next, help him try to understand why he was rejected. "You get good grades in school, and they don't get such good grades. Maybe they think you're only interested in studies, or maybe they're just plain scared of you." Get him trying to understand them, guessing at reasons why they might act that way. On an immediate level, talking about that sort of thing distracts your child from thinking about how miserable he feels. It is also a good idea if you help the child face honestly the things he might have done to promote that rejection. "When you kept bragging to them about your good grades, that probably turned them off. Maybe you shouldn't talk about grades to them—maybe you should try to get them talking about the things *they're* interested in." A problem unrecognized is a problem unsolved.

The third thing you should do to help your child cope with rejection is to get life back to normal as soon as possible. When your child has been comforted and you have tried to understand the reasons for the rejection, you should immediately get him engaged in normality. He should play basketball with his brother; he should run errands for you; he should do his chores; he should do his schoolwork. If he still looks depressed, give him a hug and ask him to cut the meat loaf; but you should still allow him some room for his private suffering. Don't insist that he forget it "because it isn't going to matter to you in six weeks." As an adult, you know that the hurt of a nine-year-old isn't going to last even that long, but the last thing he wants is to be told that the pain he is suffering is trivial.

Above all, be sensitive. Try to understand what he needs from you to get through the hard time of rejection. Eventually, he will learn to supply his own needs or find others who will help him meet them.

There is no way you will make your child entirely self-sufficient emotionally. That isn't even desirable. What you need to do is give your child enough inner strength to be able to rebound from a rejection or a loss and get back into his other relationships—and new relationships—as quickly as possible, instead of being completely destroyed by one failed friendship.

Moving

From the time your child enters junior high until he graduates from high school is when peers mean the most. It's very hard for the new kid in high school to break into the established social groups; it's also very, very wrenching for a child that age to suddenly be cut off from friends he has a strong emotional commitment to. So if you must move for business or some other unavoidable reason, make the blow as painless as possible. Try to move in the early summer so your child has a chance to get secure in his new home and begin to make contacts in the new community. If possible, let him visit the new place several times before you move, giving the initial anxiety a chance to fade. Encourage him to get the addresses of his old friends so he can write to them; let him make a few long distance phone calls. You might even allow him a trip or two back to the old town after the move, though not so much of this that he remains completely tied to the former community. If you aren't moving very far, you might let him stay in the same high school to finish out his last year or so. Even though you know from your own experience that many high school friendships don't last past graduation, you should also remember that those friendships are extremely important at the time. Just because something doesn't last forever doesn't mean it isn't valuable while you have it. Younger kids are pretty resilient about moves, as long as they aren't *too* frequent, but teenagers in some cases can be socially devastated by a move, and you should do everything you can to soften the blow.

Bad Social Strategies

There are some bad social strategies your child may learn, and you should be sensitized to them so that you recognize the problem if it arises. Psychologists Irving Weiner and David Elkind have identified four typical social strategies adopted by elementary school children: the bootlicker, the buffoon, the pseudo-adult, and the bully.

The bootlicker takes helpfulness to extremes. He tries to buy friendship with servility, flattery, bribes.

The buffoon makes himself the butt of humor in order to gain attention or approval. Sometimes this means undergoing considerable humiliation—or even physical pain, as the child is willing to do almost anything to get a laugh.

The pseudo-adult, failing to win acceptance among his peers, turns to the grown-ups around him for recognition and approval. He becomes the teacher's pet, not because he wants to but because the teacher is the only person he knows how to please. Adults see such children as excellent boys and girls—after all, they seem to respect adults, they conform to the rules, they often talk like grown-ups and perform very responsibly when adults assign them tasks. Actually, of course, they are failures at getting along with their peers, and they are miserable because of it.

The bully seeks out the company of smaller or inadequate children that he can terrorize and dominate. He cannot cope with equals, so he will rule those who lack will of their own or who are afraid of him. The bully and the bootlicker make a natural team—but it's a sick relationship.

What do you do if your own child has adopted one of these strategies? I doubt that you can attack any one of these directly. Certainly if you tell your pseudo-adult to stop spending so much time with you or to stay away from his teacher and not help so much after school, you will only be removing the one social success he has. The bootlicker is often terrified of losing what few friends he has been able to buy; the bully denies that he is browbeating anybody, and if you tell him he is showing immaturity you only make the problem worse. And trying to get the buffoon to stop being funny is pointless—if he loses his friends' laughter, he is afraid he will lose his friends.

The best strategy is simply to realize that your child needs extra help in building other social skills. Follow carefully all the other suggestions in this chapter, helping to build his self-image and giving him lots of chances to deal with other kids, eliminating any aspects of his appearance or personality that are making him repulsive to others, and building his skills in interpersonal relationships. Often it takes years to overcome your child's commitment to a bad strategy—but it can and must be done for the sake of your child's happiness.

The Solitary Child

Always keep in mind that some children have less need for social activities than others. Some perfectly healthy and normal children are loners—they like to read, collect stamps, work on model planes, sit and think. They have enough social contacts to satisfy their desires for acceptance, and they simply prefer having a lot of time to themselves, doing what they like to do. As long as this is not a pattern your child follows to the exclusion of all social life, don't worry too much about it. Let your child find his own desired level of social involvement. You only have to intervene when you can see that your child is simply not gaining any interpersonal skills at all, so that you worry about his ability to create and build strong love relationships as an adult. Then you need to gradually introduce more attractions for other children, involving your solitary child in more structured activities that force him to mingle with other kids. He may resist, but as long as you leave him some time for his solitary activities, he'll usually go along, and warm to the idea by and by.

As parents, you have the power and the opportunity to change your child's environment in such a way that he will grow socially as much as possible. The results won't be uniform, because every child is different. But you have a responsibility to give all your kids the best chance of success in life that you possibly can. Helping them develop social skills is one of the most important areas to work on.

4

How to Raise Your Child's IQ

CHILDREN ARE BORN with differences in their mental abilities. No more than two percent are mentally retarded to a marked degree, usually because of physical or genetic defects that cannot be changed significantly. But the intelligence of the overwhelming majority of children, even those with considerable disability, can be greatly affected by their upbringing, either negatively or positively.

Many people used to think that if you were born dumb or slow this was just your tough luck. There wasn't much you could do about it. And the same for smart kids: it was the roll of the genetic dice that made them that way. Like cream, the smart ones would soon come to the top and get their M.D.s or Ph.Ds or get appointed to the corporate presidency or be elected to a high office or write the novel of the decade. It was all in their genes.

However, an ever-growing body of research suggests that early environment plays a much greater role than we had ever before imagined. And environment is something over which mothers and fathers do have a great deal of influence.

In the 1960's, psychologist Wayne Dennis studied infants placed at a very early age in three orphanages in Teheran, Iran. These babies had been placed on their backs in shallow cribs with a minimum of attention. They were given no toys. They were never turned over, rarely picked up, and were fed mainly by a propped-up bottle. Almost no one talked to them. They were diapered when necessary and bathed only every other day. As they got older they were seated at a bench, row upon row, with a bar in front of them to prevent falling. They were given nothing to do.

Only fourteen percent could crawl at the age of two years. Only forty-two percent could sit alone at this age, and a mere fifteen percent could walk at the age of four. In contrast, non-institutionalized children nearly all sit alone by nine months and walk at twelve to fifteen months.

We have come to find out that as a general rule the more children per adult caretaker in an orphanage, the greater the mental retardation. The less time the adult can spend with each child, the more passive the environment and the less social, mental, and physical stimulation the infants receive.

It is estimated that a child's IQ drops five to ten points a year in such places. And it is not uncommon for the average IQ of children in such an institution to be thirty points below the population mean.

However, Dennis followed one group of children who were transferred to a second orphanage because they seemed more retarded than the other infants. In the second orphanage an amazing change occurred. The "more retarded" children began to flourish. Here they were given much more individual attention. They were held during feeding and given toys to play with. They were also "mothered" whenever this was possible. These children quickly caught up with and progressed beyond the supposedly more "normal" infants in the first orphanage.

Later, in an orphanage in Lebanon, Dennis found that by taking orphan infants out of their cribs just one hour a day and stimulating them with assorted objects and toys, the average gain in their development quadrupled. Added environmental stimulation of even one hour a day had made a profound difference in their growth and development.

Two other researchers, H.M. Skeels and Dye, transferred one- and two-year-old orphanage children to a school for retarded adolescent girls. The retarded girls were allowed to look after, talk to, and play with the orphaned infants as mother substitutes. Within two years, the children's IQ's had increased twenty-seven points, whereas the IQ's of the children remaining in the orphanage dropped twenty-six points.

One has to view these results cautiously because IQ's obtained at such an early age are not entirely reliable; but it is clear that the mothering and stimulation provided by even mother substitutes had a powerful effect on the intellectual development of the orphan infants, especially in comparison with the infants who remained in the orphanage without the extra stimulation.

Active Environments

It is only logical that a child who is raised in a stimulating, active environment will learn more—there is more around him to learn! But Siegfried and Therese Engelmann, specialists in early childhood education, found that an increase in stimulation in a child's environment not only increases the *amount* that he learns, but also increases his *capacity* to learn. It is as if the ability to learn grows with exercise: the more a child learns early in life, the more he is able to learn later on.

Other studies have clearly linked high IQs with an intensely active environment in childhood. Educational psychologist Benjamin Bloom summed up over a thousand research studies in his book *Stability and Change in Human Characteristics*, published by John Wiley & Sons, and found that the younger a child is, the greater the influence his environment will have on him. He suggests that children develop fifty percent of their intelligence by age four. In practical terms, this means that a child whose early life was unstimulating cannot make up for lost time. Lost opportunities in infancy are very difficult to replace by age five. Parents must realize that the greatest responsibility for their children's ability to learn rests with them; by the time the children get to school their *basic* intelligence is, for the most part, already formed.

Infants are learning something almost from the moment they are born, but there are certain times in a child's life when a particular skill or talent or ability is most easily learned. If that particular skill is not learned during that time it becomes difficult, sometimes nearly impossible, to learn the same skill later. The process is called *imprinting*—getting the message into the brain when the brain is ready to receive it.

Imprinting is quite noticeable in other animals. A duckling can be imprinted between thirteen and sixteen hours after birth to follow a wooden duck—or anything else about the same size—as its substitute mother. It forever remains attached to this block of wood, ignoring other female ducks or ducklings—even its own natural mother. Baby lambs separated from their mothers for a few days during the crucial imprinting period can never learn to follow the flock no matter how many years they are kept with other sheep.

Imprinting in human beings is not so obvious, but it is no less real. There is a crucial imprinting time for babies to learn to chew food. If a baby isn't given solid food around six months of age it will later reject it, vomit it out, or push it out of its mouth with its tongue.

Educator Maria Montessori maintained that the most sensitive period to learn to read is between four and five years of age. She maintained that writing skills are more easily acquired between three-and-half and four years of age than at six or seven, the age when this kind of training is typically started in school programs.

There is evidence that the human ear can become tuned or imprinted to music through experience. Children who are exposed to music in very early life appear to have greater than average music talent later on. The Japanese music educator Shinichi Suzuki has taken advantage of this fact in training thousands of preschool children to play the violin, with some learning as early as two and a half years of age. He first has the mother daily play a tape recording of several violin selections for the child to hear, starting as early as the first week of life. This music is imprinted in the child's brain. Later the child, using a miniature scaled down violin, will play these selections by ear. The reading of musical notation is taught much later.

Early Reading

The skill which most separates humans from the rest of the animal kingdom is language, and our language ability is probably the best single indicator of our intelligence. Effective language skills are the key to all other formal learning: math, science, and all humanities and social studies. If your child is not a competent reader or has difficulty understanding spoken language, he will have continued difficulty with school and be hampered in his understanding of almost all other knowledge areas. So if there is one single area of mental competence that a parent should emphasize in early stimulation of the child, it is language. Nothing approaches it in importance.

What can you do to help your child? You should talk—and sing songs—to your child from birth on. You should constantly speak in his presence, to him and to others in front of him. He will understand what you say long before he can speak himself.

Most babies start using single words at about twelve months and will have about a four-word vocabulary. At twenty-four months they will usually be speaking in three-word sentences. However, our twins, Chris and Rick—like most twins—were delayed in their speech until nearly three years of age. They chose to develop and speak their own private language which we could not understand. Despite their slow start, they later became highly fluent in English and easily learned a second language, Spanish, when they spent two years in South America in their late teens.

Being a good reader opens all kinds of doors and gives your child all kinds of advantages. Since you can give your child this early training it's hard to imagine why so many parents choose not to. You can start teaching your child to read using a home study course as early as two years of age. (In teaching our babies to read Lois made use of a special learning kit put together for parents who want to teach their preschoolers to read. For information write Career Institute, Dept 25-795-100, Little Falls, N.J. 07424.) Of course, some children won't be quite ready, but many will. This should be game-like fun, never forced. The teaching should be low-key, unstressful, and done in short time periods so as not to weary or bore the child.

Before you start this program, however, you should expose the child to readiness activities which include participation in plenty of conversation, especially asking and answering all kinds of questions, and reading aloud from the earliest years so that he will learn to listen, concentrate, and follow a story line. This will also stimulate the building of a good vocabulary. He can also learn the alphabet song, or you might help him collect a scrapbook of pictures of things that begin with each letter of the alphabet: *A* for ant, *B* for ball, etc. You can write a letter and the word by the picture on a separate page, then daily look through the scrapbook having them identify the letter and the word. This is a game most children enjoy.

When you read to him choose action-information stories with lots of pictures; fantasy-imagination material like the Dr. Seuss books and verse is excellent. Let him frequently choose what's to be read. Put him in your lap or beside you on the bed, couch, or rocker so he can "read" along with you. This is extremely helpful in creating interest and ability in reading, not to mention helping the child to bond to you emotionally.

Be sure the material you read is near the child's level of understanding, but remember that heavily illustrated adult magazines, like *National Geographic* or *Life* can be perfectly understandable to preschoolers if you discuss them in terms within the child's grasp.

If you are interested in specific helps on teaching your preschooler to read I would suggest you get a copy of Glenn Doman's *How to Teach Your Baby to Read*, published by Random House in hardcover and Doubleday-Dolphin in paperback. Another helpful book is *Give Your Child a Superior Mind* by Siegfried and Therese Engelmann, published by Simon & Schuster. These latter two authors also give suggestions on teaching your preschooler math, geometric patterns and relations, and algebra.

Doman has found at his Institute for the Achievement of Human Potential in Philadelphia that many children can read words when they are one year old, sentences by age two, and whole books by three. He has found also that many brain-injured children can read well at three years of age. This raises embarrassing questions about normal children who are not reading in second and third grade!

I always shudder when a parent brings in a twelve year old (usually a boy) who is virtually a non-reader. I grimace and hurt inside. Why did they wait so long? I know what they are going to say almost before they say it. They are at their wit's end. And so is the boy. He hates school. For too many years it has been a painful experience for him. He doesn't even try anymore. He usually finds a group of other "misfits" who have similar school problems, and they join together to commiserate with each other. They are all losers with battered egos. There's usually lots of sluffing class and petty delinquency. The kid gets off on the wrong foot and never quite gets his balance or catches up. And most of this could have been prevented if his parents, with professional help, might have diagnosed and solved his reading problem before he finished kindergarten.

The earlier the child starts remedial training the less the damage later. By training him before he started school, his parents might have solved the problem before it even began. But they didn't know.

What does it mean when a doctor diagnoses your child as a "dyslexic"? *Dyslexia* is merely a fancy word for "reading problems." Sometimes reading problems are inherited—the mind cannot make certain connections, or perceives letters in the wrong order, or cannot distinguish between the shapes of letters. Such problems occur in about twelve percent of all children, more often boys by a ratio of four to one. Usually reading problems are caused by far more manageable and correctable things.

For instance, reading problems may be caused by vision or hearing impairment, which might be corrected by glasses or a hearing aid. Even a minor hearing problem can seriously slow down language development, including reading. If the child cannot hear the word the teacher is saying, he will hardly know what is meant by the written word the teacher is pointing to. Other reading problems may be caused by faulty auditory perception, a garbling of sounds and the letters they represent, even though the child's hearing acuity is perfect.

After you have checked for such disabilities, you should check for a social or emotional problem that could be keeping your child from concentrating, or even being interested in learning. Have you just been through a traumatic divorce? Is the child abused by one of his parents? Is he adopted after years of being shuttled from one home to another? Does he have a poor relationship with this teacher; is he not getting along with the other children in class?

There are other problems that can interfere with his learning to read. Hyperactive children have a hard time concentrating long enough to read. Hypoglycemia, or low blood sugar, can also interfere with the child's concentration. Dr. Lendon Smith's *Improving Your Child's Behavior Chemistry*, published by Pocket Books, has some excellent advice on working with a child's diet to improve his neurochemistry and therefore his behavior.

Even if the child has some neurological problems, perceptual motor difficulties, or troubles with auditory or visual perception, he usually can be taught to read. The only exception to this is if the child is severely mentally retarded or acutely psychotic. Most children with mild retardation can be taught to read if given individual instruction at an early stage. This can start before school age if the child is emotionally stable and can pay attention even for brief periods of time.

The "dyslexic" youngster who has some kind of neurological damage usually has only one "channel" that is working. Maybe he has trouble decoding visual stimuli. Letters and words look to him like chicken scratches on the paper. Then you must use his hopefully normal hearing and motor skills to teach him to read.

Several methods of helping dyslexic children have been developed, but what is right for your youngster has to be determined by a careful diagnostic evaluation, and perhaps a program of individual tutoring to overcome his disability will be necessary. However, *any kind* of physical, auditory, visual, or intellectual stimulation you can give the child can only help.

In the 1960's Dolores Durkin studied children in Oakland, California, and New York City who had learned to read *before* they entered school and compared them with other children of equal IQ who had not. Then she followed these two groups of children through five grades of school. Her findings showed that the early readers not only began significantly ahead of the other children but also stayed ahead. The others never caught up.

When she tried to determine why the one group of children had learned to read before starting school and the others of equal IQ had not, she found that it had nothing to do with the children's innate ability or personality. The big difference was in the mothers. The mothers of the early readers *did* things differently and *believed* differently about how their children should be raised. They believed that they could and should teach their own child to read; they did not think it could only be done by a professional teacher. They also gave their children an enriched early environment, providing all kinds of materials to facilitate language and reading skill development. Every early reading home had some sort of blackboard. The mothers trained and coached their children in reading skills. They enjoyed teaching their children. They made time for them.

In contrast, the mothers of those children who did not start reading until they started school tended to believe that only a trained, certified teacher could teach children to read. They also claimed to be "too busy", even though there was no difference between the two groups of mothers in the average amount of outside responsibility.

Dr. Durkin's research powerfully suggests that parents and home environment can make a critically important difference in a child's intellectual growth and development. Somebody just has to care enough to invest time in the youngster.

Nursery School

I would next recommend that you seriously consider putting your child in a top quality nursery school (sometimes called a preschool) if you are financially able. The moderate expense may have a deeper impact on your child's success than his later and more expensive college education! Ideally, nursery school for a few hours a day should begin a year or two before kindergarten. I'm not talking about an all-day child care center, which is usually a babysitting agency for the working mother. The nursery school must be operated by professionals in early childhood education, and should not take the child away from home more than three or four hours a day. Of course, you will choose the best available preschool, not the most convenient one.

Before signing your child up you need to do some advance research. You'll want to evaluate the quality of the teachers, the nature of the curriculum, and the equipment available. Teacher quality is by far the most important factor. You'll want to know how the teachers relate to the children and how effective they are at teaching. What's the emotional climate of the classroom? To determine this, you should visit the preschool when it's in session and observe how the children are handled. (Don't bring your own youngster with you during this visit; make your observations without distraction.)

You should also get the names of several parents whose children attend. How do they like it? How do their children enjoy the preschool? Regarding curriculum, if all they do is engage in play activity which promotes large and small muscle development, with some arts and crafts and maybe a little recorded music, this is not enough. There definitely should be some emphasis on intellectual training, including a focus on language development, arithmetic and number comprehension, and even assistance in printing, writing, and drawing (not just coloring inside the lines). Preschools also should help the child develop creatively and emotionally, especially in learning how to relate to other children, a crucial skill.

"Teaching Machines" in the Home

Whether your child goes to nursery school or not, there are countless ways that you can give him a head start at home in becoming a successful reader. He will probably be exposed to TV programs designed to stimulate language and number skills—*Sesame Street, Captain Kangaroo, Mister Roger's Neighborhood, The Electric Company,* and *The Friendly Giant.* These are all potentially helpful, but you must not count on them for any major contribution to your child's reading progress. (See Chapter 22 on TV.) You will probably get better results from the world of electronics if you expose your child to phonograph records and tapes that combine stories and music. Nursery songs, fantasies, adventures, science, natural history, and stories about famous people are all available, often in public libraries where they can be checked out free. The very fact that they lack the visual stimulation of television means that your child will simultaneously learn to exercise his imagination and depend more on language. And though this surprises many parents, I have found that children often prefer these tapes to TV:

Books Join a library and take your child to it frequently to check out books. But he should also have some special books of his own which, like friends, he can turn to and read through again and again. Let your child choose books that interest him.

Games Play vocabulary-building games. Simple crossword puzzles, Scrabble, Boggle, categories, naming games, and charades are all helpful and useful. While traveling in your car you and your children can play the alphabet game, looking for words on signs or buildings that begin with each letter of the alphabet in turn. The winner is the one who first gets through the alphabet.

Letters Write family letters to relatives or distant friends, or to other members of the family. The children who know how to write can add their own messages; younger children can tell you what to write for them. It's a lot of fun when answers come back, and children realize the enjoyment of communicating with people outside their daily contacts.

Tape Recorders   Encourage your child to use a tape recorder to send "spoken letters" to friends. It's also helpful with the pronunciation of words and in the teaching or learning of music lessons. Record his best rendition of a tune on the violin, piano, trumpet, or whatever instrument he is learning to play; then play it back. Even young children love to make up stories, tell them into a tape recorder, and hear their own tales spoken back to them in their own language.

Converse, Don't Just Eat   Have lively and informative family conversations around the dinner tale. This is a great time to ask questions and raise all kinds of interesting topics.

Periodicals   Subscribe to both a morning and evening newspaper, as well as strongly visual magazines like *Life, Sports Illustrated, National Geographic,* and *Popular Mechanics.* Let your child feel that these magazines come as much for him as for you. You might also give him good comic books as rewards when his chores are done well or his behavior has been good. These combine interesting visuals, which children love, with highly interesting printed language. Many comics are well done and provide excitement without gore and titillation.

It's a good idea to subscribe to one or two excellent children's magazines that come especially for your child. Several that I would recommend are: *Humpty Dumpty's Magazine* (ages three to seven) 52 Vanderbilt Avenue, New York, NY 10017; *Jack & Jill* (ages four to ten) 1100 Waterway Boulevard, Indianapolis, IN 46206; *Child Life* (ages four to twelve) 1100 Waterway Blvd., Indianapolis, IN 46202; *Children's Digest* (ages eight to twelve) 52 Vanderbilt Avenue, New York, NY 10017; and Golden Magazines (ages eight to twelve) North Road, Poughkeepsie, NY 12601.

Family Books   You should have an encyclopedia in the home. For school-age children the best of the lot, in my opinion, is *World Book Encyclopedia,* right up through the twelfth grade. Another good set is *Compton's Encyclopedia.* These are well written in readily understandable language. If you habitually turn to the encyclopedia when questions come up and show your child *how* you look up the answer, he will soon learn to delve into the books himself to satisfy—or stimulate—his curiosity.

Every home should also have a good dictionary for school-age children. *Webster's New Collegiate Dictionary, The Random House College Dictionary,* or the *American Heritage Dictionary of the English Language* are inexpensive, will serve the whole family, and are not forty-pound monsters or multi-volume sets that discourage the younger children. There are also several dictionaries designed for younger school-age children. One I recommend for grades three through nine is *The American Heritage School Dictionary.*

You should also have several kinds of atlases and teach your children how to read maps. *The Rand McNally Road Atlas*, published in paperback, is inexpensive and always useful for showing children where things are or what route you're following on a trip. *Goode's World Atlas*, also paperback, has over 300 pages with many colored illustrations and maps. Children's encyclopedias often come with atlases. I also recommend that you have a free-spinning globe of the world in your home. As your children hear or read about news events happening in other countries, they are going to want to know where these countries are located and their relationship with the rest of the world.

Handwriting Training Handwriting is an acquired skill that requires a fairly high degree of eye, arm, and hand coordination. Hammering nails, catching balls, scribbling, putting together puzzle pieces, filling in color books, and cutting with scissors are all excellent activities which will help improve the child's handwriting and general motor coordination. To begin direct practice in handwriting, you first teach your child to write his name in capital letters. Then help him write simple nouns describing familiar things in his environment such as *dog, cat, ball.*

Private Practice As your child gets older and becomes more proficient in writing, you might encourage him to keep a diary—a marvelous way of increasing his verbal fluency and expressive skills.

Age Levels of Books Since you know it's a good idea for a child to be surrounded by books and magazines from an early age, you should plan on plenty of shelves and lots of display space. After all, if grocery store owners can put everything out in the open to attract you, you can certainly do the same for your children. But what book will be right for your child? Certainly you don't want to bore him with material far too juvenile for him; you also don't want to frustrate him with advanced material that will only turn him off to reading.

Fortunately, books are often labeled by age group. In a good children's section of a bookstore or library there will be distinct categories. The earliest children's books will be mainly pictures and the name of the item pictured. Alphabet books fit in this category. Soon, however, your child will graduate to books that tell simple stories but with a lot of illustration. Also, quite a few heavily illustrated books are exactly right for you to read to your three-year-old, and just as appropriate for a six-year-old to read to himself.

Librarians and good children's bookstore clerks can also be helpful, or write to the American Library Association, 50 East Huron Street, Chicago, Ill 60611, and ask for their free list of Caldecott Medal Books and Newbery Medal Books. Just enclose four first-class stamps to cover postage and include your return address. If you don't live close to a bookstore or library where you can browse with your children to let them find what interests them, you might want to write to Scholastic Books Service, 904 Sylvan Avenue, Englewood Cliffs, NJ, or 5675 Sunol Blvd., Pleasanton, CA, for their free Reader's Choice catalogue, which lists hundreds of good paperbacks for children that you can order by mail.

Little children aren't picky about plot. A two-year-old can have as much fun going through the Sears catalogue with you, labeling pictures, as he will have with a Caldecott winner. And long before a young child really understands the meanings of words in nursery rhymes and songs, he will love listening to them and even doing hand motions along with them. Your child will constantly surprise you by being ready for things you would have thought beyond him.

Toys and Play Space

Toys can be invaluable aids to a child's mental and neurological growth if selected wisely. They should be appropriate to the child's age, interest level, and degree of physiological maturity. An erector set for a one-year-old would be a waste of money and dangerous to the extent that the child might swallow some of the metal parts. A rattle or cradle-gym for a five-year-old would be contemptuously discarded in about five seconds as boring, unchallenging, and inappropriate.

Toys provide a powerful stimulus for play, and through play the child learns to test out, explore, and master his environment. This brings great pleasure and a sense of satisfaction to the youngster. The play of a new infant tends to be solitary in nature. He is not mature enough to engage in sustained social interaction. This means that toys, in particular, can play a vital role in his growth and development. The new infant must have a great deal of sensory stimulation: to hear a variety of sounds, touch all kinds of objects, observe, taste, and smell everything he can. Play is serious business. It's essential to learning.

Generally speaking, the simplest toys are the best because they encourage greater use of the imagination. Fifteen building blocks of various sizes and shapes provide years of stimulation and enjoyment for the child, while an electric robot which a child can only watch doing it's tricks is soon boring. Many a parent at Christmas has watched in dismay as their child ignores the expensive toy and plays with the box for hours, letting it become a fortress, a train, a house, a mountain. Children put simple toys together in an infinite array. They tend to break complicated toys down into their constituent parts—it's the only fun thing to do with them!

Research at the Harvard Preschool Project on the development of competence in young children suggests that it is unwise to keep a baby caged up for long hours in a playpen, crib, jump-seat, or high chair unless it's for a nap or as a temporary safety restraint while mother goes to borrow some eggs from the neighbor. Instead of confining your child, childproof your home by putting safety latches on forbidden cupboards, gates at the doors of forbidden rooms, and valuable and fragile items out of sight and out of reach. Then let the child have the run of the house. Being confined long hours in a playpen limits the child's opportunities for movement and motor growth. Instead of penning the child while preparing a meal, Mother might pull out four or five pots and pans, several ladles, and some large spoons for the baby to play with on the floor beside her. While Mother works at the sink or counter the baby "works" on the floor, with a flow of friendly words coming from Mother and grunts or single-word comments coming from the baby.

Balls of various sizes are another must for every child. Because each size looks different, bounces differently, and feels different, they provide endless hours of interest for all children. Dolls, teddybears, and other stuffed animals are toys that all children (of either sex) delight in. Many small children prefer cloth or furry textures to cold plastic or rubber, though the latter are more chewable and washable.

Most of our children also had a favorite "security blanket". This was a small, furry, soft-feeling blanket which they would haul around with them, chew on, and be very attached to. It seemed to fill a deep need to have something warm and soft to rub their face against or put their arm around. We never made a big issue of this since it obviously gave them a lot of comfort.

Here are some appropriate toys for various ages and growth stages:

FIRST TWELVE MONTHS
 1. Rattles
 2. Brightly colored mobiles strung above or across crib or playpen
 3. A cradle-gym (suspended above the crib) with different objects hanging down from it, such as small balls, teething rings, etc., which the baby can grab, kick, or look at
 4. Rubber squeeze toys that make noises
 5. A musical carousel or musical mobile that responds to the baby's touching or pulling
 6. A stainless steel mirror suspended above the crib so the baby can see himself
 7. Rubber teething rings which the child can put in its mouth and chew on
 8. Strings of large plastic beads to bang and chew on
 9. Floating toys for the bath
 10. Large colored balls
 11. Washable cloth books with pictures of familiar objects
 12. Old magazines and newspapers to tear, crumble, feel
 13. Pots and pans, wooden ladles, and other utensils to bang, stack, feel, hold lift

14. Soft animals and dolls to squeeze and cuddle

15. Foam rubber blocks and blocks with bells inside

16. Push-over toys that pop back up to standing position when shoved

17. Phonograph records for mother to play for baby: these should be simple melodies, very rhythmic, with clearly sung lyrics

18. Talking toys which the baby can activate by pulling a lever or string

19. Baby bouncers

20. Small nest of unbreakable plastic bowls

21. Colored sponges for in and out of bath-tub play

22. A "busy box" (container filled with all kinds of interesting things to handle, feel, play with: small toys, an empty tape spool, a small plastic bottle, a spoon, a jar lid, a metal mirror, small pictures. This can be purchased commercially or made up yourself, but remember that everything will go in his mouth so don't have anything that he might choke on or that might poison him)

23. And the best toy of all: you. Nothing will ever be as stimulating and fascinating as interacting with Mom or Dad

TWELVE TO TWENTY-FOUR MONTHS

1. A peg-board

2. Rocking horse

3. Large cardboard boxes of various sizes to crawl in and out of

4. Outdoor sandbox and small shovel and pail

5. Small rocking chair

6. Straddle toys (fire engine, animals on wheels, etc.)

7. Push-pull toys

8. Small doll carriage

9. Music box (crank it and music comes out)

10. Playdome (to crawl up and on)

11. Balls, books, phono records, dolls, furry or rubber or plastic animals

12. An outside playhouse

13. Toy cars, trucks, tanks

14. A pet dog (cats may scratch this young child)

15. Hammering and pounding toys

16. Toy xylophone

17. Outside water toys: plastic boats, coffee cans, cups

18. A small slide — inside or outside

19. A toy telephone that dials and rings

TWO TO THREE YEARS

1. Balls, books, phono record, dolls, furry/rubber/plastic animals, blocks, rocking horse, playdome, and slide left over from year one

2. A small tricycle
3. Clay and play-dough
4. A blackboard with white and colored chalk
5. A bulletin board to pin up all kinds of things
6. Crayons, lots of paper, blunt scissors
7. Pencils, felt-type pens with washable ink
8. A small desk or table and accompanying chair
9. Sled
10. Wagon
11. Outside swing set including climbing equipment
12. Counting toys and number puzzles
13. Flashlight
14. Garden tools
15. Housekeeping toys
16. Fingerpaints
17. Inexpensive cassette tape recorder or player
18. Rhythm instruments (bought or homemade) such as drums, cymbals, bells, triangles, tambourines
19. Simple puzzles
20. Play furniture, dishes, cooking utensils, small broom, carpet sweeper (either sex)
21. Take-apart, put-together toys
22. Dress up clothes for pretending and make believe (either sex)

THREE TO SIX YEARS (PRESCHOOL PERIOD)
1. Advanced versions of nearly all that have gone before, including balls, records, books, blocks, outside play equipment
2. Toys that allow imitation of adults at work: doctor, detective, space explorer outfits
3. Carpentry and garden tools, including wheelbarrow
4. Large-scale "ride-em" toys (scooters and wagons)
5. Art and craft materials: all kinds of paper (colored and white), crayons, chalk, easel, washable paint and ink, finger paints, felt-tip marking pens, glue, scotch tape
6. Simple board games
7. Trampoline (with supervision and careful teaching of safety rules)
8. Games that teach numbers: dominoes, telling-time, dice
9. Simple jigsaw puzzles
10. Kaleidoscope
11. Ice skates, sled, beginner skis
12. Hand puppets
13. Wading pool
14. Easy construction sets (Tinkertoy, Lego, etc.)
15. Coloring books

16. Toy trucks, autos, planes, trains, bulldozers
17. Knock-down dummies and punching bags
18. Dollhouses
19. Etch-a-sketch
20. Ant farm
21. Cuisenaire Rods (parents' kit) which enables parents to teach their children math as a game—order from Cuisenaire Co. (12 Church Street, New Rochelle, New York 10805)
22. Assorted puzzles and matching games (most sold commercially print on the top the ages which are appropriate to the games' difficulty and maturity level)
23. Rubber stamp set, so child can put letters together to make up his own stamp
24. Jump rope
25. Climbing ladders and monkey bars, swings

AGES SIX TO TWELVE
1. Jigsaw puzzles
2. Tetherball, table tennis, badminton, tennis equipment, archery, croquet, volley ball, football, baseball, basketball
3. Model kits for planes, boats, cars
4. Handicraft sets for leather, embroidery, beadwork, jewelry, metal
5. All kinds of card and board games. Scrabble, chess, checkers, dominoes, Monoply, Anagrams
6. Two-wheeled bikes
7. Magic sets
8. Camera
9. Chemistry and science sets, microscopes, telescopes, gyroscopes
10. Stilts
11. Trampoline
12. Kites
13. Sewing and weaving materials and equipment
14. Toy typewriter, printing outfit
15. A real musical instrument (guitar, drum set, ukelele, flute, xylophone, piano, or recorder)
16. A pet animal (this might include not only a cat or dog, but also a rabbit, gerbil, guinea pig, pony, bird, or turtle)
17. Transistor radio, phonograph player, tape recorder
18. Skis, skates, ice skates
19. Books for stamp and coin collection
20. Plus more mature versions of those items mentioned at the earlier ages: books, records, outdoor swing and slide sets, tools

In playing with toys a child develops small and large muscle coordination. He improves his perceptual-motor skills. He sharpens his vision. He learns the names of things. He does research on all the sensory qualities of the world he lives in—seeing, hearing, smelling, tasting, and touching everything he can lay his hands on. He compares the hardness and softness of things. He constantly compares everything he experiences with what has happened and has been experienced before. He learns to manipulate his environment. Neural fibers throughout the whole brain are being constantly activated and their growth stimulated. Memory traces are being filed away in vast numbers, improving his general competence.

According to Jean Piaget, probably the best-known specialist in child development in the world, it is from all the simple isolated acts like grasping, glancing, sensing, and feeling, as they accumulate and become organized in the brain, that later mature intelligence springs. Piaget also states that the more a child has seen and heard, the more he wants to see and hear.

The evidence is overwhelming that providing the preschooler with a vast range and spectrum of stimulating experiences will increase his intelligence. But doesn't this raise the danger of pressuring the child or pushing him beyond his capabilities? Couldn't this generate anxiety and maybe even be the foundation for the development of a neurosis? If done improperly it certainly could. If the small child is hounded and badgered with "stimulating experiences" it could eventually be a turn-off for him. But if it's done in the context of a joyful parent-child relationship, as fun, as play, as another game, the child will actually develop an ever-increasing appetite for such experiences. But remember always to terminate the activity a little *before* the child has had enough, whether it is reading together, playing records, a trip to the zoo, shopping, or playing ball.

Experiences for Teenagers

As your youngster gets older, he will tend to have a mind of his own. More and more he will want to have a voice in decisions that affect him. You may wish to give him experiences he feels indifferent or even negative about. He may not want to go along. It will require tact and diplomacy as well as shrewd leadership ability on your part to get him involved.

Here are a number of activities I have found that help stimulate a young person's imagination, mental competence, self-confidence, and inner discipline:

1. Participation in *any* athletic sports program generates self-discipline and self-assurance, which in my experience always has generalized to other more intellectual areas. It helps the youngster to compete, to organize his resources to accomplish some goal. There is a "cross-over effect".

2. Get your youngster employed. Each job he has will teach a great deal, not just about office work, supermarkets, landscaping or whatever area he is working in, but also about responsibility and getting along with others. For this reason, it is often wise not to have them work for you.

3. Many junior high schools, high schools, colleges, and universities have summer programs for juveniles, involving creative writing, drama, sports, math, history, social sciences, dancing. Sign them up for something that would interest them—just for fun.

4. Put your child on an "outward bound" or survival training experience. Make sure it's not one loaded with juvenile delinquents—some of these programs focus on rehabilitating kids who have been into heavy drugs or violence. Also check the leaders' qualifications and experience.

5. If your finances can handle it, put your child into a "study abroad" program for six or nine months. In some cases you can participate in an exchange program where your child will actually live in a foreign home.

6. Subscribe to two newspapers (morning and night) and as many magazines as you can afford, such as *U.S. News, Fortune, Sports Illustrated, Consumer Reports, Readers Digest, Harpers, Book Digest, Popular Mechanics, Newsweek, Time,* plus some special interest magazines that focus on family hobbies and interests.

7. Travel to interesting places. And do advance research if you are headed for a site with historic or current significance.

8. Encourage your child to participate in contests, run for office, try out for special scholarships, join school clubs in areas of interest, submit articles for the school newspaper, get in the school play. Don't be afraid to push a little here, but never give him the feeling that your love for him depends on his success. It's the trying that counts most.

9. Have a collection of games around the house that promote vocabulary growth, memory, number skills, powers of concentration.

10. Every night at dinner bring up current hot issues in the news, the latest scientific breakthroughs, what's happening in your line of work, or something of general interest you just read. If the kids tend not to join in or are somewhat nonverbal at times like this, then let Dad and Mom stage a conversation about any issues they want their children to "accidentally" hear.

Will all this guarantee that your children will be geniuses? Of course not. Nor will it mean that they will be "better" than other children. What this does guarantee is that your children will rise to their highest possible level of competence. You will be arming them with the mental tools to achieve their goals in life. You will be giving them the verbal skills to let them communicate well with other people. You will be teaching them that their minds are fertile, creative, competent, logical, that they can learn and remember what they have learned. Parents using wise strategies at the right times can powerfully stimulate their children's imaginations and intellectual growth. I see it happening all the time.

5

Effective Sex Education: Nurturing Affection and the Capacity to Love

YOU CAN TEACH the basic essentials of procreation to any reasonably bright six-year-old child in about thirty minutes. This includes the facts of menstruation, sexual intercourse, fertilization of the female ovum by the male sperm, the nine-months pregnancy cycle, plus the birth process itself. And you can illustrate this lesson using tactful diagrams or pictures from almost any home encyclopedia. If you want to include, for the benefit of the older children, a few words about venereal disease, abortion, contraception, tubal ligation, and vasectomy, add another half hour.

If you are still concerned that your youngsters may be sexual illiterates, let me remind you that, in addition to anything you and the school might teach them, they are also getting a daily massive media exposure—from popular movies, *Reader's Digest*, and Ann Landers to nearly every book on the fiction bestseller list and many nonfiction books, too. Then there are the hard-core pornographic pictures, written material, and dirty comics passed around furtively in the local high school, junior high, or even elementary schools. In fact, one can hardly go through a supermarket checkout counter without noticing the magazine cover condensation of some celebrity's latest sexual experience. This may be about an aspiring actress barely into puberty or a woman the age of one's grandmother—if it's slightly kinky it sells better.

In fact, never in history have young people been exposed to so much sexually oriented information.

Nobody would argue that children and teenagers don't need to have responsibly presented factual information on human sexuality and reproduction presented to them as they grow up. But that's not enough. I find that merely possessing knowledge about sex and its technology is no assurance or guarantee of a person's good sexual adjustment and happiness. Most of the teenage girls who get pregnant out of wedlock know about contraceptives; they choose not to use them. Lack of information is often not at issue. It is faulty attitudes, inappropriate feelings, and bad sex experiences that do most of the damage.

Some sex educators, unfortunately, treat sex education apart from these issues. They downplay values, personal responsibility, and the total complex of male-female relationships. They think that technical manuals and massive information doses alone lead to a kind of sexual super-maturity and personal fulfillment.

Teaching Young Children about Sex

I've observed that from the time children start to talk until the beginning of school or maybe a little later, most have a refreshing, unashamed innocence about their bodies. It is at this time that you will find them asking many questions honestly and openly about their origins.

At this age the child usually spends more hours with the mother and often has a close emotional bond with her. Thus, Mom usually will be thrust into the role of the child's first sex educator; but both parents should be prepared. When the child asks the tough questions, be sure to answer. But do it at his or her level of understanding. Probably the child will be less embarrassed than you about it all. But you need not engage in over-kill. An answer of a few sentences will usually suffice; half-hour lectures are not needed. If your answer stimulates a further question, answer briefly and directly. Use words and terms you feel most comfortable with. It's your attitude and feelings as much as what you actually say that will influence and stay with the child.

Often when Mother is pregnant, a young child will be excited by the expectation of a new arrival. This offers you a marvelous opportunity to allow your child to feel the unborn baby kicking in your "stomach". You can answer simply and honestly the stream of questions about pregnancy, birth, and conception that the child will ask. There are many picture books or home encyclopedias which will allow the child to see what their unborn brother or sister looks like at any period during the pregnancy. Thus it is possible to make mother's pregnancy an exciting adventure and educational experience for children. I would also recommend reading to the young child books such as the beautifully told, tastefully illustrated *The Marvelous Story of How You Were Born* by Sidonie Gruenberg (published by Doubleday).

In addition to answering the young child's natural curiosity about reproduction and birth, children should be taught at an early age how to cope with child molesters. This instruction should start at about the time they are first walking to school or the store alone. You tell them never to accept rides, gifts, or candy from strangers. You explain that some of these people (ninety percent men) are sick, and sometimes they try to do improper things like undressing children or taking off their own clothes. They should be avoided.

Often this can be taught in the context of a newspaper article about a molestation. Or it can even be a personal experience of one of the parents or a neighborhood child which would illustrate the point. While you don't want to traumatize your children or exaggerate the danger in discussing it with them, you shouldn't minimize it either. A small anxiety they can handle, while a brutal molestation could leave permanent scars that might never be entirely erased.

Children with low self-esteem and little self-respect are especially vulnerable to the molester's blandishments, and remember, the victim could be your son just as well as your daughter. You should also instruct them that if they are ever approached improperly by anybody, they should immediately let you know. Frequently child molesters are neighbors or even relatives. Such a person may abuse and intimidate the child, threatening her if she tells. The child should know ahead of time that she must resist all improper advances and inform you about it as soon as possible, and you will protect her from retaliation.

This is especially important because molesters are repeaters, and they can be teenagers as well as men in their sixties. They may be regular church-goers or atheists; they may be single or married. If successful once with a child, there is a high probability of the molester coming back for more, in a compulsive, obsessional fashion. Good judgment, fear of being caught, and conscience all seem temporarily absent when a molester approaches a target child, and worse may happen the second time.

The situation is entirely different, however, if there is sexual experimentation between two of your pre-teen children who are near the same age. Usually, the one who initiates the sexual encounter is interested, excited about sex, and unable to control his naive sexual curiosity. You should not sanction any repetition of the act. Kindly explain to him that his behavior simply cannot be permitted; point out even if you have already done so beforehand that the proper use of sex will come later in life. Let him know that you find his sexual activity inappropriate, but that you still love and care about him as a person. This also offers you an opportunity to give your child some explicit factual information about sex and to present your own values with a broad perspective of how sex fits into the grand scheme of man-woman relationships. If the situation persists, see a counselor.

Setting an Example of Healthy Married Love

Why doesn't the mere possession of the facts about sex guarantee healthy sexual adjustment? Because healthy sexual adjustments can never be considered apart from the total man-woman relationship. If you want to teach your children healthy attitudes about sex, one of the most important things you can do for them is to demonstrate a healthy, loving relationship in your marriage.

Children need to see parents showing love, affection, respect, and loyalty to each other. Seeing you argue occasionally does not hurt if there is usually a successful outcome, and quarrels need to be more than balanced by good times and good days. Thus, the greatest gift a father can give his children is to demonstrate his love for their mother, and vice-versa. I'm convinced that this will do more than almost any other single thing to instill healthy sexual attitudes and feelings in children.

If, despite an otherwise healthy relationship, there are continuing unresolved sexual problems or blocks, the parents should see a counselor who has specialty training in counseling sexual difficulties.

The primary, most crucial commitment in the family is spouse to spouse; the parent-child commitment comes second. If the bond between husband and wife is good, everything else can flow from that. Sure, the children need lots of love and attention, but if the wife consistently puts her husband second or third on her priority list, his interest in her will eventually lessen. He may feel rejected, become depressed, work two jobs, stay late, or find someone else. Eventually both the wife and her children lose. And it works similarly the other way around, when a husband puts his job or his friends before his wife. If his work is always number one in his life he may become prosperous or famous, but he may lose his wife's and children's love.

This never happens overnight, of course. There are certainly times when a man has no choice but to invest all of his energy in his work to save a dying business or get through school or hold three jobs to pay for the second mortgage on the new home. Or the wife's career, children, and social life may stretch her to the point where life is no longer fun and she's chronically under stress. That condition cannot go on indefinitely without an eventual major disturbance or blow-up in the marriage.

I have seen a legion of men and women, unloved and neglected in their marriages, who wither and go stale. They become vulnerable to an affair, get chronically irritable, or are too often angry or hard on their kids. They often pull into a shell and have a continuing low-grade depression, or they may turn to booze, physician-prescribed drugs, or other sex partners. These eventually are all dead-end strategies, resolving nothing, and only create other problems. Some frustrated spouses try more positive strategies and seek new careers or further education. This may not be a bad solution, but it doesn't cure the dull aching void inside, and the kids always get the short end of the stick one way or another.

Dad and Mother need to like each other, be friends as well as lovers. They need to show loyalty, put each other first, have a good sexual adjustment. This teaches the children, day after day and year after year, how it is possible for a man and woman to relate to each other. It can be a practical demonstration of how parents can negotiate, handle stress, and mesh their personalities in such a way that they don't lose their identities. Being loved, they can facilitate each other's unique personality development. They can experience growth with an inner sense of fulfillment unknown to the unmarried or badly married. Remember, parents need love just as much as children do. The kids need to see them getting love as well as giving it.

*Commitment to the Marriage and Spouse** I see seemingly compatible couples end their marriages in divorce because of lack of commitment, while other couples with fairly major problems of incompatibility survive and wind up eventually with quite good marriages. Why? Simply because they have *decided* to make it work. Even if you have many marital problems that need resolution, you can still consciously decide to love each other. Love is a daily decision! And if both husband and wife make that decision, they can overcome considerable differences of personality and temperament, but the commitment, will, and energy still have to be there for it to work.

Effective, Positive Communication This means more than just speaking words to each other. Many couples communicate a great deal—negatively through chronic fighting, criticisms, put-downs, and expressions of rejection which scar deeply. In fact, such a couple may communicate too much! This kind of negative communication separates people. Effective communication must include positive verbal exchanges—happy talk as well as pleasant negotiation. It means dealing with feelings in open and honest but non-attacking ways.

To experience negative feelings is no crime, but you are still responsible for what you *do* with your feelings and how you handle them. Thus it would be permissible for a wife to share with her husband that she has some negative feelings towards him. She might comment that some of the things he has done have caused her a great deal of distress. But she need not yell or scream at him. And she need not call him vile names or attack his masculinity or family or friends, or do other things that might be very damaging. Likewise, the husband can share his feelings with his wife without attacking her personally. He need not call her names or repeatedly point out her deficiencies in hurtful, denigrating ways.

I have found that good communication skills can be learned. It is easiest to learn to communicate while growing up, but if you didn't learn then, you can learn now through an effective therapy experience or through various communications training workshops for couples. It won't be easy, but it's possible.

Dealing with Conflict Responsibility This involves two techniques: First, diffuse your immediate explosive anger. This can be accomplished by such simple expedients as taking a walk, taking a very hot or cold shower, or otherwise disengaging temporarily while each partner cools off. Second, engage in thoughtful, committed, reasonable negotiations so tnat you can find some mutually acceptable solutions to your problems. Good negotiations can end in any one of three ways: acquiescence, compromise, or stalemate.

*I am indebted to marriage counselors Dr. David and Vera Mace for many of the ideas presented here.

Acquiescence means that one partner "gives in" to the other's wishes. The wife, for example, may wish to visit her mother on their vacation. The husband is opposed to this and would prefer to do other things, but because he loves her and is committed to their relationship he may on this occasion agree to do something that he really doesn't want to do. This, in a sense, is a gift of love. The rule here, however, is that there should be reciprocity in this approach. What is sauce for the goose is sauce for the gander. On some occasions the wife may acquiesce, but she shouldn't do it all the time; the husband should take his turn, too.

Compromise is a negotiated solution in which some of the needs of both parties are met. Each of you gives up something; each gets something. Sometimes a compromise is not exactly fifty-fifty, but the "tilt" should not always be in favor of the same spouse. There should be reciprocity over a period of time, so that in the long run it works out that both parties feel they have justice—a fair share of the goodies as well as chores. But it's dangerous to keep an exact tally sheet—this always degenerates to keeping score, and soon turns a marriage into a war.

The third valid result of negotiation is to agree to disagree. You simply "put it on the shelf". Some issues cannot be instantly resolved, and what frequently happens is that with time and the discovery of new data or with changing circumstances, natural solutions later emerge—the problem solves itself.

If you agree to disagree, you should recognize frankly that for the time being you see things differently. Neither of you is yet willing to make a commitment to go along with the other person on the matter. This is not a disgrace. It should be candidly admitted.

Perhaps you are surprised that I have spent so much time on the parents' marriage relationship in a chapter on sex education of children. Yet in my experience this is exactly the way it has to be. You really cannot effectively deal with sex outside of the context of the total man-woman relationship.

While it is true that some men and women are great actors in (and out of) the marital bed, I have found that they usually cannot continue indefinitely to be a turned-on sex partner unless the relationship ultimately offers them something more than genital tumescence. Good sex techniques alone cannot sustain a relationship any more than candy bars alone can sustain your physical health. Good sex is facilitated by the totality of a good relationship, and many sexual adjustment problems stem from problems in other areas of the marriage.

How do you teach children about things like this? Easily. You teach them that sex is part of a whole, part of an integrated relationship. If you teach them anything less you have failed.

Pornography: Sex Miseducation

One interesting phenomenon in the area of sex education has been the vast increase in sexually-oriented material available in all media. Hard-core cinema and porno bookstores are established in most U.S. cities. However, despite the illusion of sexual openness, the old misinformation is simply being replaced by new and no less harmful mythology under the guise of freedom and liberation. Furthermore, there is a very real anti-female bias in most of the pornography that is produced. Extremely sexist, it gives false information, both covert and overt, about human sexuality and especially about female sexual response.

Pornography is produced almost entirely by males for male consumption, usually by people operating on or beyond the edges of the law. This trend to dehumanize women in media sex has been duly noted by both militant feminists and more conservative, anti-ERA women—one of the places where both camps agree.

Women almost never go to see porno films by themselves. When they do go it is out of curiosity, and usually at the behest of a boyfriend or husband. And in most cases it's a turn-off experience as they watch the sexual exploitation of other females.

For some males porno viewing can become voyeurism, a minor sexual deviation, and when men get into this to any degree I often find three things happening to them. First, there can be an *addictive* phenomenon. Some men get hooked on this kind of thing and keep coming back for more and more for sexual stimulation. Second there is *escalation*, wherein it takes increasingly stronger and rougher material to give the man his sexual turn-on. And third there is an increased risk of *acting out* the sex acts that he sees, often disturbing the marital relationship as his wife becomes unwilling to perform increasingly bizarre or degrading acts.

I also see some porn as actually being anti-sexual and giving considerable misinformation about sex. Since sustained porno viewing is increasingly becoming a required "macho" experience for adolescent and young adult males, it has to be considered as one important part of their sexual experience and education. With pornography repeatedly presenting females as dehumanized sex objects, healthy relationships with women could become more and more difficult for them to establish, and women have a right to be concerned.

Sociologist Diana E. H. Russell comments,

Pornography is vicious, anti-woman propaganda. It tells lies about us. It degrades women. Pornography is not made to educate but to sell, and for the most part, what sells is a bunch of lies about sex and women. Women are portrayed as enjoying being raped, spanked or beaten, tied up, mutilated, enslaved, or they accept it as their lot as women to be

victims of such experiences. In the less sadistic films women are portrayed as turned on and sexually satisfied by doing anything and
everything that men order them to do, and what this involves is for the
most part totally contrary to what we know about female sexuality;
i.e., it is almost totally penis-oriented, often devoid of foreplay,
tenderness, or caring, to saying nothing of love and romance.

Susan Brownmiller sees much woman hatred in pornography, and she
wrote in her *Against Our Will*, "Pornography, like rape, is a male invention,
designed to dehumanize women, to reduce the female to an object of sexual
access. The gut distaste that a majority of women feel when we look at pornography comes from the gut knowledge that we and our bodies are being
stripped, exposed and contorted for the purpose of ridicule, to bolster that
'masculine esteem' which gets its kicks and sense of power from viewing
females as anonymous, panting playthings, adult toys, dehumanized objects
to be used, abused, broken and discarded."

Some may argue that women such as Russell and Brownmiller are just
uptight feminine extremists, but I don't think we can so easily dismiss their
concern. I've seen too many sexually unhappy couples where the woman has
been treated as an object or thing, where she has been manipulated, conned,
and used. This is always damaging to the relationship as well as devastating
to the woman's self-respect.

Where do men learn these attitudes? We do live in a sexist culture, and I
think some types of pornography provide a lethal type of sex miseducation
for a boy to feed on. It stimulates him sexually and pairs this arousal with a
lot of false images and feelings about females, raising the possibility that he
may need to *act out* some aspects of deviant pornography in order to be sexually satisfied.

In summary, if you wish your children to have healthy sexual attitudes
and adjustment, consider the following:

1. Be sure your children have been exposed to accurate information and
knowledge about human reproduction and human sexuality. Teach them at
their level of understanding. This starts when they can first talk and ask
questions.

It may be done through informal conversations and having books lying
around the house which have appropriate sex education information in them.
The children, in privacy, can pick them up and read them.

However, it is vital for parents also to formally educate children at inter-
vals during childhood. If parents do not want their children to collect misinformation from peers, popular literature, and pornography, they must
assume responsibility for conveying accurate information—along with their
own values. In order to do this, however, most parents must educate
themselves to fill gaps in their knowledge due to their own inadequate past

education. Personal reading will also desensitize many parents so they are more at ease in discussing sexuality.

It is also important to consider that one of every two couples has some sort of sexual dysfunction or difficulty. It may be difficult for many of these couples to convey a positive attitude toward sexuality unless they seek out some kind of help to overcome their hang-ups.

2. Model a healthy, loving relationship in your own marriage. This allows the children to see and witness firsthand how men and women can live together peacefully and lovingly. It also demonstrates how Mom and Dad work through their occasional conflicts. In other words, put your own marriage in order. If you have sexual hang-ups, get counseling and help.

3. Give your children a good self-image and help them to be comfortable with their sexual role. Develop their self-respect. This comes from their having proved competence. I have found that having an inner sense of self-worth will be a powerful contributor to your child's ultimate sexual adjustment. Women in particular who don't like themselves nearly always have sexual adjustment problems.

4. Be cautious about your kids' exposure to pornography, especially your male children. At least share with them your concerns about the "hidden messages" of this type of material—let them know that the greatest danger of most pornography is not that it is "dirty" but that it is dishonest about sex.

5. Teach them good sexual values. Knowledge of mere technique without values can produce monsters. You must teach them a concern and sensitivity to the needs of other people, a respect for their individuality, and a refusal to exploit them.

6

Conscience and Moral Values: Keeping Your Kid Out of Jail

OUR DAUGHTER JANICE was seven months old and got around the house mainly by crawling when I noticed that she had a special fascination for looking at and touching appliance and lamp plugs stuck in the baseboard electrical outlets. I felt vaguely uncomfortable about this but said little until one day I noticed her pulling at a plug with her hand covered with saliva.

As she put her little fingers in and out of her mouth and then touched the electric plug, I instantly went to her side. I explained with some intensity and feeling in my voice, "No, Janice, stay away from there. You could really hurt yourself. *No, no, no!*"

I then put her in another corner of the room, giving her a plastic toy to play with. But ten minutes later, with one eye on me, she again began fiddling with the lamp plug.

"Janice!" I said, sharply and emphatically.

She jumped back from the plug and quickly scurried away with the guiltiest look on her face I'd ever seen. She was very obviously aware, even at seven months, that she was engaging in forbidden behavior and instantly desisted when caught and confronted. She had a conscience, or at least the beginnings of one.

How does the conscience develop—or fail to develop—from this weak beginning stage? An example: Lori, age nine, complains tearfully, "Mother, somebody's taken my lunch money out of my purse! It was two quarters and a dime. What'll I do for school lunch today?"

Fifteen minutes later the exact change is found in thirteen-year-old brother Jimmy's back pocket. Since he has taken money before, he quickly became a prime suspect for Mother. "Jimmy," Mother says angrily, "how did this money get into your pocket?"

"How would I know? Quit accusing me! Maybe somebody put it there just to get me into trouble."

Later discussions with Jimmy when Dad comes home bring further protests of innocence, all said with emphatic sincerity, while looking his parents right in the eye and even shedding a few tears at their disbelief.

The matter closes with that, but both parents feel uneasy. They know Jimmy has been caught before in a number of outright lies. They murmur,

"What kind of son do we have here? Where did we go wrong? Has he no conscience?"

What Can Parents Do?

Various studies have repeatedly shown that all young people, even non-delinquents, break a lot of rules because of immaturity, ignorance, poor judgment, or "just being their age." They do many things which our statutes would define as illegal and punishable offenses.

This does not necessarily mean that they are sociopathic—that they have no conscience. It does mean that parents have to keep on teaching ethics or moral behavior. Parents have to clearly define and label improper behavior. If a child steals money out of your purse, you can't pretend you didn't see it or don't know. Parents have to take a stand and draw a line *repeatedly*. Teaching moral values and ethical behavior takes many years.

Also, it's critically important that Dad and Mother behave morally and responsibly themselves if they expect their children to do likewise. With children, it's "monkey see, monkey do". This is more than just a catch phrase. It accurately summarizes a vast amount of research in the area of modeling and imitative learning. If Dad regularly beats up his wife and kids, guess what most of his sons will do when they get married? Most child abusers were themselves abused. So the rule is: If you want your children to have good values, model them yourself. Then, have a good relationship with the kids so they identify with you and your values. They will unconsciously incorporate most of these into their own conscience.

A Look at Delinquency

Close to half of all felonies (serious crimes) are committed by persons seventeen years of age or younger. Although adolescents account for only one-seventh of the population, they commit a vastly disproportionate amount of crime. Also, adolescent criminals are primarily male. Females account for only ten to fifteen percent of serious teenage crime. Most people who commit criminal offenses are neither apprehended nor jailed; those who go to jail are usually repeaters. For example, the recidivism (or repeat) rate for murder is sixty percent. For robbery, rape, and assault it is seventy-five percent.

Many young delinquents are severely behind in reading skills, and in most cases this backwardness cannot be attributed to low intellectual ability. They frequently have a history of anti-social behavior, and their pattern of interaction with their parents tends to be undisciplined, inconsistent, primitive, hostile, and full of conflict. Their families tend to be larger and in the lower socio-economic classes.

In my experience there are six kinds of delinquent children, and it is important, if we are to be helpful to the child who misbehaves, to know what type he or she is. Treatment strategies which are appropriate for one kind of delinquent are often entirely inappropriate for another.

1. *Just fooling around*   Such a youngster engages in a lot of normal foolishness and mischief-making which parents sometimes overreact to and mislabel as delinquency. This may involve coming home late, truth stretching, occasionally cutting school, kicking over neighborhood garbage cans, or sneaking into the back door of a movie house without paying. It might include constantly teasing brothers and sisters, letting the air out of somebody's tires, setting off a stink bomb at the high school dance, and minor experiments with drugs. The prankster might borrow the family car without a license or permission, spray paint a neighbor's fence or a school building, or set off illegal firecrackers outside the church windows Sunday morning.

All these behaviors are disturbing and irritating and sometimes approach petty vandalism, but they are still relatively minor. As the youngster is consistently apprehended, disciplined, and required to make restitution, he almost always matures out of such habits and settles down. Though upsetting and distressing for adults, these pranks ordinarily do not indicate acute pathology and do not often escalate into more serious criminality. They merely reflect high spirits, irreverence, and a willingness to risk and dare, often in association with like-minded companions.

The best parent strategy for dealing with these high jinks is to make sure the youngster suffers certain and just consequences. Penalties should fit the nature of the misdeeds and should keep recurring as irrevocably as death and taxes. If your youngster kicked over garbage cans, he must clean up; if he does it again, he must clean up again. But parents should still maintain their good humor and continue to work on and develop a good relationship with the youngster. They should make sure to have happy times with him or her at mealtimes, for instance, or on family outings.

Parents should also encourage such a child to work. Boredom and lots of free time invite him to amuse himself—often destructively. You may also want to discourage his association with friends who clearly influence him negatively.

2. *Parent-kicker*   This youngster's antisocial acts are, at the core, a way of retaliating against one or both parents. Somehow his relationship with his parents has degenerated over the years into a war. Often parents are taken by surprise when, in early adolescence, their child suddenly becomes hostile. They don't realize that he has been resentful for years and only now is beginning to show his strong negative feelings. Sometimes these parent-child wars become so intense that the child should be placed for a while with a relative or in a foster home; sometimes the child simply runs away.

For example, Bruce reminded his mother of her hated ex-husband, who had deserted her years ago. Bruce had the same narrow eyes, whiny voice, and deceitful way about him, and she concluded, "Like father, like son." Afterward she readily admitted that in raising her two children she greatly favored Bruce's younger sister, and even when Bruce was a small baby she would savagely punish him when he cried or became upset and colicky.

Bruce keenly felt the rejection and antagonism. As the years went by he learned to get back at his mother by infuriating her with a great variety of mischief. Eventually he started running away, only to be caught and returned to receive further abuse and violent condemnation. In time the mother-son conflict became unbearable for both.

In another example, Jenny was the third of three girls in the Mattson family. Her father had always wanted sons. When she was born the disappointment was especially keen for him, and he never forgave her for it. He was a stern and unloving man who was not given to praising or seeing anything positive in his wife or daughters.

Jenny soon found that there was nothing she could do to please him. In time she did learn his sensitive spots and became remarkably adept at provoking anger in him. She would use provocative language around the house, became sexually promiscuous, and stole money from his wallet to buy drugs. She learned to enjoy triggering his anger as he found out about her delinquencies; it pleased her to see his face purple with rage.

Since these vicious parent-child circles take years to develop and become deeply imbedded family habits, they often take considerable time to change. In my experience, the prognosis for this type of problem is directly related to the age of the child. That is, the younger the child when treatment of him and his parents begins, the greater the chances for change.

With the "parent-kicker", the child's improper behavior is merely a symptom of a disturbed parent-child relationship. Often when the child is moved into another family situation where his basic emotional needs are met, where he experiences reasonable controls plus a lot of love and friendship, his behavior miraculously improves. Sometimes this is the only solution that works.

3. Bad buddy Clinicians sometimes refer to this as the dyssocial personality. There is nothing basically wrong intellectually or emotionally with the child except for improper learning—from association with delinquent buddies or, more rarely, from being raised in a delinquent family. In other words, the child has a conscience, but it's tuned into the norm of his antisocial peers or shiftless parents. His loyalty is to them, and he lives by their rules.

What was learned can usually be unlearned; this kind of child can be rehabilitated. A fictional example would be Oliver in Charles Dicken's *Oliver Twist*. He comes out of Fagin's den trained to steal, lie, and cheat, but given a change to a better environment he learns better habits.

It often works the same way in real life: Frankie's father died when he was three. His mother, a good woman with failing health, had to work long hours at low pay to support him and his two sisters. It seemed his mother was never home except when sick, and a woman in an adjoining apartment would look in occasionally to see if everything was all right. TV and the streets were his main recreation.

In time he associated with a gang of boys. They called themselves the "Hit Men". They engaged in a variety of petty vandalisms and stealing, getting into fights and giving the local girls a bad time. Boredom and depression they countered by using alcohol and drugs.

His mother died when he was fourteen, and he was sent to live with distant relatives on a farm in Ohio. He made the change in life styles remarkably smoothly. He enjoyed farm work, especially taking care of animals, and prospered in the much smaller high school that he now attended.

After finishing twelfth grade, he attended a trade institute. Eventually he became an electrical contractor, married, and fathered two children. He is currently living in a small Ohio town, where he is a member of several civic organizations. He is a regular attender at his wife's church and is regarded favorably by all who know him as a responsible citizen and good Republican.

Since this type of delinquent responds to a change in environment, it may necessitate a move for the family to get away from a delinquent area, or it might mean sending him to live with an aunt or uncle for several years or some such similar strategy.

4. Organic In this case the child is brain-injured or mentally retarded, with a sometimes explosive temper and poor control of his emotions. His delinquencies are due primarily to impaired intellect and poor judgment.

Unfortunately, he is often teased and tormented by other youngsters in the neighborhood because he is different or because he seems helpless. Sometimes he becomes mean, like a dog that is repeatedly kicked. Such children have to be protected, supervised, and in some instances institutionalized. However, this is very rare.

They should be given training in simple skill tasks so they can become productive citizens to the extent that this is possible. Some can learn to do simple labor for pay, but usually they need to be under somebody's protection and supervision. Their so-called delinquent acts are strictly incidental to their basic organic or brain problems.

5. Psychotic This youngster is mentally ill, insane, or psychotic; he may hallucinate, feel that people are out to get him, and at times have very irrational thoughts and ideas. One such young boy, fourteen years of age and intellectually very bright, shot and killed both of his parents. His explanation was, "I had to. They tried to stop me from shooting the superintendent of the school."

This young man spent several years in a state mental hospital. He later was released when it was found that he responded well to medication, one of the phenothyazines. This frequently is very helpful in dampening the symptoms of psychosis and clearing the person's mind. He subsequently married and had a son. However, he has found that to function responsibly and without the symptoms of his psychosis he has to take his medication daily.

While not all psychotic youngsters might go to such extremes of violence, they still can be very disoriented and confused in their approach to life. They need help, medication (usually), supervision, and protection.

6. *"Bad seed"* This type of youngster is often called a "primary psychopath". His delinquency is characterized by a life-long repetition of anti-social acts, virtually unaffected by any therapy. This deviance is noticeable at a very early age, often even before starting school.

Usually male, the "bad seed" keeps on committing antisocial acts whether he is caught and punished or not. Neither fear nor conscience works to stop him, and it isn't just conscience he seems to lack—he is also unable to learn any of the positive, prosocial behavior patterns. He is unable to love anyone consistently. He is irresponsible, undependable, and unable to learn from experience. He feels no shame, no guilt.

"I scream at him," his father says. "I yell at him, I punish him, I beat him. Sometimes you might say I'm guilty of child abuse. But nothing touches him. He still persists in his behavior."

Such a child is utterly self-centered. Whenever he feels an impulse, he carries it out. He can't bear to postpone any pleasure—he must be satisfied now. He lies without any obvious motive, yet he can be very charming, very likeable, and he is an expert at manipulating and exploiting others. While he can get very angry or irritated or frustrated at times, he seems unable to experience anxiety—the anticipation of future unpleasantness—which is one of the main emotions that prevents most people from committing illegal acts.

However, he is almost never psychotic or mentally retarded, showing no sign of being "crazy". In fact, he is often bright, glib, articulate. He can be an ardent lover for one night, but he is a disappointing husband and father. He is often sexually promiscuous, and if he gets pleasure from drugs and alcohol he will use and abuse them as often as he likes.

To date no treatment really works with the "bad seed". Sometimes he mellows with age. Sometimes he will seem to show remorse, even to the point of tears, but it is all for show. He isn't sorry. He just knows that he can get what he wants by crying occasionally. He promises a lot but rarely delivers. To listen to him, to believe him, to depend on him is a fatal error. The *only* way to understand him is to look at what he *does*, never to what he says.

In the last ten years there have been a number of independent, crucial, and seminal research studies focusing on this type of psychopathy.* They have all had similar findings, pointing to the genes as an important cause of the problem, though environment can certainly influence it too. (The same is true for alcoholism and schizophrenia; they have also been found to have hereditary components.)

Mednick and Hutchings carried out a study of criminals who had been adopted to see whether the natural father and the adoptive father also had criminal records. There was a much stronger correlation between criminality in the natural fathers and criminality in their sons than between criminality in adopted fathers and their adopted sons. In other words, a child could withstand criminality in his environment much better than he could withstand criminality in his parentage or genes.

How do you identify a child who will later be a psychopath? Sociologist Lee Robins studied the childhood patterns of 526 adults, many of them diagnosed as psychopaths. She compared them with 100 normal adults and found that the following symptoms of future adult criminality tend to appear in childhood: theft, incorrigibility, running away from home, truancy, associating with other delinquents, school discipline problems, being held back in school, fighting, recklessness, impulsivity, reading difficulties, slovenliness, bed wetting, motiveless lying, being unloving, and showing no guilt. No *single* sign was a sure predictor of adolescent or adult psychopathy. Nearly all of these symptoms are found occasionally in normal children. But she found that a sheer number of these signs in childhood was predictive of psychopathy in adulthood. Thus, the more signs, the greater the risk—and many of the signs tend to show up before the child begins school.

Robins also found that parents who were alcoholic, psychopathic, hysteric, and of low social class have a higher risk of having a psychopathic son. She found that a broken home or death of a parent by itself was not related to criminal psychopathy, nor was the level of neighborhood delinquency where the child was raised very important in such cases—another indicator that it is genetic factors more than upbringing that lead to this special condition. This does *not* mean that environment plays no role as a contributor to delinquency. It does, but genetic factors probably play an even greater role.

Most human beings are law-abiding and reasonably prosocial. Why? There are two key behavior patterns that most of us learn very early in life: "resistance to temptation" and "guilt" are both important factors in keeping

*These include the work of such scientists and researchers as Lee Robins, S.A. Corsin, Robert Hare, Hans Eysenck, Sarnoff Mednick, Paul Wender, Barry Hutchings, James Satterfield, Daisy Schalling, Charles Spielberger, and Samuel Guze, representing many disciplines from many areas of the world.

most of society relatively free of crime. Both of them depend on anxiety—resistance to temptation is the result of anxiety after *thinking* of performing a forbidden act but *before* actually carrying it out; guilt is the anxiety felt *after* performing the forbidden act and *before* punishment.

Psychologist Hans Eysenck, among others, suggests that conscience is a "conditioned fear response". Mother gives Jimmy a hard smack or a verbal reprimand when he has done something wrong. This is a *negative* reinforcement, and in Jimmy's mind bad behavior becomes linked with punishment or pain. Thus, when the child is tempted in the future, the very thought of performing a forbidden act arouses anxiety—unconsciously Jimmy expects something bad to happen, and the only way to get rid of that anxiety is to decide not to perform the deed. Jimmy is able to resist temptation.

Furthermore, Jimmy's conscience doesn't apply just to specific acts he was punished for in childhood. At thirty he is unlikely to be tempted to steal bubble gum from the supermarket, but the learned anxiety about doing bad things can apply to his temptation to siphon off funds from the corporation or his temptation to enter into a sexual relationship with his partner's wife that he knows would hurt many people. He learns to feel anxiety about performing any act that he knows is disapproved of by the people important to him—peers, parents, church, society in general.

Conscience is not strongly linked to acts of congresses or legislatures, however. It is linked to attitudes of parents and peers. A child with a very strong conscience about stealing and lying may have no conscience at all about speeding or breaking traffic laws, since his parents and peers engage in those activities and treat them indulgently. (It hardly needs saying that children learn their parents' *real* value system much more readily than they learn their parents' *professed* value system.)

While conscience formation is almost entirely unconscious, it is painfully logical. Some parents believe that the stronger the punishment they inflict on their children the more it will help them develop a conscience, but too much punishment can have the opposite effect. If a child feels that punishment is brutal and unfair, it may only teach him anxiety about being around the punishing parent. In other words, along with appropriate punishment, conscience formation depends on a close, loving relationship with parents. If a child hates or fears his parents, he isn't too likely to adopt their attitudes toward right and wrong as his own—he is more likely to rebel *against* their attitudes.

Another factor that is very important in creating resistance to temptation is the *promptness* of punishment. If punishment is delayed until a long time after breaking the rule, the child will learn to go ahead and perform the act—*then* feel anxiety about the coming punishment! This anxiety after the act is *guilt*, and while guilt can be valuable in helping people avoid antisocial behavior, it is not as good as resistance to temptation.

Guilt can, however, work to help a person resist temptation, but only in a backhanded way. If a person feels guilt intensely enough and starts feeling it as soon as he has broken a rule, the guilt begins to function as a punishment all by itself. And since it begins promptly, it gradually serves to condition resistance to temptation—in order to avoid the pain of guilt, the person does not perform the forbidden act in the first place. In other words, if you tell your erring child, "Just wait until Dad gets home, and then you'll get it," the punishment won't be very effective—except, of course, that the child will learn to dread having Dad come home!

The "bad seed," however, does not easily develop such conditioned fear responses. He feels no dread of punishment because, on an unconscious level, he never makes the connection between past punishment and future actions. Anxiety plays no significant role in his life. Furthermore, he doesn't even respond very well to rewards. Anything that requires him to *anticipate* the long-term results of his actions gets nowhere. He only learns to get immediate gratification—stealing the item he wants, seducing the woman at hand—and avoid immediate pain—he doesn't perform crimes in front of policemen; he doesn't beat up his younger brother while his parents are watching.

This absence of anxiety may have a bio-chemical cause. We know, for example, that ACTH fractions (chemicals produced by the brain) control aversive conditioning to some extent. There is also evidence strongly suggesting that lack of conditionability or inability to experience anxiety is genetic and inherited. This does not mean that this kind of a criminal doesn't clearly know the difference between right and wrong—he does. The core issue underneath is that he doesn't care.

We must also mention a related condition: the hyperactive child (See Chapter 23). This child is over-active, has a short attention span, is distractable, impulsive, irritating, and does poorly in school despite average intelligence. His condition also is inherited. Since a significant minority of these children may exhibit psychopathic traits, it is important that they be treated for their hyperactivity with appropriate medication and possibly diet. The evidence clearly suggests that treatment of their hyperactivity reduces possible tendencies toward psychopathy.

I believe, then, that conscience development, and therefore a person's likelihood to behave ethically, depend on four general factors.

1. Having an adequate neurology and biology, which guarantees enough intelligence and conditionability to allow the development of a conscience—in other words, good genes.

2. Having parents who explicitly model ethical behavior, along with promoting a healthy, loving relationship with their child. This enables the child to learn what his parents' real values are and encourages him to adopt them as his own.

3. Being carefully instructed in a value system, with stress on understanding the consequences of his own actions. Logical reasons need to be given to the child for why he should or shouldn't do certain things, including the Golden Rule or a family ethical code. Parents need to take advantage of opportunities for such informal but explicit teaching.

4. Being involved in a reinforcement system, where good behavior is consistently rewarded and antisocial behavior is consistently discouraged or punished. See the chapter on discipline for many specific strategies here.

Of course, parents who have taught their children to develop consciences may—and probably will—have the frustration of seeing their children do things, particularly in their teenage and young adult years, that are in direct violation of the moral code the parents tried to teach them. This isn't a signal for parents to beat their heads against a wall, moaning about how they have failed in raising their children. In all likelihood, they have succeeded—their children have adequately developed consciences and are able to resist many temptations and even feel guilt about their transgressions. What has happened, however, is that a different ethical system has come into play. They are more strongly influenced by their peers or other role models at this stage than they are by their parents. Usually, however, children will return to their parents' value systems to one degree or another. A daughter's idea of how to be a mother depends strongly on her own mother's behavior. So, if children have been responsive to ethical training and conscience development in early childhood, the aberrations of their teenage years and childish rambunctiousness are not cause for alarm.

Unstinting love, consistent and judicious punishment and reward, a good example, and careful teaching will almost always result in what most parents want: a child who has become a responsible, law-abiding, good adult. There is a great deal of truth in the maxim, "Raise up your child in the way he should go, and when he is old he will not depart from it".

7

How to Teach Your Child to be Responsible

MOTHER, VERY EXASPERATED: "Darleen, your bedroom is a pig sty! How can you stand sleeping in there? When I saw it a few minutes ago I felt like throwing up. And you know good and well that it's supposed to be cleaned up before you go anywhere—yet last night you just took off! I'm fed up with your complete irresponsibility."

Father, gruffly: "Ted! The lawn is still unmowed—the grass and weeds are so high our yard is the neighborhood eyesore. I can't even see the house from the street! When I advanced you six dollars on your allowance last week you promised that the lawn would be cut within twenty-four hours. And look at it now—nothing! Don't promises mean anything to you?"

If I were to rate each of our nine kids on a scale of one to ten on their natural inclination to be responsible, it would vary from about two to ten. And yet they all have the same set of parents—Lois and me. Children are just born with different temperaments and dispositions. Expect it.

Some are like race horses—they just love to grab at a challenge or new job and seem to be born responsible. They have so much initiative it's almost impossible to hold them back. Others, also good kids from the same good family, need an electric cattle prod just to move them from one room into the next. They don't seem willing to carry out any task unless you stand over them while they do it. Parents should be aware that there is a natural variation in personalities. You didn't necessarily "fail" with one child and "succeed" with another.

What exactly is responsibility? I think it means making and keeping commitments without being constantly prodded and reminded. The responsible child—and adult, for that matter—can be depended on to do what he says he'll do. Self-motivation is at the core. But self-motivation, by definition, can't be forced on anyone. There are ways to encourage it, however, with skills and confidence you can help the child build step by step.

Why bother? If your kid is reasonably obedient and well-behaved, doesn't sass back and always means well, isn't that enough?

Maybe. It certainly seems to be enough for many adults. Almost every employer I talk to identifies this as one of his major problems—irresponsible workers. You can't depend on them. You are never sure if they are going to

82

show up for work, let alone complete the tasks assigned to them. That seems to be average behavior, and if your child is like that he'll fit right in.

But then, you're not reading this book to find out how to make your child average. The average child becomes average without much help from anyone. You want to help him be the kind of adult that others learn to depend on; that employers quickly learn to trust. Even a reasonably competent employee who is dependable soon gets promoted. Instilling responsibility is one of the best things you can do to help your child be a winner.

1. Start small. You don't expect a three-year-old to be able to mow the lawn on a regular schedule. But a three-year-old might be able to handle the regular responsibility of unloading the silverware from the dishwasher and putting it in the silverware tray. True, the job will take more time than if you did it yourself, but the objective here is to teach your three-year-old there are jobs that are his alone—that he can do them well and is expected to do them regularly.

As the child's capacity for learning and carrying out responsibilities increases, you need to help him stretch those capacities. Has he learned to tie off the garbage bags and put new ones in the wastebasket? Does he perform that job faithfully, with only occasional reminders? Then add to it—let it be his job to carry the tied bags outside, or even to take them out once a week to the curb for the garbagemen to pick up.

2. Start early. Don't wait until your child is fifteen to insist that he clean up his room. It's far too late then. Give each child, even preschoolers, as much responsibility doing daily chores as he can handle—no more, but certainly no less!

3. Don't do for the child what the child can do for himself. As soon as he learns to put his blocks in the box, insist that he do it himself every night before going to bed. As soon as he knows the difference between shoes and socks, he should be expected to put them in their place when they're taken off him at night. When your children are old enough to dress themselves they must be allowed to dress themselves—even when you're in a hurry, even when they have a tendency to put together dreadful color combinations. Later you can teach them to do it better, just so they are always practicing doing it.

4. Let him experience the natural consequence of his irresponsibility. If he fails to come home by dinnertime at six-thirty, insist that he go to bed hungry. If he doesn't do his work around the house, he doesn't get paid his allowance—no exceptions allowed for whining and wheedling. If he dents a car fender, he pays the insurance deductible for repairing it—and the increase in the insurance premium, if there is one, for the privilege of continuing to drive the family car. Sometimes the experience can be painful. Suppose he has put off studying for a test and then comes to you frightened saying, "I just forgot and now I'll flunk the test—can't I stay home today and study so I can make up the test tomorrow?" You will do him no favor if you give in. You'll just be teaching him that someone will always cover for him if he doesn't do what he's supposed to do. Much better to let him take the test, take his chances, and learn what happens when he "forgets" to study—though of course there's no harm if you help him study for the next one and let him know that you *do* care whether he succeeds or fails.

5. If you have an allowance system where kids get money for just being alive and dwelling in your house—abolish it! Get rid of the welfare state in your home. Let them earn *all* their money. If they want extra for a movie, skiing, a rock concert, or a new pair of pants, don't just give it to them. Instead, give them a job they can do to earn it. They may complain sometimes, but it's hard to think of a more valuable lesson to teach your kids than the cold hard fact that possessions and entertainment cost money, and money comes from work, not parents.

Often parents use money as a way of trying to win their children's approval and favor. A quick dose of cash does often earn a hug and a "You're super, Dad!" But you should know that you're not really super at all, and that hug was bought, not earned. You'll feel a lot better about the hug you get when your kid is twenty-five and just got a promotion and comes to you and says, "Thanks for teaching me how to work when I was a kid!" That's earned love, because you gave your child what he needed, not what he wanted.

6. Deliberately and repeatedly present your kids with situations that require them to make choices. Let them decide which chore they will do *from among several you make available.* This allows them to fit it in with their particular schedule or tastes—while it guarantees they will choose a chore you want to have done. You select the situations; they make the choice.

When you take your young son to the barber, let him tell the barber how he wants his hair cut; that won't hurt anything. When your daughter needs a winter coat, let her choose from among three or four possibilities in your price range so that the choice of color and style is hers. You can talk to her first about what's important in buying a coat and what to look for, but let her choose it—and live with the choice afterward. And when your child receives a party invitation, let him decide whenever possible if he wishes to go. This doesn't mean that you don't give him an occasional nudge, but if you want him to make wise decisions later, when he's on his own, get him in the habit of thinking for himself now.

7. If your child fulfills a commitment or does a job well, always notice and appreciate it. Use lots of sincere and animated praise and rejoicing over his

good performance. But the reverse is true: don't let a broken promise or undone job go by without comment or discussion. Follow through. Insist on completion or some equitable resolution *every time*.

Some parents are so afraid of their child or so want to avoid hassle that they pretend not to be aware of even his most glaring deficiencies. They look the other way. They fail to make sure the child feels the consequence even when there has been a serious goof. All this does is guarantee that the goof will be repeated. By their inaction, the parents label this as acceptable behavior.

Make sure your mercy doesn't slide into license. If you set a pattern of obtaining reasonable compliance to family rules and work standards in preteen years, then you won't be constantly struggling to keep your kids in line later.

8. Dad and Mother need to set an example of responsible behavior themselves. They need to follow through on their commitments. It's good for the kids to see Dad and Mom help each other, working happily together on routine chores like those the kids are expected to do. It's also good to show that people who love each other, help each other: when one of the kids has an extra big pile of dishes to do on his Thursday evening turn, Dad might help out so the job is done sooner. Parents can model a positive and joyful attitude toward work, which can be contagious with the kids. Work isn't bad. It's not a punishment. It solves problems, earns money or gratitude, accomplishes things. It's also a great therapy for each of us: making or finishing something makes us feel good. It's our gift of love to people we care about.

What I'm talking about is the much-maligned "Protestant work ethic". Oddly, the idea that work is good and necessary isn't particularly Protestant—there's not a society in the world that has lasted long or accomplished much that didn't put a high value on accomplishment. If you value work and take pleasure in doing it, your kids will adopt the same attitude, by and large, and their lives will be better for it. Work isn't everything, but without work not much of anything will ever be accomplished.

9. Use charts to monitor work done and assignments carried out so there is no confusion about who did or didn't do what. They also provide you and your kids with a track record over a period of time, clearly showing if a child is improving or standing still in his performance of responsibility.

10. Children will tend to be more responsible if they can be a part of the family decision-making process. Hold weekly family councils with a formal agenda—new business, old business, polite and open discussion, and all the rest. Post the agenda on the refrigerator with the understanding that anybody can add items to it for family consideration. Everybody gets heard and treated fairly. However, this doesn't mean a pure democracy. You, as parents, are still the final authority. But if you carefully take your children's desires and opinions into account, compromising where you can and explaining the reasons when compromise is not possible, they will understand family decisions better—and feel a deeper stake in their outcome.

11. Establish a rule that chores and homework come before play and TV. Then strictly abide by it. And work should be done in advance if the youngster is going on an outing or away from home overnight. Any other course almost guarantees procrastination or abandonment of responsibilities.

12. If your child's chores aren't performed well enough, use the apprentice system for a while by having the child work *with* you. Do the job together for a few weeks, so you can repeatedly demonstrate exactly how you want the job done and what level of performance you expect. This can be fun for both of you and a chance to become better friends even as you prepare your child for independence. But be careful not to be too critical at first. Better to have a few clumsy but happy efforts that gradually improve than to insist on miserable, tearful perfection the first time.

Remember—responsible kids aren't produced overnight. It's a step-by-step process that takes many years. These techniques do work. All that's required is a consistent effort by patient, loving parents who respect their kids too much to let them be infantile when they are ready to be nearly adult.

8

How to Protect Your Child's Mental Health

HOW DO WE RAISE STRESS-PROOF KIDS, who, when they get banged around and battered, will show grace under pressure and somehow survive? How do we best generate ego-strength and sound mental health in children? How do we best protect their mental health?

It is clear, in an ironic way, that some stress and challenge can strengthen children. Too much can destroy them. There is a delicate balance. As loving parents our task is to give them skills and knowledge so they can successfully face and meet life's challenges and slay some small dragons; it is not to over-protect them. At the same time we must not let them be overwhelmed by stress or anxiety or trauma which is beyond their capacity and ability to cope with. We are preparing them for adult living—that requires making them strong and resilient—but they can't get strong unless they have practice at solving and overcoming smaller, then larger problems.

When our teenage daughter Connie went on her thirty-day wilderness survival experience (a family tradition for all of our children), she unfortunately did not have time to break in her new hiking boots. Too late she found they didn't quite fit her, and within a few days her feet were covered with terrible blisters and open sores. This wilderness experience, sponsored by a local university, required her to hike with a pack over 300 miles of extremely wild and torturous desert and mountain terrain, capped by a 23-mile marathon run. Her leaders suggested that she be taken off the program and returned home because of the condition of her feet. But Connie is not a quitter. She has great pride and an inner toughness. She obtained a pair of oversized cheap canvas tennis shoes, hoping her feet might heal if she wore only them, but their soles were thin—inappropriate for traversing such rocky, bruising terrain. She hung on, enduring a lot of pain, to the end—even winning the 23-mile marathon. She slew her dragon. Although her feet have long since healed and the pain is gone, she'll never be quite the same again. Every child should have such an experience—but geared to their capacity to cope and successfully handle it.

One afternoon on a transcontinental flight, 36,000 feet above our great Midwest, I had a lengthy conversation with my seat companion, a regional sales manager for *Encyclopedia Britannica*. We were discussing what it took to be an effective encyclopedia salesman. He mentioned that in his experience it took more than just sales ability—even though this was very important. It also took an extra inner toughness to survive the drought that occasionally every salesman faces, a time when nothing works, when no matter what you do you come up empty-handed.

The really good salesman can endure these occasions; he has an inner faith in himself. He knows someday the tide will change. This man is like a rubber ball—when he hits bottom he can always bounce back. There are other salesmen who are more like eggs. When they hit bottom they splatter, and they never quite put themselves together again. It is the former quality, not the latter, which we work to instill in our children.

The Things You Alone Can Do

Briefly I'd like to list some obvious preparatory things parents can do to strengthen their children—some even before they are born.

1. First, marry someone you love and are compatible with who also has good genes—who comes from good stock. Genes do make a difference. Certain kinds of emotional instability and mental illness are at least partially inherited. I hate to say it that bluntly, but it's true. Look not only at your beloved but also at his or her parents, grandparents, and other family members. Give your kids a good genetic inheritance or endowment.

2. Second, mothers, when you are pregnant, give your growing fetus super-nutrition and avoid toxic substances like powerful medications, excess alcohol, smoking, X-rays, and drugs that could brain-damage your infant-to-be.

Scientific evidence suggests that malnutrition, especially in the last three months of pregnancy and in the baby's first two years of life, can: (1) reduce the overall size of the brain; (2) damage the cerebellum; (3) reduce the overall number of brain cells or neurones in the brain; (4) reduce the amount of lipid available for myelination of the axons (this damages inter-neurone connections); (5) disturb certain enzyme levels which adversely affect the operation of important neurotransmitter chemicals in the brain. Unfortunately, this kind of brain damage has been found to be permanent and irreversible.

Thus, a sixteen-year-old girl, pregnant, living on junk food, could unwittingly suffer from malnutrition which might significantly affect the brain development and later mental health of her infant. The same thing could happen to an older woman on a fad diet during the latter part of her pregnancy.

Also consider that a mother's breast milk is nutritionally the most perfect food possible for a new baby, which would argue for breast-feeding of the infant as another safeguard for the baby's developing brain and later mental health.

3. Third, maintain a solid, stable, loving marriage. If necessary, get marriage counseling from the very best therapist in your area. We can't point out too often that a vast number of behavioral science research studies as well as clinical observations keep coming to one overwhelming conclusion—children born into a stable, loving home environment have tremendous advantages over those born into highly conflicted, unstable families. If the mother's energies are mainly going into surviving the trauma of a horrible marriage, she will have much less to give her children. She will be stressed, short-tempered, and have more erratic judgment. The children will sense her insecurity and depression and be infected by her emotional distress. Neuroses are highly contagious. A mother can, in time, become partially or greatly incapacitated by a chronically assaultive, critical, demeaning husband—just as a shrewish, vituperative, nagging wife can emasculate and drive a husband out of the home, into a depression, or both. In all instances, the children eventually become the losers.

Repairing ruptured marriages is my specialty, and I know that you don't have to have total compatibility to have a great marriage. I also know you both can be a little neurotic or crazy and still work out an excellent relationship. I've repeatedly seen it happen. But you *do* need commitment to each other and to the marriage, adequate communication skills, and the ability to deal with anger healthily. While these latter two can be learned, the "commitment" has to come from the heart, reflecting your deepest values and personal priorities.

4. Next, properly inoculate and vaccinate your child to guard against childhood diseases which might affect his or her mental and neurological growth and health. Some parents worry about the safety of these vaccines, but the federal government through the FDA has become super-cautious about licensing the sale and use of all drugs and vaccines. They all have to pass rigorous tests and inspections, making the risk of disease far greater than any supposed risk of the vaccine. This is especially true where Americans and their families travel so much and get exposed to so many more and different kinds of viruses and infectious diseases than ever before.

Just as an example, take measles (rubeola). It can kill. It can cause mental retardation, learning difficulties, or even knock the edge off of a child's IQ. In the case of German measles (rubella), it can damage the fetus of a pregnant mother. The inexpensive vaccine for these diseases can give long-lasting, usually permanent protection against getting it later. Why take a chance? Most state departments of public health will give varieties of protective shots to children without cost if the parents will just bring them in.

5. Hide or correct all physical defects: crooked teeth, funny noses, ears that flap, facial blemishes, etc. This will improve the child's body image, bring fewer taunts and jeers from peers, and in general help the child feel better about himself. By helping the child to be more socially acceptable to other children, you will be protecting his mental health by reducing social stress.

My college friend Larry had a sister about ready to enter the University of California at Berkeley, where we were both enrolled. She was very attractive in all respects except for an over-sized unshapely nose—making everybody smile when they saw her. Larry insisted that before starting her freshman year in college she have some plastic surgery to alter the size and shape of her nose. She did, and the results were stunning. Nobody laughs when they see her beautiful face now. And she felt great, since most of the people she then met had never known her before the nose operation. Even those personal friends in her remote home town applauded the results and quickly adjusted to her new more beautiful appearance.

The Things Your Child Must Do – with Your Help

One of the things that makes psychology an inexact science is the fact that no two individual human beings are the same. While chemists can count on one oxygen atom behaving exactly like every other oxygen atom, we who try to alter the lives of unhappy human beings find, time after time, that what works with one person does not work with another. Even identical twins respond differently to the situation of being twins!

This means that in your own family you are going to find each child bringing his own unique set of problems and joys to your life, so the strategies you developed with the first child might not work at all well with the second.

More important, though, is the fact that ultimately the child's responsibility for his life rests with himself. His responses to the problems he faces in his life will be his own, not yours. Nevertheless, you still have a chance to influence his life powerfully by the way you help him face the crises of his life. If you anticipate the struggles he will face you can make those struggles easier—not by removing them, which would only weaken him in the end, but by forearming him. Help him develop the personal resources to face those stresses and win.

Hercules, the hero of Greek legend, faced Eurystheus, son of the king of Argos, and learned of twelve terrible trials he would face. Eurystheus required Hercules to accomplish twelve seemingly impossible labors, including such things as killing Hydra, the poisonous nine-headed serpent; cleansing the Augean stables in one day; capturing the mad bull which had terrorized the island of Crete; and killing the savage Nemean lion.

If he actually accomplished the labors, however, Hercules stood to gain much. He was doing penance for an earlier misdeed, and that would be forgiven; but even more important was the prize of achieving immortality by becoming one with the gods. Contrary to all expectations, Hercules accomplished every single task set for him to do. It is interesting that the Greeks did not think it was cheating for Hercules to get a little help from the gods along the way. Without that help he couldn't possibly have succeeded—so why shouldn't the gods have helped?

There are some universal tasks or trials that every human being must face at some time in his life. Unlike Hercules' twelve physical labors, these human crises are developmental and psychological: it is not brawn that will win out, but rather mental and moral strength; the reward is not immortality, but rather happiness and self-respect during this mortal life.

If children came into the world with no one to help them develop the mental strength and moral courage to meet these crises, few would be met. But they aren't alone—they have parents, and with your help they can win each battle as it comes along. The result of victory is a winner—a child who will later become an adult who is depended on by others and who can depend on himself. The result of significant failure is a loser—an adult who can't cope, who has neither the will nor the wisdom to set a direction in his life and follow it. Never sure what he wants but positive that he is incapable of getting it, he is unhappy, frustrated, and difficult to live with.

Hercules faced twelve labors. Your child will face ten. A successful resolution of each will protect his mental health.

1. Emotional bonding to the mother This occurs in the first year of life. In the absence of a mother it could occur with a nurturing father, but in ninety-five percent of the cases the mother will play the key role here. By holding, caressing, cuddling, talking to, and possibly nursing the baby the mother communicates in a thousand ways her love and affection for the infant. The infant powerfully senses and feels that this is a good world to be in. Lack of bonding can be profoundly damaging; but with successful bonding the mother instills into the deepest recesses of the infant's psyche a sense of security, a sense that "I am a worthwhile person," a sense of trust and hope. This kind of foundation will later permit the individual to endure much stress and adversity but still have hope and refuse to give up. The mother builds a foundation and reservoir of psychological strength reaching to the very core of the infant's unconscious personality.

2. Acceptance of self This follows closely after the bonding experience with major emphasis in the second to fifth years of life, though continuing throughout life. Here the child learns to accept himself as a worthy person who has a right to be here. He learns that his body is his alone, that he is a separate individual; he learns how to move, how to make his body do his bidding, how to perform increasingly intricate and difficult physical tasks. He also learns to act on his environment, both physically and verbally, "helping" other people and things change because of what he does to them. In short, he becomes not just a reactor but also an actor in the world. And in the process, because his individual will is accepted as worthy of attention by his family and others, he learns that he has a legitimate place in life. He learns to accept himself, respect himself; he faces life with a confidence that he can change things around him. These are the beginnings of developing a positive self-image and self-respect which later will be so crucial to healthy, social, emotional, and intellectual growth.

3. The Civil War called sibling rivalry Every child in one way or another faces this mythic battle—to share mother (especially) and dad with another sibling. It's a war that can't be avoided, and the successful resolution involves reaching a level of maturity where one can share the parent's love—to give as well as take. This process involves compromise, negotiation, and truce-making with rivals.

It is true that some "only" children or those widely spaced do not have the opportunity to work through this growth stage or developmental "crisis". This is not necessarily to their advantage. Its essential core involves sharing, admitting equals into one's life space, and dealing with the issues of self-centeredness and narcissism. The "only" child who is denied that opportunity to struggle with these issues at an earlier time in his life with brothers and sisters will still have it to face later, particularly in his marriage.

Parents can do a great deal to help or exacerbate these problems involving conflict and competition among their children. They can also add fuel to the fire. See Chapter 10 for numerous ideas for parents to help their children resolve conflicts in this area.

4. Control of impulse or self-mastery This involves a continuing struggle between the id and ego, between natural appetites and rational self-interest. It may involve getting control of an outrageous temper, a weight and diet problem, out-of-control sexual aberrations, intemperate use of drugs or alcohol to the point where their use becomes self-destructive. It can also involve such entities as a festering self-pity and certain kinds of neurotic depression which the individual masochistically wallows in.

As an example, I've seen men struggle with the problem of sexual exhibitionism. They are repeatedly caught and punished. Their wives divorce them. They lose their children. They lose their jobs. Their compulsion to "exhibit" rules and ruins their lives. It's the same with many alcoholics, narcotic addicts, wife abusers—impulses, not reason, govern their lives. The personal cost to these people and to those who love them is enormous. Every human being is faced with the challenge to control some of his irrational, often destructive, impulses. No one is exempt.

Parents who set reasonable limits help children gain mastery over their impulses. They teach their children the skills of resistance to temptation and delay of gratification. The children learn that desire alone is not reason enough for an action; they learn to think before they act because they have learned from their parents' discipline that actions have consequences.

5. *The accommodation to authority* A major task or challenge facing nearly all young people, peaking during adolescence, is how to deal successfully with authority and authority figures. Most of us at times don't want to obey rules set up by others. We don't want to be told what to do; we want to make our own decisions. We want to have our own way. Yet if society is to survive, we have to enter into agreements with others for our mutual protection and benefit. Many adolescents in their fierce desire for freedom and independence feel that they are above the law or would like to be. They are restless at the restraints imposed on them and their behavior.

The initial testing of authority begins in the home with the parents representing the position of the "establishment". Since the family represents society in miniature it is here where many protracted struggles occur between the generations. Each new crop of kids and their parents experiences this same conflict or struggle.

Some individuals never do learn to deal with the authority issue responsibly and rationally. They live and die bitter, truculent, uncompromising, angry, frustrated, and in a state of continuing rebellion toward their associates, spouses, employers, the religion of their childhood, and even sometimes themselves. Many are thus divided and torn within. They are truly unhappy individuals. They are unaware that we are all—necessarily, simultaneously—followers sometimes and leaders other times. This isn't necessarily bad. For us to have some sort of social order where others can serve us requires our cooperation and reciprocity where we serve them also. The mature individual learns to abide by mutually-arrived-at constraints or rules that protect us all from tyranny and loss of freedom.

6. *The crisis of competence* At some point or several points in each of our children's lives they must learn some skills exceedingly well. They need to become competent. They need to know how to discipline themselves so they can produce a product that is marketable, brings recognition, and pleases others. They may be the best paperboy in the district; they may be a fabulous tennis player, or football tackle, or marathon runner. They may have a special talent in designing and making clothes, cooking gourmet foods, repairing cars, writing, rappelling impossible mountains, or selling more shirts at J.C. Penney's than any other clerk. Some children never learn this—to be competent at something. They fumble their way through school and life, accidentally drifting into a career which they often don't really like then get trapped by car payments, a pregnant wife, a big mortgage on the house. Many live lives of quiet desperation or boredom—never really pleased with themselves.

Parents can make a major contribution to their children becoming competent through subtle suggestions and introducing them to all sorts of growth experiences. A number of the other chapters in this book deal with this issue practically and specifically.

7. Developing a healthy sex-role identity This begins in early adolescence and is that period of time when the individual clearly recognizes that he is a male or man, female or woman. It requires an acceptance of one's biological sexual nature. It means fashioning a masculine or feminine identity or persona which the youngster can feel comfortable with—but which is also acceptable to friends and those one works and lives with. If this gets messed up it can cause much grief to the teenager.

Edith, whose parents were divorced, hated her mother and over-idealized her father—an uncouth, boisterous sort of man. When I saw Edith she was sixteen and a social outcast in her school. Unconsciously identifying with her father she wore very masculine clothes, used loud, rough, vulgar language, and paid little attention to her hair. This was in imitation of her father. Though basically friendly, she was repeatedly rebuffed by both boys and girls in her middle-class high school. Edith was neither fish nor fowl, and her confusion over her sex-role identity made her adolescent social adjustment exceedingly difficult and painful.

However, our male and female sexual roles need to be flexible. Rigid sexual stereotyping causes problems. If your son grows up believing the lie that masculinity only goes along with athletics, while art or music are effeminate, what will it do to him to discover that he doesn't really excel at athletics while music and art provide him with pleasure and success? Does he have to doubt his manhood? And if your daughter believes that being a leader and a good administrator means that she isn't feminine, what will it do to her when she finds her greatest satisfaction is in getting jobs done and directing the activities of other people in a common task? In short, what if your kid comes up against a stereotype that isn't true in his own case? The solution lies in the parents teaching and modeling the fact that there are many, many ways for a man to be manly and for a woman to be womanly.

8. Bonding to and establishing a committed relationship with an individual of the opposite sex This requires a mature capacity to commit oneself to a long-term relationship involving friendship, love, affection, and positive sexual experiences. It requires successfully negotiating and resolving differences in personal style and values, developing a capacity to give and take, and to assert oneself while permitting uniqueness in one's partner. It involves forming a nuclear family similar to the one the individual came from. To do this properly requires remarkable skill, personal discipline, wisdom, and flexibility. This new social unit—husband, wife, and possible offspring—is the core unit of our whole society, and how it fares determines the viability and eventual fate of our whole civilization.

9. Serving others Many children never learn to give or serve others. For them it's always take, manipulate, and use. I know with a certainty that when any of us freely gives something in the service of others, subtle inner changes occur within our psyche or basic personality that ennoble and strengthen us. In an old-fashioned sense we are blessed. We become something greater and better than we were before. Our friends and family see us differently—in a more tolerant light. Anyone who has ever contributed significantly of themselves, especially their time, to a worthy social cause, a community project, their church or synagogue, or to help sick or disadvantaged people will know what I am talking about. If the contribution has amounted to what is a real sacrifice in time, talents, or means, then the impact on our psychological selves is even more profound. For example, every member of Alcoholics Anonymous who has served an alcoholic brother in time of need knows this special feeling. There is real magic in service. It changes us for the better. It gives us an inner balance, an extra dimension as a human being. And it also protects our mental health. I don't know for sure how this happens, but I see it in those individuals who serve their fellow man and are unselfishly their brother's keeper.

10. The Search for values and the meaning of existence Even though I feel that it is vitally important for parents to share all they know with their children in the area of their values, in the end each young person has to make much of this search and journey alone. They can be raised in a church and dutifully attend for years, but that doesn't guarantee anything. The young person will have to come to grips individually with these kinds of issues. We all need to have some sort of higher value or creed to live our lives by. Personal expediency is a blind alley that leads nowhere except to self-indulgence, and this doesn't really satisfy. The successful resolution of this search for values, of a personal ethic, will lead eventually to a higher order of emotional maturity and mental health.

PART II
SOLUTIONS TO THE FIFTEEN MOST COMMON PROBLEMS PARENTS FACE IN RAISING CHILDREN

9

Not Minding:
Discipline that Works

A MAJOR DISASTER OCCURRED in a large number of American families, starting in the 1950's. It was called by many names, most frequently "permissiveness" and "family democracy". It was a noble experiment based on the mistaken notion that young children are basically wise and good and perfectly able to determine their own destinies without parental interference. To punish, to insist on order in the home, to exert control over your children was called authoritarian and anti-democratic. To spank, even in love, was seen by some of these "experts" as a serious form of child abuse.

These mistaken theories, widely read by middle class parents who wanted to give their children the best possible upbringing, sounded reasonable, democratic, and just. But the effect was that parental authority and control were lost; being a good parent now meant letting your kids do their own thing. They knew better than you what was good for them.

With a new vision and surge of hope, a legion of trusting parents raised a generation of children who tended to be ungrateful, demanding, lacking in impulse control, directionless, self-indulgent with alcohol, sex, and drugs, and who later found difficulty staying married (or, for that matter, even staying with someone very long *un*married). In short, many of these parents found that their children became exceedingly obnoxious adults. Brats: spoiled and selfish. It's no wonder that many of these children, seeing the grief they caused their parents, now have hesitations about having children of their own. Having and raising kids can be a nightmare. They ought to know—they were there—but it wasn't really all their fault.

The experts kept telling parents that all their child needs is love, understanding, and acceptance—and it will all work out. He'll grow up to be a beautiful, responsible person, and if this is not happening then you're just not giving him enough love. Or perhaps you have to learn to talk his language. Haim Ginott called it "childrenese" in his book, *Between Parent & Child*. But *discipline* was still a dirty word. Even Dr. Ginott (much of whose material I like) preached against parents insisting their kids do chores assigned to them. He felt it might have an undesirable influence on building their character. (He actually said that.) He also suggested that parents not supervise or check their child's homework unless asked—that's the child's and school's responsibility, not the parents'. In other words, if they go down the tube—tough! Whatever you do, *don't* interfere!

John Holt, a famous educator and author of *How Children Fail,* suggested in a later book, *Escape From Childhood,* that children at any age should have the right to choose their own guardian, have a guaranteed income, control their own learning, have legal and financial responsibility and do essentially anything they want to do.

If you think that sounds crazy, consider the recommendations of another, the influential British educator, A.S. Neill, in his famous book *Summerhill.* He flatly states that parents have no right at all to insist on obedience from their children. A child, according to him, should be required to do nothing until he chooses. In fact, he believes children shouldn't be asked to work until they are eighteen. Punishment should never be used, and children shouldn't be taught any religion because this would be inflicting parents' values on their kids. Even giving a child rewards is seen by Neill as being degrading and demoralizing because it's an unfair form of coercion. He not only recommends eliminating all authority in rearing children but also has attempted to do just that with resident students at his Summerhill school. The children there are not required to get up in the morning, attend classes, do homework, take baths, or even wear clothes (though most do).

Somewhat akin to Neill, though not quite so extreme, is Dr. Thomas Gordon, author—promoter of the well-known Parent Effectiveness Training program. This is national in scope, with more than a quarter of a million parents having been through his program. While he teaches some excellent skills in listening to and negotiating with a child, he also rejects the notion of disciplining children and goes so far as to say, "In fact, I have become convinced that [discipline] is actually a very dangerous belief; it alienates parents and children and contributes toward the deterioration of parent-child relationships."

I am personally convinced that these theories have wrought utter havoc and brought much sorrow to large numbers of American families. This is especially so among the middle and upper classes, who tend to pay more attention to the experts and read more about such matters.

I've seen in these parents, again and again, a paralysis of will, an uncertainty of what to do when their children become abusive, tyrannical, destructive, and manipulative. I've repeatedly seen parents function as servants and children as masters. The monkeys are too frequently running the zoo. These parents become desperate, angry, frustrated, and trapped, though they desperately want to do the right thing.

I have seen some gentle and loving parents pushed and goaded to the point of exploding—even physically assaulting their children. But then, immediately afterwards, they feel terribly guilt-ridden and either withdraw and "throw in the towel" or try to make it up to the kids through money, gifts, and favors. This only makes matters worse. They now look the other way while their children get away with murder. They cover up and excuse serious misconduct because they have to make it up to their kid somehow. They have, by their loss of self-control, given their children a bigger whip with which to beat them: guilt. And these selfish and confused and undisciplined children don't hesitate to use it.

While all of this can be extremely irritating and disconcerting to the father, it can be a total disaster for the mother, who is usually closer to the children. It can drive her to valium addiction or alcoholism and sometimes may even break up the marriage. I can never erase from my memory the faces of the hundreds of these mothers that I've seen, etched with permanent tension and worry lines.

Being a good parent isn't a popularity contest. Psychologist Haim Ginott has commented, "A parent must like his children, but he must not have an urgent need to be liked by them every minute of the day." He notes that some parents are so afraid of losing their child's love that they dare not deny him anything; he becomes a tyrant ruling over anxious servants.

Pediatrician Benjamin Spock has stated, "Parents can't feel right towards their children in the long run unless they make them behave reasonably, and children can't be very happy unless they are behaving reasonably."

By setting reasonable limits and boundaries on your child's behavior and firmly enforcing them, you are helping your child establish his own inner controls and self-discipline over his antisocial impulses.

Psychologist Lee Salk has commented that in his experience, "Children actually like discipline—even enjoy it, because they feel more secure and protected when their parents set rules and regulations and enforce them consistently. Some parents think that any attempt to limit the child's freedom of expression will only cause frustration, repressions, and possibly neuroses. I do not agree. In fact, I believe just the exact opposite. Everyone has to learn to channel their feelings and actions in a socially useful way. To do so requires learning to accept some frustration in a way that does not infringe upon the rights of others."

The notion that the exercise of parental power is bad developed out of psychoanalytic theory, which suggested that the cause of most neuroses was the suppression or repression of the child's primitive natural impulses. So the belief among many well-educated and conscientious parents was, "Don't repress or traumatize the children. Be very cautious about saying 'no' to them. Don't frustrate. They will grow up neurotic if you do. Allow them to grow up unhampered and like a rose or apple tree they will ultimately become productive people and produce beautiful fruit." Most of the hypotheses proposed by psychoanalytic theory remain to this date unverified or rejected scientifically, and most behavioral scientists do not regard these theories very seriously anymore.

If Parents Don't Do It, No One Can

In my experience the notion that a family operates best as a pure democracy with everybody having equal votes doesn't work out practically. The further notion that we should eliminate authority figures in families is naive and romantic and could cause disastrous consequences to children raised under such a system.

Psychologist Stanley Coopersmith points out that every social group, no matter what its size, must establish patterns of authority and delegate power, status, and responsibility to its members in order to function effectively, *and this includes families*. In family organization parents clearly possess greater material resources, knowledge, experience, skills and strength than do their children. This remains true until the children are well into their adolescent years and beyond.

Dr. Coopersmith states, "The general notions of family democracy and permissiveness fail to consider that children have less knowledge and foresight than their parents, that discussions based on ignorance tend to be aimless, and that *parents are ultimately responsible for the conduct of their young children.*"

In my experience, the single most crippling problem American parents have in raising their children is lack of firmness and confusion about their leadership roles in providing guidance to their children. Love is not enough. Love has to be tempered and balanced with discipline and control if you want to produce great kids. This is where many parents become incapacitated—when their authority is challenged. A fifty-pound bundle of sass intimidates and often wins out over two mature parents in the battle of wills, even when the child's preferences are clearly self-destructive. When this happens, everybody loses.

Your children can't respect and love you back (no matter how much love you give them) if you are weak and indecisive. If you don't believe me, look around at families where this occurs. The kids manipulate and use their parents, but respect and affection are not there. And, ironically, as they get older they feel contempt and anger at their parents' failure to protect them from their own immaturity and poor judgment.

It is in the nature of all children to push and test their parents' will and firmness even at the earliest ages. It's the universal struggle against authority—a necessary and expected part of growing up. The trick for parents is to remain reasonable, just, and loving, but not yield to improper intimidation and pressure. If Jack or Jean or Billy break the rules, which they are well aware of, then sure punishment or consequences *must* follow. And we make sure this happens because we love them. This is a vital learning experience, necessary for their healthy development into decent adult human beings.

In raising nine children we've faced the whole range of personality types.

You name it, we've had it. We've been loving parents and have always encouraged our children's independence. But we have also been tough and unyielding in some of our confrontations with them. And in looking back, this was one thing we did right, despite our mistakes in other areas.

With each of our children there was, at some point in their growing up, a real donnybrook over some issue involving authority and their right to break the rules regardless. They pushed us to our limit to see if we could be intimidated and manipulated. On occasion there were tears, threats, shouts, every emotional weapon that children have at their disposal. However, Lois and I are very united on such occasions as this. And though they stormed and blustered, we stayed strong and didn't yield (but were very giving and merciful on other occasions).

Then it was over. The rules still applied fairly to everybody. The children were not damaged; there was peace and good will; they were reassured by our strength. We found that this temporary contest of wills didn't injure our love for each other. If anything, it improved it.

Every parent at one time or another will have this experience. The firmer but calmer you are, the less often it will happen.

Dr. James Dobson, author of two excellent books on discipline, *Dare to Discipline* and *The Strong Willed Child*, published by Tyndale House, has refreshingly commented about his own role as a parent: "It is certain that I will make mistakes and errors. My human frailties are impossible to hide and my children occasionally will fall victim to those imperfections. But I cannot abandon my responsibilities to provide leadership, simply because I lack infinite wisdom and insight. Besides, I do have more experience and a better perspective on which to base those decisions than my children possess at this time. I've been where they're going."

These notions about the necessity of a balance between love and discipline in raising good kids is also backed up by research. These are not just clinical hunches or something found in my unique therapy experience.

The Harvard Preschool Project has been studying the origins of competence in young children since 1965. Its director, Burton L. White, has stated: "In the homes where children are developing well as contrasted to the homes where children are developing poorly, we have always seen mothers running the home with a loving, but firm hand. The babies in these home situations rarely have any question about who is the final authority. In homes where children are *not* doing well, however, there is often an ambiguity with respect to the setting of limits and who is going to have the final say on disagreements."

The Harvard research suggests that the combination of firmness and structure with love appears to give the child a maximum of security as well as the most opportunities for healthy growth.

In the 1960's, University of California psychologist Stanley Coopersmith conducted a series of studies on children who were high, medium, or low in self-esteem. He found that the greater the child's self-esteem, the more likely he or she is to be a success or winner in many areas of personal functioning (see Chapter 2). What kinds of families do the high self-esteem "winner" youngsters come from? Dr. Coopersmith found striking evidence that the parents of the high self-esteem children were more strict. They ran a "tight ship" and had a clearly defined and comprehensive set of rules for their offspring, which they enforced zealously. They were also more accepting of their children and allowed more initiative and independent action by them *within* the framework of their family rules.

As Dr. Coopersmith puts it, "Limits and rules are likely to have enhancing and facilitating effects" on the children. These findings suggest that parents who have definite values, who have a clear idea of what they regard as appropriate behavior, and who are able and willing to present and enforce their beliefs are more likely to rear children who value themselves highly. And, interestingly, these kids also have greater respect and affection for their parents.

Home: Preparation for the World

In homes where kids can do pretty much what they want, standards and expectations are unclear and ambiguous. The kids never know where they stand. It is a confusing world. It makes it more difficult for them to establish their personal identities, and it may make it more difficult for them to know how to get along with others outside the family, what the rules of society are and how to play the game of life. No one has really sufficiently instructed them. Many of these spoiled and self-indulged young people, in my experience, are insecure. Others are somewhat immature and selfish and not really very happy. They have usually had their way, and it is hard for them to be giving and cooperative, leading to many adjustment problems for them in later life.

Discipline, tempered by love, teaches a child how best to behave in order to survive in society. He learns to engage in socially acceptable behavior so that he isn't rejected by others. Suitable discipline helps him develop an identity, an internalized set of values and ideals, a conscience, an inner ethical sense. It teaches him to delay and put off the immediate gratification of his impulses, to defer instant pleasure for later pleasure in a socially acceptable manner. It also helps him channel potentially destructive impulses into healthy creative outlets.

If parents don't assume this responsibility, if they don't set and consistently enforce reasonable and just limits, the child is apt to interpret this as parental indifference: "My parents don't care." This makes the child anxious and reduces his capacity to develop inner controls. Not only that, but the child will more likely be personally obnoxious and objectionable, risking social rejection. He will also be harder for the parents to love and enjoy.

Spanking

I know fine families that spank and others, equally good, that don't. And outstanding kids can come from both. If it is done appropriately, I see no harm in it. However, even in "spanking families" there may be some compliant children who will never require it at all.

On one occasion I mentioned to a lady that I had occasionally swatted or spanked my younger children. With a haughty, condescending air she sniffed, "Well, frankly—I've never touched mine." But I happened to know that she locked her kids up in dark closets as a way of shaping them up—a practice that I feel had much more potential for harm or trauma. I can see it now, frightened little kids screaming and banging at the door—terrified by the darkness and their inability to get out.

Spanks or swats on buttocks or upper thighs are especially effective and non-traumatic for preschoolers—a brief sting, a temporary discomfort. And it sure beats lengthy lectures by a mile. No injury is done, but the child instantly knows that what he's done is inappropriate: running into the open street, loosening the handbrakes on the car, turning on all the burners on the kitchen stove, striking matches in the bedroom. The important thing is that they fully understand the reason for the punishment; otherwise it will be a wasted experience.

As children get older, into school, I find spanking becomes less appropriate and less needed. Dr. James Dobson, an expert in the area of child discipline, also feels that spanking should be relatively infrequent in the preteen years of six through twelve. The occasional exception, as he sees it, would be the strong-willed child who absolutely demands to be spanked. In this case Dr. Dobson feels his wishes should be granted. This is the willfully disobedient child who dares you to set limits and brazenly challenges your authority and leadership role with a flagrant disregard for family rules. The issue here is revolution—a contest of wills.

Using physical punishment in the teen years is pretty much forbidden. There are a lot of risks, especially when so many other effective methods are available. For one thing your kid may be as big as you and hit you back! And in any pitched battle you might well lose—a humiliating prospect for all concerned. Even if you win, your child's humiliation can be serious and lasting, so in most cases it's not worth the risk of permanently damaging your relationship.

One exception to this rule occurred with a very mild, non-abusive mother. She never spanked or hit her kids. She nearly always turned the other cheek.

One evening when her sixteen-year-old daughter was vilely abusing her with filthy language, Mom, finally unable to take it any longer, clouted her daughter across the mouth with the back of her hand with great and righteous anger. The daughter was so shocked that she never abused her mother with bad language again and, in fact, gained a great deal of respect for her. But it was the shock, not the pain, that taught.

Those child experts who oppose spanking altogether have legitimate concerns about the potential for child abuse. This is indeed a very serious problem in some families. Unfortunately, those parents who seriously abuse their children with physical violence are usually people who were themselves abused as children, and they in turn are producing another generation of child abusers. Such parents should seek professional help to overcome their violent tendencies. If neither spouse will initiate this, neighbors should contact welfare authorities before the children sustain permanent injuries and the parents go to jail.

However, just because some people are guilty of child abuse doesn't mean that all parents are, or that there isn't an occasion for a swat or two to correct and guide children. It all depends on how it's done and the spirit behind it. Each set of parents can best decide about this matter as befits their particular values, temperament, and personal preference. If a parent finds himself spanking brutally, without self-control, or in moments of great anger, he should immediately forbid himself ever to strike his children under any circumstances. If he cannot stop, he should immediately get professional help.

To discipline means to *teach* or *train*. It involves learning the rules for living with other people. Punishment, while part of discipline, is different. It is the price we pay for breaking these rules.

Here are the very best, most effective methods I know for teaching and training children in each stage of life. But remember, discipline without love can be as useless and damaging as love without discipline.

Infancy: The First Year

In the first year of life, the newborn infant goes from total dependency in the mother's arms to crawling, then walking, then speaking several words and understanding many more. As the baby becomes mobile, he feels an insatiable curiosity to explore his environment. It is almost impossible to spoil a child this age with too many hugs, kisses, smiles, or too much attention. You can give him all you've got without fear of ruining his personality. This is also the age of mother-infant bonding, the time when he will learn whether this is a safe world to live in. So how do you discipline an infant?

"Child-proof" Your Home Discipline in the first year consists mainly of giving the baby gentle direction and teaching him to avoid a few simple dangers as he becomes mobile and scoots around the house. To save yourself from getting gray hairs and having constantly to say "no", you should "child-proof" your home, or at least the rooms where the baby will be moving around. This is also called *environmental control.* Put up barriers like temporary gates to keep him out of forbidden or dangerous areas. Take away little knick-knacks or anything delicate or destructible that might be within his reach. Then you won't worry, and he won't accidentally knock over or ruin something valuable. Remember, anything he can grab will go into his mouth.

A playpen may be a good idea for brief periods, but it shouldn't be overused because even the youngest babies at the start of the crawling age need a much larger area to practice their motor development. You might choose to give your child the freedom of the kitchen and family-room area, where one parent or the other can keep an eye on him while carrying out other tasks.

Diversion and Distraction Use diversion and distraction to get your baby out of something he shouldn't be into or to make him give up something he shouldn't be playing with. Maybe he has been banging on the sauce pan and you need it now or the noise bothers you. Give him an egg beater or a rubber bear. Make a big fuss about the new toy, and the sauce pan will be instantly forgotten. Children this age are easily diverted to new interests, and it will take only thirty seconds of your time to get him out of trouble and into something else.

This technique avoids confrontations and unhappy, frustrated babies. There are no negatives, and it works. You may also wish to pick the baby up and remove him to another spot. Then give him a squeeze, smile, friendly words, and a new diverting toy as you point him in another direction out of mischief.

Teach, Instruct, and Lead Believe it or not, small babies can be taught—especially as they start moving around. When your baby does get mobile and puts his wet, gooey little fingers on the electric lamp plug, you need to say firmly, "No." Shake your head, "No." Look serious. At the same time remove his hand from the plug and say something like, "Hurt, hurt, that will hurt. Stay away!" Then pick up the baby and remove him to another part of the room. It will take five or six trials for most babies to learn not to touch the plug. Punishment for a baby this age is really inappropriate. All it would do is disturb your relationship with him. He is incapable of doing any real wrong, except occasionally getting underfoot.

Dealing with a Fussy Baby Babies this age will cry frequently—even happy, contented babies. Almost always they cry because they are uncomfortable. They may be hungry, need burping, have a soiled diaper that's irritating them, be colicky, have a new tooth just beginning to break through, have an earache, be coming down with a cold or infection that makes them cranky, or they may just be tired and worn out.

You should *never* scold or punish a baby for crying. You *should* find the cause and give them comfort. You can easily keep them clean, diapered, warm, and fed.

Colic (digestive upset) may require help from your pediatrician. Better yet, nurse your baby. This will give him the nearly perfect formula. He may still have occasional digestive upset but it will be much, much less frequent. Lois nursed all nine of our children and found it a very great experience for both mother and child. Sore nipples at the start may slow you down for a few days, but they quickly toughen and that problem is soon solved. Sometimes an ointment helps.

For teething, give him a rubber ring or similar object to gum on. You might occasionally rub some topical pain reliever on his gums; several brands are available at all drug stores without a prescription. Give him a lot of comfort during his misery. I think it's imperative that every mother have a rocking chair so that when the baby is fussy she can hold him and rock him to sleep. This is a very soothing, comforting experience for the baby.

Each mother will quickly learn to identify the baby's different distress calls, so she will know instantly whether it's time to eat or he needs burping or a new tooth is coming through. Some babies are "easy"; others are more whiney and hard to comfort. That is merely part of their inherited temperament, and both kinds can grow up to be great people. There are, of course, special children who have neurological or bio-chemical problems, such as the hyperactives, and you will need special help from your doctor to get you both through a difficult time.

When you're giving the baby all the comfort you can and there's no identifiable cause and he is still crying at 1:30 in the morning, it's not going to hurt to put him in another room, close the door, and allow him to cry himself to sleep. Parents need rest, too. By morning the colic (which is probably what it was) will be past and both of you will be feeling better. But remember, *never* punish a baby for crying. Try to find the cause and correct it. In some cases he will simply need to cry it out. If in doubt, call your doctor.

Toddlerhood: Ages One and Two

This is the roller coaster, hell-on-wheels age. They are now fully mobile and bursting with energy. But they are still very immature, self-centered, demanding, not at all considerate, and haven't caught on to the rules yet. In addition, there will be two periods, around eighteen and later at thirty months, when they will answer everything with "No." If you don't take their *no*s too seriously you can easily outwit them. You are smarter than they are.

It's also a funny age and a funny time; you can have a marvelous time with a child this age.

However, their Niagara Falls of energy will be hard on Mom. Dad should help out and take over, especially in the evening just before dinner, and maybe at bedtime, too. Mothers need support and tender, loving care during this hectic period.

"Child-proof" Your Home   What applied at the earlier age applies even more now. The secret here is that if you do a good job of "child-proofing" your house you eliminate fifty to seventy percent of potential future discipline problems. However, now you have to check every room in the house and every area of the yard because they will get into everything. And they just don't have the maturity, impulse control, or good judgment of an older child. You wouldn't expect a monkey to drive a car, and neither should you expect a child this age to be wise and responsible. If you do a good job of environmental control, it will spare you much grief and greatly increase the pleasure of having your child living in your home. If you have to follow him around all day constantly saying, "No, no, no, stay out of this, stay out of that," I guarantee you'll wind up with a neurotic child and an ulcer.

Milk is going to get spilled, food will accidentally get dumped on the floor, things are going to get tipped over. Expect it. A humorous motto at our house when our children were very young was: "Milk—four cups to drink and one to spill". So get your house and yard in shape. It'll save you a nervous breakdown and the cost of ten visits to the analyst.

Make Use of Alternate Outlets   This is a preventive strategy. It's designed to eliminate potential discipline problems before they happen. With high-energy kids, you need to provide safe outlets for their urges, frustrations, and high spirits. If you don't, they'll find their own outlets—like using your new couch as a trampoline or the upstairs bathtub to flood the lower floors. Suitable play equipment and outside or basement space are absolutely vital for large muscle exercise and the discharge of all their tensions. Rocking horses, "Big Wheels," small trikes, pounding and building toys, packing boxes, sand boxes, wading pools, building blocks, small punching bags, and even trampolines (with supervision) can save wear and tear on the house and on your nerves, besides being therapeutic, educational, and physically healthy for the child.

If your funds are limited, you might get old cardboard packing boxes free from the furniture or appliance store. Children will play by the hour with these. You can blow up an old used truck innertube, which is great fun to jump on. You can get all sorts of building blocks from the site of a construction project for free—in fact, they might even pay you for hauling them away!

Teach, Instruct, and Lead This becomes even more important than at the earlier age. Here you teach them a few important rules (to be added to as they get older) such as, "Stay out of Daddy's study", "Don't run into the street", "Never, never play with the gear shift on the car", or "Stay out of Daddy's tool chest".

When they break a rule after it has been clearly explained to them, you give them several stinging slaps on the thigh or buttocks. They'll briefly cry and be angry with you, but there are certain dangers like running into the street, playing with matches, or hitting their brother with a toy truck that warrant this quite harmless but very effective type of punishment. The child is, of course, in no way injured, though he does feel the sting and instantly gets the message that this behavior is inappropriate.

It's critical that the punishment come right after the bad deed and that the child be fully aware of what it was that he did wrong. You don't wait until Dad comes home or three days from now to punish. It must happen right after the infraction. Some toddlers will learn the rule after just one such confrontation; others with a more rebellious spirit will require more eyeball to eyeball, hand to bottom confrontations to get the point.

Use Diversion and Distraction This still works very well, just as it did with the one-year-old. To get him out of something he shouldn't be in or to give up something he shouldn't have, you can divert his attention by merely picking him up, giving him a big hug with some affectionate talk, and then, when his "cup is full" a few moments later, putting him down elsewhere out of danger or out of trouble. Give him a toy or something to occupy his attention, then go on your way.

Ignore It or "Chair" Him If the toddler is obstinate, noisy, threatens to be destructive, or is bullying, you should initially *ignore it.* Most of the time such behavior can be like a quick storm—in a few moments it will pass. It's not worth making a big hassle over. Don't jump the gun and over-react because it's primarily his age and a reflection of his immaturity.

If, however, the child persists after one or two (at the most) warnings, quickly and firmly place him on a chair and tell him he cannot get off until he has quieted down. It's important that you be in control and assume an active leadership role. Explain that he can get off as soon as he has behaved himself or quieted down for one or two minutes. When he complies, let him go about his business. But he must demonstrate one to two minutes of peace on the chair, and you must make it clear that you won't start timing until he is behaving properly. In some cases it may be necessary to take him to a "time-out room" in a quiet part of the house. This can be a bathroom or bedroom where he will stay until he has been quiet and peaceful for from three to five minutes. Then when his time is up (you should use a kitchen timer so that he can hear when the "impartial machine" says his three minutes are over), you welcome him back into your presence with congratulations on his getting control of himself. All is forgiven, and you start anew.

Preschool Age: Three through Five Years

This is a great age to have the child in your home. He is now more co-ordinated, he's learned some of the family rules, he is more responsible, he is very playful, he can communicate with you, he has a tremendous curiosity and is always asking questions, and he is, for the most part, loving and responsive to you as a parent. He's really great to have around.

The only exception to this is if you have one of those special high-energy kids. Then the task is to keep the child challenged and provide sufficient outlets for Mr. Super Energy before mother collapses from exhaustion and nervous fatigue. Most mothers I know offer up a prayer of thanks when such a child enters school.

Even if you don't have a hyperactive child, I think a high quality pre-school, if you can afford it and one is available, does a lot of good things for children. It deals a body blow to discipline's greatest enemy: boredom. Bored children seem to gravitate to trouble. That's when kids are most likely to fight, quarrel, tease, and torment each other—even good kids. "Idle hands are the devil's workshop." Trite but true. A nursery school keeps explosive kids busy for a few hours—productively busy, far better than television. And you'll still have plenty of time to love your child.

The Power of Modeling A child this age watches every move you make. He wants to be big and grown up like you. He'll imitate you in a thousand ways, unconsciously adopting even your subtle voice inflections and intonations. So if you want him to have good table manners, for example, then you must model it for him again and again, meal after meal. If you want him to be polite with others, you must be polite with each other and with him. Screaming and yelling begets screaming and yelling, and when they have kids of their own, the probability is very high that they'll repeat in the next generation what they've witnessed and learned in this.

The notion "Do as I say but not as I do" doesn't work. If you lie to your kids repeatedly, no matter how you instruct or discipline them regarding truth-telling, your *behavior* has already sanctioned their lying. Be sure your behavior jibes with your verbal messages. Otherwise you are wasting all your effort at instruction and discipline. Model the behavior you want your children to engage in and eventually it will become a part of them.

Teach, Instruct, and Lead Children at this age have a voracious appetite for knowledge. They want to know what the rules are. They are uncritical and guileless. They are impressionable and teachable. Their occasional naughty behavior will be mild and will usually occur as part of their natural curiosity. Punishments, when necessary, can consist of mild scoldings or several swats on the legs or buttocks. With some children reason and a "talking to" will be all that is necessary to correct bad behavior.

It is time to start teaching your child to work. At this age it may be unwise to ask a child if he would *like* to help, because that gives him a choice. If he says no, where does that leave you? It is better to say, "This is what we are going to do today," suggesting the decision has already been made or, "I need your help; you hold the dustpan while I sweep."

Sometimes working briefly along with the child will prime the pump and get him moving with the job. In the beginning, with a new type of work or chores, it is important to spend enough time with him, explaining and instructing so he will understand exactly what standards of performance and quality are expected from him. If you show enthusiasm for what is being done, the work can be a kind of game or challenge to him.

Try the "Time-out Room"   This technique works best—especially with pre-teen children—in dealing with teasing, fighting, whining, sassing, temper tantrums, and attempts to damage or destroy toys or property. It cools everyone down, preserves a child's self-esteem and the parent-child relationship, and avoids long arguments and fruitless no-win discussions.

When the child persists in this type of behavior, escort (or carry) him to a "time-out room" where he is removed from everyone's presence. A bathroom is a good choice because there are no people, toys, TV, books or other distractions there. It's a very dull place to be, yet is large and bright and familiar enough not to be frightening.

Tell him that as soon as he has quieted down for five minutes and can behave, he can rejoin you and the family. Use a kitchen timer. Put it where both you and he can hear it ring after five minutes. However, let him know that the timer doesn't start until he has quieted down. If he persists in shouting or making noise let him know you will *add* time to the "time-out", and come hell or high water stick by your guns on this issue. No matter what it takes, you have to win this battle of wills every time.

"Time-out" really works because most children's misbehaviors are designed to get your attention, punish, or annoy you. By removing him from your presence, "time-out" has just the opposite effect. Bad behavior no longer pays off. And you needn't scold or harangue him because your actions speak much more powerfully than your words.

A modification of "time-out" for more minor offenses is to put a child on a chair or stool in the corner of the room where you are working, as you did when he was younger. The punishment is mild—but it still works. It also allows you to talk peaceably to the child while you continue to get dinner ready or clean the cupboards or sharpen the lawnmower.

For "time-out" to work you need to use it *every* time the child engages in obnoxious behavior, location permitting, and both parents should know the program and each back the other up when you use it. You're on the same team; you need to make sure you're running toward the same goal.

Use Positive Reinforcement Every time your child does something good or right, reinforce it. The Law of Reinforcement has never been repealed: "Behavior that is rewarded tends to get repeated". This is probably the most powerful tool in disciplining children. Rewards can range from hugs, smiles, praise, a squeeze of the arm, or a pat on the back to stars on a chart, money, treats, or some form of public recognition.

Why do you think an Olympic swimmer trains five years to win a five-minute race?

However, praise and reward have to be justly earned; otherwise they lose their value, meaning, and power to motivate. Positive reinforcement, honestly done, works miracles—not only with kids but with your spouse as well.

Elementary Years: Ages Six through Twelve

This is another beautiful age to live with children. They are, for the most part, innocent and open. Mom and Dad are still heroes and good guys. Kids this age are fun to go on trips with, and they still laugh at and enjoy Walt Disney movies. They're eager to learn—full of questions and curiosity. You can still help them with their homework. They may get into occasional mischief, but most of it is prankish and good-hearted. (There are, of course, exceptions.)

It is important to keep this age group busy and occupied—especially in the summer. Give them camp experience, swimming lessons, tennis lessons, enjoyable summer school activities; let them spend a month with a relative on the farm or out of town. Try to keep them out of each other's hair. In other words, *prevent* discipline problems.

This doesn't mean you don't take into account what their wishes and desires are. You do. But fill their lives with interesting and challenging activities and experiences.

Teach, Instruct, and Lead This age group is still highly receptive to parent counsel—especially if it's done with love, tact, and skill. Continually teach and share with them all you know. Verbal punishments—scoldings—may be needed occasionally, but physical punishments (if used in the past) should be gradually phased out with the increasing age of the child. Spankings should be used only for flagrant, willful, major violations of family rules, and if it doesn't work, other disciplinary techniques should be tried. In extreme cases of persistent, rebellious misbehavior, a professional counselor should be consulted.

Use Modeling and Imitative Learning Techniques This is still a powerful influencer. Again, it's monkey see, monkey do. If you want to teach your children to be friendly, outgoing, sociable, and gracious, then model and demonstrate this yourself. Invite friends over for joint family picnics, dinners, evening socials. Introduce your children. Let them see how you do it, over and over again.

If you want your children to be tidy, organized, and good housekeepers, first you must be that way. Parents who have nasty tongues and tempers tend to produce similar children. If you want kind and compassionate children, then they need to be treated kindly and compassionately. The better your relationship with your kid, the better the chance he'll adopt "your ways".

The If-Then Technique Tell your child, "*If* you finish mowing the lawn, *then* you can go swimming," or "*If* you don't tease Robyn for a week, *then* I'll let you go skiing Saturday and pay the lift fees," or "*If* you'll help me get dinner tonight, *then* I'll let you buy some ice cream for the picnic." A reward is given *if* a desirable behavior occurs. It's optional with the child. He has a choice. This minimizes argument. If the child chooses not to do the "if" behavior, his decision should be honored, but the parent can usually choose a reward that will make his acceptance of the proposition more likely.

The "Time-out Room" This can still be used with an out-of-control child, especially in the lower years of this age group, but it's best to do it *before* you get mad or "at the end of your tether". It's very important that you maintain self-control in the face of his tantrum, teasing, or fighting.

Positive Reinforcement Some parents complain to me that rewarding kids for good behavior amounts to bribery. This, of course, isn't true. Bribery is a crime that involves "buying someone off" to violate a public trust or moral obligation. A basic fact of adult life, which we are preparing our kids for, is that good, responsible behavior almost always gets rewarded—on the job, in our relations with friends. I can think of no better place to teach them this universal law than while growing up in our own families. Which is better, to be constantly crabbing and yelling at your kids because they are not getting their unpaid work done, or to regularly give them a fair allowance for chores done on time and up to quality standards?

Remember, rewards don't have to be money. They can be special privileges, a trip, a date with parents, a visit to the library, an overnight stay with a friend. Any time you see your child doing something good—sharing a toy or a candy bar, being helpful, doing work on his own, being polite—really lay on the praise and approval, including lots of hugs and smiles. And be sure you do it with *all* your children; the ones who are not usually good need the praise and affection all the more!

Another powerful reinforcement tool is the star-chart, or point system. It works best with children of elementary school age. It might look like this:

BECKY	Mon.	Tues.	Wed.	Thurs.	Fri.	Sat.	Sun.
Bed made	10	10					
Leaves for school on time	10	10					
Brushes teeth without being told	5	10					
Went to bed without complaining	0	10					
Fed and watered dog	0	10					
Was kind to Julie	10	10					
TOTAL POINTS	35	60					

Each day you might give ten points for each behavior done properly. Partial points can be given for a job partially done. In a particular situation, your youngster could earn sixty points on a single day if everything were done properly. I find that it works better to use a large number of points, like ten or twenty.

Next, you work out an agreement where points can be exchanged for money, TV time, treats, and privileges of all sorts. For this to work, you need to pay off quickly and frequently—no long delays. It should be done weekly—even daily, depending on the age of the child. If the child has one area where he is especially weak or keeps slipping, you can double or triple the points earned for its accomplishment each day.

Behavioral scientists have conducted thousands of experiments using rewards as a means to teach children. One thing they have found is that it is extremely effective in the *early* stages of training to reinforce every step of good behavior your child takes toward a desirable goal. Reward every time.

Then, *later*, these reinforcements can be spaced out. This is called intermittent reward. It works great!

Logical Consequences Many times, instead of inflicting punishments or giving rewards, you can allow the child to experience the natural consequences of his good or bad behavior. For instance, when sixteen-year-old Jimmy gets a twenty-five dollar speeding ticket, his parents don't bail him out but permit him to pay for it out of his own meager savings. Or when Annie fiddles around and doesn't finish her homework assignment by the appointed hour, she doesn't go to the movie with the family that evening because she *must* use the time to do her homework.

Another example: After being called twice to dinner, Harold still fails to show up from downstairs. His plate is removed and he misses his meal. There is no scolding or long harangue about the matter—he just goes to bed hungry. He will not starve to death; a short fast will be therapeutic.

With logical consequences, the child always has a choice and knows ahead of time what the consequences are for a particular behavior or misbehavior. With this system there is no need for parents to be angry. The child is already sufficiently penalized by the natural consequence.

Logical consequences require less talk and more action on the part of the parents. Be firm but kind. Natural and logical consequences quickly help the child learn to be responsible. This method works best where the child's misbehavior is an attention-getting mechanism or a matter of sloppy or bad habits. It would *not* be appropriate where there is real danger to the child, such as keeping him from darting into the street; or where the child suffers from some acute mental or emotional illness and tends to be irrational. However, for most school-age children, most of the time, it works.

What if the children don't seem to care if they miss a meal or don't get to go to the movie with the rest of the family? In most cases this is just a bluff. Disregard their indifference. Smile politely and let the natural, logical consequences continue to occur like death and taxes. In the rare cases where the child really doesn't care, then next time adjust the consequence so that it involves something that the child *does* care about. Whatever the consequence is should be something logically related to the misdeed. Then let it be quickly over and done with.

Over-correction When the child's misdeed has harmed someone else, have him make extra restitution. If he has scribbled all over one wall, he cleans *that* wall off *plus* two more. A local judge has regularly sentenced highway polluters, caught throwing garbage from their cars, to working four Saturdays with a road crew cleaning up debris in the freeway barrow pits—cleaning up not just their own garbage, but other people's as well.

If the child has the bad habit of dumping his jacket on the floor each night when he comes home from school, have him pick it up *five* or *ten* times in a row and put it in the closet. This involves repeated positive practice to reinforce in his mind what to do and not to do. Don't get angry. You may even smile and talk kindly about something else while the child practices picking up and putting away his jacket.

Scolding or Jawboning Jawboning or scolding tends to be a favorite middle-class child-control technique. It leaves no observable scars, but in many ways it can be even more painful than physical punishment.

Sometimes, however, it is helpful and necessary in correcting children—if it is used wisely. Obnoxious children may require powerful verbal confrontations about their highly unacceptable behavior. They need to feel some psychic pain. Better a little pain now than a lost job or failed marriage later. And I'm convinced that in most cases a certain amount of "jawboning" will not ruin your child's life.

Some parents, who may have been damaged themselves in their own childhood, may be verbally destructive and abusive to their children habitually. I've seen some parents engage in a constant flow of verbal assaults and degrading remarks to their children. Eventually almost any child will wither under this barrage of abuse. Both self-esteem and ego can be injured. The child can also be made chronically anxious and filled with much undeserved guilt. In some cases a child, as a defense, may develop a "deaf ear" and turn his parent off altogether. The harangues become a type of "static" which he tries to tune out and ignore, but this can result in constant evasions and poor communication, and the whole process of discipline and child-rearing becomes disturbed.

I would suggest that you also avoid making a lot of threats to any child. It puts negative ideas into the kids' heads. It's like saying, "I dare you." But it's certainly permissible to give reasonable warnings: "Becky, I'm really upset; if you don't put your bike in the garage at night I'll have to lock it up for a while." Be prepared to follow through if the bike is still left out or you'll lose your credibility.

If you expect the best from kids and let them know it, they'll tend to live up to your expectations. If you expect the worst and tell them so, then that's what you'll get—the worst.

Adolescence: Ages Thirteen through Eighteen

For any kind of discipline to really work with a teenager, you need a warm, firm relationship with him. There needs to be some spark of love and respect. That greases the machinery of family interaction and togetherness. But plan ahead. Cultivate his love and friendship *before* he gets on the wild roller coaster of adolescence. And make sure that the major confrontations on discipline are over with before the teen years—what can be accomplished fairly easily with a ten-year-old is often impossible with a fourteen-year-old, at least without causing serious harm to the relationship.

Adolescence is the time of letting go a little, of giving your kids increasing responsibility, of preparing them for adult living. But they are still living in your house and there are some family rules that still apply to them. If they break them with impunity, it sets a destructive example for your younger children. This makes things a little awkward and tense at times.

You should bargain, reason, and negotiate with them on rules. They are nearly your equals, but you are still their legal guardians. You have every right to expect reasonable behavior while they are still in your midst. And no matter what their age, they still need wise counsel. If they feel good about you, they just might listen.

Each teenager is unique. At one time or another almost any of the previous discipline techniques may work with a particular boy or girl. Review all that has gone before if you are struggling to find the right approach to help your son or daughter. However, for most teenagers these are the three techniques of discipline that usually are most appropriate:

Logical Consequences We've already discussed this approach in the previous section, but the fatal mistake many parents make here is to abort the natural consequence when their child has goofed. Some well-meaning parents again and again bail out their child who keeps continually goofing.

A father I know had a terribly spoiled, bratty son who kept getting into trouble. He'd get a girl pregnant and the father would pay the girl off. He wrecked a car while drunk, injuring an old lady; the father hired a sharp attorney who made black look white so the son wouldn't lose his driver's license or have to accept responsibility for what he had done. The son borrowed large sums of money from his Dad to support a dissipated lifestyle, and never paid or even intended to pay him back.

I think the father felt guilty about producing such a son, so he was unable to be firm or insist on responsible adult behavior. The country is full of guilt-ridden parents like this who actually cripple and destroy their children by their predictable "rescue missions". Instead of helping, they turn their children into social infants.

I can hear some parents saying with horror, "Do you mean I should let my child go to *jail?*" What these parents forget is that children rarely start with a serious offense. If the child is caught shoplifting and the parent takes him out of the store and does nothing more than lecture him, why should the parent be surprised if three years later the crime is car theft or burglary? Instead, the child should be exposed to the natural consequences of this act. A confrontation with the store manager and a commitment to sweep floors or carry bags in the store for a period to make up for the shoplifting will go a long way toward preventing later, more serious offenses. Even letting the law take its course when the child is young, so that he gets a taste of juvenile court and mild punishment might scare a child enough to help him realize that he can do things bad enough that no one, not even his parents, can bail him out. After all, the whole point of discipline is to turn the child into a responsible adult who can get along in society. Criminals are adults who *can't* get along in society. If your teenager has serious behavior problems, you will find that as long as you are trying to help the child overcome his weakness, society provides a lot of support for you. It's a rare store manager who won't go along with you in helping curb a tendency toward shoplifting; it's a rare juvenile court judge who won't consult with you and find the most effective way of turning your child from further serious offenses.

You should also be attuned to your child's real feelings. Was his serious offense just a lark, done for fun? Then you need to make sure he senses the damage his action does, both to himself and to others—take the fun out of it. Or was his serious offense done as part of a group? He might very well have disapproved strongly of the action and already be scared to death about having been involved in such a thing. If he is truly repentant and has no history of such actions, you might want to keep the punishment milder and avoid public humiliation.

But you should not automatically take your child's side. Too many parents, when they get a report from school that their child has been caught vandalizing, charge down to the principal's office armed with more wrath than good sense to abuse the principal for having slandered their child. "He's a good boy," they insist, "and I know he'd never do such a thing." The truth is that teachers rarely have any motive for lying. They may have misinterpreted, but usually if the school is alarmed enough about your child to report his misbehavior to you, you should take the matter seriously and discuss it with them. They are potentially your allies in helping your child achieve responsible adulthood. You won't gain points with your child by automatically bailing him out of trouble. He is more likely to think you're overreacting—or to start regarding you as a "sucker".

Old-fashioned Rewards and Penalties Rewards can be given for getting work done, boosting grades, not teasing younger children, not using bad language around the home, or getting a Scout advancement. As discussed before, a reward can be anything that works for a particular youngster, but pay off promptly and specifically. It has more effect that way.

The use of penalties or taking away privileges works best when:

1. The loss of privilege is fair and reasonable—the severity of the penalty matches the offense.
2. The penalty occurs immediately or very shortly after the offense occurs.
3. The penalty is logically related to the offense, if possible (i.e., she can't use the car for a week after getting a speeding ticket; homework isn't done so he can't look at his favorite TV program now on the air). Also the penalty should be meaningful to the child. A fifty-cent fine is not meaningful if the youngster has a thousand dollars in the bank.
4. The parent is firm but kind with no lengthy hassles or continuing arguments. Refuse to argue. Just act, and be friendly.
5. The parent is consistent in applying the penalty. You can't overlook the offense one day and punish it the next. In other words, the rules must be clear and consistently applied—no double standards. The rules can become

more lenient and change, of course, as the child gets older and is able to assume more responsibility.

What is a privilege for one child will not be for another. So wisdom must be used in choosing and exacting penalties. However, it's important not to engage in overkill.

Taking the bike or car away from Robyn for thirty days instead of three is not ten times more effective. In fact, it's usually counterproductive or even *less* effective as a punishment. Why? The three-day loss of the bike or car makes your point very powerfully. But it means that in three days you can use the vehicle again as an effective deterrent or lever.

Let me list some lost privileges which I have found to be most potent motivators for teenagers:

Can't use the phone for three days (this really hurts).

Can't use car for three days or the coming weekend.

Grounding for three to five days—go nowhere but school and home.

Loss of money or allowance when work not done.

No TV or stereo use for three days.

A trip is called off.

A good rule on penalties: Don't use any that you can't enforce.

Nonpower Negotiations This, in a sense, is a nonauthoritarian approach to any problem which you might be having with your teenager. It involves "active listening" followed by peaceful negotiations using techniques popularized by Dr. Thomas Gordon.

When you have a concern or problem involving your teenager, such as a need to assign chores, to limit his use of the car, or curb his coming in too late, you should bring this concern to the child with an "I" message. Frankly own up to having a concern or problem that you wish to resolve: "Hey, John, I'm really bothered by your constant quarreling and bickering. It's really getting to me." Rather than saying "shut up" or making threats, bring the problem to the child so that he has an opportunity, through negotiation and discussion, to introduce solutions. He may then be more likely to assume responsibility for his actions.

Some Final Comments One extremely dangerous booby trap is for husband and wife to sabotage or undercut each other's disciplining of a particular child. This is dynamite and can blow a family apart. I've seen it happen many times. It can be the beginning of the breakup of a marriage. It often happens with remarried couples who bring children from a previous marriage into the new family.

Dad and Mother have to plan their strategy of discipline ahead of time when they have a child who is out of control or presenting serious behavior problems. If they cannot arrive at any reasonable agreements and stick by them, then they should instantly see a seasoned, wise counselor.

Lois and I usually saw things pretty similarly with regards to disciplining the children. We occasionally ran into trouble when one of us got "out of sorts" with a particular child. Then our spirit wasn't very loving towards that youngster. Sometimes there was frank irritation and resentment, so the discipline had an uncomfortable edge to it. This didn't inspire a helpful cooperative response from the child. A kind of tension built up between parent and child that became increasingly unpleasant. It was like an infection that kept getting worse.

Our solution, which worked well, was for the one of us who was having the problem with the child to back off or totally bow out of any further disciplining for a while. The other parent took over entirely in this area. This allowed us to then mend our fences and improve our relationship with the youngster. But it required full cooperation between us as husband and wife and good communication as well as a major commitment to each other and our family.

It worked. And over the years each of us had a turn at being close or sometimes briefly distant from one child or the other. But we healed the wounds and had many happy experiences with all of our children.

In summary: Discipline is good and necessary. You can't raise healthy, "winner" children without it. Its purpose is to teach and train the child to cope with a difficult world. It essentially involves correcting, strengthening, and perfecting the youngster. If done well it will help give him effective healthy inner controls and self-discipline, so that as an independent adult he can organize his energies to accomplish freely chosen goals.

The ultimate aim of discipline is to free the person from the irrational and impulsive side of his nature—not to repress or tyrannize him, but rather to give him powerful habits of focus, direction, work, and good judgment, adding up to great personal power. Good discipline produces strength, not weakness; creativity, not banality; responsibility, not self-indulgence. It can also produce the character out of which the capacity to love and sacrifice can emerge.

10

Sibling Rivalry

COMPETITION, HATRED, OR VIOLENCE between siblings lies at the root of some of the oldest and most powerful stories in literature. The Bible begins with Cain murdering his brother, Abel, and continues through the rivalry between Jacob and Esau to the brothers of Joseph selling him into slavery in Egypt. The mythical founders of Rome, the brothers Romulus and Remus, were no better—Romulus won sole control of the city by killing poor Remus. The Greek goddesses Artemis, Athena, and Aphrodite, all daughters of Zeus, were bitter rivals.

And sibling rivalry isn't confined to myths. Great wars have been fought between brothers trying to win kingdoms; many domestic tragedies have been caused by long-lasting quarrels between siblings. While your children may not sell each other into slavery or start a civil war, you may find yourself listening to comments like these:

"Mommy, why does Jerry always get the biggest piece!"

"Don't I ever count around here?"

"Dad, make Jill move over. She got to sit by the car window last time!"

"He always sits by the window on the long trips, and I only sit by the window on the way to the store!"

Russ, our oldest, was three and a half when Janice was born. He was quite frank about not liking to have her around. He was used to having us exclusively to himself, and he was in no mood to share. Today, as adults, they have a great relationship—but back then she was an interloper.

In my experience, the adjustment to a new baby is hardest for the older child who is between eighteen months and four-and-a-half years. Such a child is already talking and has a bonded relationship with his parents, but he is not in school yet and has not matured to the point where he can have outside friendships; his dad and mom are ninety percent of his universe. He's not going to give up his world, not without a fight!

Does this mean you have to have your second child within a year and a half? Or space your children at least five years apart? I doubt it.

There are some distinct advantages in having your children in clumps, only a few years apart. In their teens and young adult years it helps them to be closer, to support each other in their social life. Our Russ and Jan were close enough in age to be friends as well as siblings. They lined up dates for each other many times. Their early rivalry for our love and attention had disappeared with maturity.

Sibling rivalry is an almost universal early-life crisis. It confronts all families with more than one child. It requires the older child to learn to share some of the parents' time, attention, and love—to cut the pie into more pieces.

This isn't bad. It's good. It's the beginning of a social conscience. The youngster learns to be part of a social network. He learns you must give in order to get. Learning to share may not be easy, but it's necessary for healthy adult living—and early family life is the best time and place to learn these lessons.

Parents can help their children make this difficult adjustment—or they can make it harder, make the rivalry more painful and intense. In some families sibling jealousy is like a raging fever, and it continues for years, to the very deathbeds of the parents and the children. Probate lawyers often see this as they struggle through dividing up estates among children who hate each other.

I attended a funeral of a lovely lady who had six surviving married children. As the speaker recounted her great love and many sacrifices, the family unitedly wept in sorrowing memory. Two days later they met at her humble home to divide up her personal effects and her ancient worn furniture. Two of the married daughters in their thirties got into a name-calling and hair-pulling fight. At issue was an old beat-up chair worth not more than ten or fifteen dollars. This sad spectacle occurred on their deceased mother's front lawn in view of the entire neighborhood. The years had not dimmed their ancient rivalries and jealousies.

Sibling jealousy and rivalry is, to some degree, to be expected in every family. The arrival of the second child will provide a larger trauma for the firstborn than the arrival of the third or fourth. Once the youngster gets used to the idea of sharing his parents with one sibling, it becomes a little easier to accept the next children to come.

Occasionally I see a child who has a pathological hatred of his brothers and sisters. He is vicious and destructive to the point of being dangerous, and he can injure and maim just as well with words and psychological warfare as with his fists. This must never be tolerated. When this does occur, I usually find that the parents are crippled by some kind of guilt feelings. They are afraid of the child. They say *no* only hesitatingly and are unable to take decisive action. In almost every such case the parents need professional assistance to deal with their pathologically hate-filled child. If you have such a problem, don't wait too long to get help.

You Can't Package Love in Identical Parcels

In every family there are some children who are cuter, more attractive, and more responsive to love than others. It's a temptation to establish favorites—perhaps unknowingly. The less lovable children are very tuned into the fact that there is no way they can compete with the favored Danny or Julie. They see Dad's eye light up every time Julie waltzes into the room. But Dad hardly notices them except when they've failed to close a door, left a coat on the floor, or have made too much noise—then his face is hard and rejecting, not the kind of attention they would prefer.

How do responsible parents handle this dilemma? Haim Ginott suggests that it is impossible to give exactly equal shares of love to all of your children, and I agree. In fact children do not really yearn for equal shares of love—they need to be loved uniquely, not uniformly.

One day many years ago I had a chat with Dr. Merritt Egan, a remarkable man who for many years was a pediatrician in Salt Lake City and then became a child psychiatrist. He and his wife Marsha have eleven amazing children. Somewhat kiddingly I asked him once who his favorite was. Without blinking an eye or hesitating a second he said, "The one closest to me."

Mormon colonizer Brigham Young had twenty-seven wives. This has always been somewhat exhausting for me even to contemplate, but the historical documents and diaries suggest he had remarkably good relations with most of these women. Sure, there were one or two marriages that didn't work out, but his batting average was still higher than for most of us.

How did he do it? Somehow, each of these women was made to feel that she was his favorite. I think we have to do the same thing with our children. Each is our favorite. Whichever one we are nearest to at the moment is the one who feels most loved by us.

In some cases we have to go out of our way to make sure we are near to each of the children at some time or another. Take one shopping with you. Dad, on a business trip, can invite a child along from time to time. The opportunity to talk heart to heart often occurs after midnight, when everyone else is asleep and a teenager comes in after a date. As each child comes home from school, similar opportunities present themselves. You can ask questions gently, not to pry. You can share your caring. You can tell them in words that you love them; sometimes there may even be an embrace.

Such moments, from early childhood to young adulthood, are remembered a lifetime. Each child knows in the deepest recesses of his soul that he really matters to his parents. The children know that they don't have to compete neurotically for your time and attention. They can share their parents' love because they know they will always receive all they need. Remember, sometimes it's the child who is least lovable that needs it most. If you properly nurture him in his early years, then he won't later become an obnoxious, impossible teenager that turns everybody off.

. So the first commandment in dealing with sibling jealousy and rivalry is to make sure you fill each child's cup with love. This can never be done exactly uniformly; it must be done uniquely for each child. Stop counting and measuring—life will become impossible for you if you do. Be spontaneous. Seize each occasion as it arises, and take full advantage of it.

At certain ages and times some of your children will get more of you than at others. Usually this balances out over the years. That's the way all their relationships through life will be; it's a lesson they need to learn. But you can still reassure them that no matter what happens, no matter where they are, there is still a special relationship, a bond, a caring and love that nothing can erase. Even when they make mistakes or disappoint us, they still *belong* to us.

How do you show love if you're the cool sort? Parents are the product of their past, just as their children will be. I once heard about an old man, married thirty-seven years, whose wife complained that he had never told her he loved her during all that time. "When we first got married I told you I loved you," he said. "When I change my mind, I'll let you know."

I come from a "cool" family, We were intellectual and rational. There was love there, but it was never expressed in a "sloppy", open, demonstrative way. We loved each other and knew it by a special kind of ESP and subtle nonverbal cues; it was not considered good form to do a lot of hugging and kissing.

My wife, Lois, has no such inhibitions. Her family was more affectionate and demonstrative. She expresses feelings openly and honestly.

One day, as a fairly new bride, Lois approached me apprehensively. She hesitatingly told me that her mother felt I didn't like her.

I was rather stunned. Lois's mother was a very gracious, warm, friendly, affectionate person. I really like her. I considered myself lucky to have such a lovely mother-in-law.

As Lois and I discussed why my mother-in-law felt I didn't like her, the answer emerged: I never hugged and kissed her when we greeted each other. This was the style she was used to in her family.

I must confess it took me about ten years to learn how to kiss my mother-in-law. It really wasn't that bad.

My non-demonstrative style slowed me down in expressing love openly to my children. I loved them, but they weren't really sure of that; I didn't say so very often. But people can change, if they wish, and I did—not totally, but now each of my children knows very clearly how I feel about him or her.

Love is a daily decision. And, freely expressed, it is the single most powerful antidote for sibling rivalry and jealousy I know.

"Why Can't You be Smart Like Joanie?"

Second, third, fourth, and later children never have quite the same problem with jealousy that the first one has, but that doesn't mean they won't
ever feel jealous. You can help ease childhood jealousies by not comparing
your children with each other. If you constantly say, "Charles! Why in the
world can't you keep your room neat and clean like your sister Samantha?" it
will make Charles resent Samantha. It may harm Samantha, too, as it suggests to Samantha a way of lording it over Charles. She may start keeping
her room clean just to aggravate her brother! She wins doubly—she gains
parent approval as she puts her competitor down, but her smug smile will not
go unnoticed by her brother as Mother berates him. To retaliate he might
even be prompted to go in and mess her room up, fomenting a brother-sister
feud that could go on for years.

It really isn't fair to compare one child's performance and behavior with
another's. Each is at a different age, physically and mentally, and each has a
unique mix of talents, abilities, and inadequacies. Samantha may simply enjoy being tidy, while Charles's creativity demands a delicious disorder!

My Child, the Super-Spy!

Discourage tattling. Firmly refuse to allow children to habitually come
to you with long recitals about a sibling's bad behavior. As Thumper Rabbit's
father said in the film *Bambi*, "If you can't say something nice, don't say
anything at all." You may need to remind your children of this many times.

Remember—I refer to habitual tattling about relatively unimportant
matters. If you reward such behavior by paying serious attention to it or,
even worse, punishing the child who was told on solely on the strength of the
tattler's testimony, you can bet the child will tattle again and again—earning
his brother's or sister's undying hatred and not really gaining the love he
wants to have from you.

There are things, however, that children *should* feel free to tell you. If one
of the children is bullying or being cruel to the other children when you
aren't there, his victims should know that you care about them and will take
steps to protect them. The difference between good telling and bad telling is
one of degree. If a child doesn't often tattle, when he reports something
serious you should take it seriously. But if a child makes a habit of telling on
brothers and sisters, particularly about relatively trivial matters (or in-
vented ones), you should discourage his tattling immediately.

Another situation where you need to have children talk about each other
is when a specific wrongdoing has to be investigated. For instance, the pud-

ding you prepared for a charity banquet is half gone. You're already twenty minutes late, but you specifically told the children the pudding was not for them, and you can't let them get away with it. The trouble is, they all want to put the blame elsewhere.

"Mother, it was Tanya who got into the pudding. She got it out of the fridge."

"She's a liar; I did no such thing! I found it on the counter!"

"Shut up; you're a pig; you ate most of it; I saw you!"

"I'm not a pig. You're a pig, and last Saturday I saw you take stuff out of Mother's purse!"

The children are ready to come to blows—or tears. You know you have to put a stop to the quarrel before it becomes serious. The easy way is to make a snap decision about who was wrong—or decide to punish everybody, just to end the argument. The trouble with this is that even if you happen to hit on the pudding-eater, he'll believe you are "against" him, that you are "on their side". It promotes bad feelings among the children. And if you punish them all when only one was really at fault, the others will resent the guilty one deeply. What can you do?

First, postpone the discussion. Go to the banquet. Don't punish anyone when you don't know the facts. End the argument by ceasing to be an audience for it.

Later, when you do discuss the matter, take the children aside one by one, so that you can hear each child's version of the story without having the others call him a liar or find out who's "telling on" him. This minimizes the possibility of the children feeling rancor or hate toward one individual, and you aren't forced into a position of seeming to agree with that hatred.

When you have all the evidence, and you're sure who was at fault, you can decide what the punishment should be for each child. They don't even have to know what each other's punishment is—it's strictly a matter between you and each child.

Small children can be furious with each other at one moment, and the next moment the argument is forgotten. You need to know when to make a big deal out of the problem and when to simply separate them for a few moments while they forget to be angry with each other. Above all, don't keep bringing up the past, reminding them of past arguments and old wounds.

"My Big Sister Is My Best Friend" Actively foster bonding among the children. This can be done in a variety of ways.

Let them plan a surprise birthday party for a brother or sister. Through your contagious excitement and subtle leadership you can make this an "everybody wins" experience. Encourage an older child to read to a younger child. Pay an older child to be regularly in charge of a small child at bedtime. He might help the little one into his sleepers, assist him in brushing his teeth, and lie down with him to get him to sleep, if necessary. Again, everybody wins. The older child doesn't feel exploited or resent spending the time with the little one. Junior gets the attention of his older brother or sister while Mother can catch a breather and spend some time with her husband or other children at that evening hour. Of course, if the older child wants to do it for free, so much the better!

"At Least Fighting Is Something to Do" No matter what age they are, keep your children busy. Bored children get into each other's hair. During summer vacations insist that all of your older children be employed. Some parents will even give a kickback to a neighborhood grocer to hire their youngster. If it's necessary, it's money well spent. Summer camps, workshops, trips, visits (say, for a month) with relatives, or working in community youth programs should fill your children's summers so they don't spend all their time annoying each other just to have something to do. High energy, muscle-flexing children lying around all day looking at TV quickly become explosive. It's like leaving spilled gasoline on the floor waiting for someone to light a match. Weekends also need to be carefully filled with activities.

The Private Interview Once a month have a special private interview with each child in a private place where there are no interruptions, no phones ringing, no other children demanding attention, no visitors knocking on the door. It should last from thirty to sixty minutes. You might bring some food along to loosen things up—popcorn, diet drinks, or whatever their favorite might be. One or both parents can be present; either way can work well.

The interview should be low key. It's a time to listen to the child. It's a time to see how he feels about school, his friends, you. It's a time when you ask him if he has any suggestions about changing family rules or habits. This is his hour. Treat him as you would treat a client you are trying to make a deal with—as if he were the most important person you know!

When you first start this, your kids will be a little suspicious. What's the hidden agenda? What are you *really* getting at? They may not feel like talking a lot at first, but by the third month they'll love it. Call it by a catchy name: PFI, for instance. Personal Family Interview. You explain that you just want to be better parents. You want to find out what they're thinking and feeling about things.

It may sound corny to them, and they may act sophisticated and pretend that they don't need it. They really do, and they want you to persist. All children like private time with their parents. But remember to listen; don't lecture. And don't let things bog down—plan beforehand ten helpful questions you might ask them to get things rolling.

The sooner you put these rules into effect in your household, and the younger your children are when you start, the greater the impact on them.

These strategies really work. In a year you will notice a major change in your children's relationships with each other. You also have to pay the price: some of your time. Everything really good or great costs something. But which price would you rather pay? Some of your time now—or watching your children drift apart years later?

11

Lying

MOTHER STANDS BY THE FREEZER, looking at Charley and Martha. "All right, which one of you finished up the ice cream? I was saving that for when the Andersons come to play bridge tonight. You *know* you're not supposed to take anything out of the freezer without asking me first. Who did it?"

Charley and Martha both shrug and shake their heads slowly with innocent, slightly bewildered looks on their faces. It's just as much a mystery to them as it is to Mother. That is, except for the streaks of ice cream on their chins and upper lips.

Why do children lie? Not surprisingly, they lie for pretty much the same reasons adults do.

1. To conceal guilt and avoid punishment or other unpleasant consequences: "I didn't take any money out of Sarah's pocket! Quit blaming me for everything that goes wrong!"

2. To avoid ridicule, disapproval, "loss of face", or personal embarrassment: "I know I turned that assignment in—the teacher lost it and now he's blaming it on me."

3. To impress others in order to win acceptance or approval: "My dad makes over a hundred thousand a year, but he doesn't like showing it off. That's why he drives that old car."

4. To get others into trouble, because of jealousy, competitiveness, vindictiveness, or to put down a rival: "Mom, I saw Robbie punch Jenny while you were gone."

5. As a deliberate hostile act in a parent-child struggle: "You're so sure I broke the window, well just try and prove it. Nobody saw who did it. So what are you going to do about it?"

6. Then there is the delinquency-prone, conscienceless youngster who will lie for no reason at all. In its extreme form, this habit can lead to major adjustment problems as the child grows into adolescence and adulthood. We refer to the whole complex of behavior that includes motiveless lying as sociopathy, psychopathy, or the "anti-social personality". According to the best available research, this seems to be a form of personality disturbance, long-term and untreatable, and it may well be partly genetic and biological in origin. The individual in such a case knows perfectly well that he is lying, but he doesn't much care—and is even indifferent about the consequences when he is caught in his lie.

The Conscience

Consciences grow slowly, and in relation to the child's age in years and general maturity. We usually don't see a fairly mature and active conscience emerging in a child until ages six or seven, at which time most children understand what telling the truth means—though, of course, that doesn't stop them from fibbing occasionally.

There is some suggestion that conscience may be stronger and develop earlier in girls than in boys. (The occasional child who appears to lack a conscience entirely is discussed more fully in Chapter 6.)

Even *with* a developed conscience, however, children still have to be repeatedly taught and trained in truth-telling, as well as property rights, temper control, courtesy, generosity, loving, forgiving, and all the other social amenities. And, of course, they will frequently fall short and sometimes have to be taught the same lesson again and again.

Children vary remarkably, even in the same family, in their ability to experience guilt, remorse, and concern about lying and wrongdoing. Sometimes fairly normal, decent teenagers lie habitually in order to handle a neurotic mother or overbearing father, or to deal with parents who expect too much of them.

"Why aren't you studying? You know your average was barely a *B* last time, and here you are goofing off again!"

"My homework's all done. They didn't assign any today."

Lying is easier than getting a boring half-hour lecture on the importance of keeping cupboard doors closed, putting the top on the Listerine bottle, not borrowing Agnes's jacket or lipstick, or whatever other "crime" an incessantly nagging parent might have discovered. "It wasn't me." "She told me I could." It makes the teenager's life tolerable, even though he or she knows lying is wrong.

Little children are often easy to catch in a lie. They don't realize they are making facial expressions and gestures that give them away completely. But teenagers have caught on. They know how to make a lie sound plausible, especially if they have been forced into lying as a family survival technique.

Parents who habitually make mountains out of molehills, nagging their children mercilessly about trivial matters, are inevitably going to have children who not only lie but are good at it. Is the left-on light, the unwashed dish, the undone homework so important that it's worth inviting your child to lie about it? Perhaps sometimes it is. But not habitually—because habitual, long-winded, or cruel nagging rarely stops the children from doing the things they're being nagged about. It *does*, however, stop the children from taking responsibility for their own actions.

There are two things you can do to combat lying. First, long before there's any serious lying problem, you must cultivate the habit of truth. And second, you must look behind the lie to find the reason for it—and treat the problem, not the symptom.

Creating the Habit of Truth

To begin with, you have to believe in honesty yourself. If you habitually lie in order to cover your errors or avoid embarrassment, you're going to have a hard time convincing your children that *they* shouldn't lie. But convince them you must, because the problem with lying is that if you catch the child in a lie and punish him, you can't be sure whether next time he'll tell the truth—or just tell a more convincing lie!

If your daughter is constantly lying to impress her friends, eventually they catch on and the word spreads. People begin doubting anything she says, and it's impossible for her to be trusted. If your son always evades trouble with a lie, eventually he will be assumed to be guilty even when his protests of innocence are true. Furthermore, habitual lying gets under the skin.

Liars begin to think of themselves as liars, to be distrustful of others because they may be lying, too. Thus the child who lies frequently risks losing love and acceptance from those he cares most about.

Children need to be warned explicitly that this is what lying does, and not just when they're caught in a lie. When they admit to a minor wrongdoing or take the responsibility for their own embarrassing situation, you should make it a point to tell them how good it is that they are being honest about it. "Of course I have to punish you for using the car without permission, but I'm glad that you admitted it—because now I know that when you tell me you *didn't* do something wrong, I can trust you to be telling me the truth." Or, "Johnny may be mad at you for using his train without permission, but I'm proud of you for telling the truth."

When parents run across someone whose honesty is worthy of note, they should point it out to their children. "Did you notice that the shoe salesman could have made more money by selling me that really expensive pair of shoes? And yet he told me that the soles tended to wear out really quickly and couldn't be replaced easily. Talk about honesty! I'm going to come back to this store again!" Or, "That boy didn't have to come and tell us that he ran over our rosebush on his bicycle. He could have just ridden off and we would never have known. I'm going to call his parents and tell them just how wonderful their son is!"

Examples like that aren't lost on children. They catch on pretty quickly that honesty is a better way to please their parents than lying.

However, you have to remember that while you're praising honesty, you can't let every other character attribute take care of itself. When your son runs over the rosebush, you don't just say, "Well, since you were so honest about it, we'll forget it this time." You say, "I really appreciate your being honest about it, son. Now get the shovel and let's dig it up and plant a new one. The new one costs $6.98. Who do you think ought to pay for it?" Otherwise, you let their honesty become just another strategy for getting out of punishment. You need to let them know that honesty doesn't avoid punishment—but it does increase love and trust and respect between them and you. You don't want your kids to think, "My parents don't care *what* I do, as long as I tell 'em."

Curing the Habitual Liar

You may already have a problem with a child who lies—or despite your best efforts to create the habit of truth, one of your children may suddenly begin to lie habitually. What do you do?

First you look at the pattern of the child's fibbing or lying. *When* does the child lie? What kind of lies does he tell? Go through the list of reasons for lying and try to figure out which of them fit best. Sometimes you have to be brutally honest with *yourselves*: Your child might be lying because you're constantly pushing him into no-win situations where his only escape is lying. Or he may be lying in direct imitation of you, telling his friends exactly the same kind of lie you tell *your* friends. Study the pattern of the child's lying, and be pretty sure you understand what's going on before you take any other action.

If the child is lying simply because he's too young to understand the consequences, you can do several things. First, work to establish the habit of telling the truth. At the same time, you can discipline him mildly for lying. Not with long tirades; not by branding him "a filthy little liar". Rather you should say, "You can't ride your bicycle for two weeks. One week is because you rode it right through the newly planted lawn after we told you not to. The second week is because you lied about it. When you lie, it doesn't make it any easier on you—it makes it worse." Lessons in truth-telling combined with mild discipline help the child understand the importance of honesty as he matures. But remember—because the child is immature, it may take many repetitions of the same lesson before it really sinks in and becomes part of his personality.

If you don't understand why the child is lying, of course, you shouldn't work on the lying problem at all. Instead, do just what a professional counselor would do. Deliberately take some pressures off the child—remove an unwanted responsibility, or stop pressuring him to improve in some other area. Then try to get closer to him; find out what's going on inside his head.

This might require a brief trip away together or some low-key conversations around bed-time. Not accusing conversations: "I know you've been lying to me—now I want to know why!" Make the conversations exploratory: "Becky—you've looked kind of tired and sad lately. Anything I can help with? You know we all have our ups and downs. Once when I was twelve I had a best friend who really let me down. I felt like somebody had cut off my arm. Have you had some real disappointment lately? It helps sometimes to talk about it. Maybe I can help."

You can tell from the child's reaction whether you're barking up the wrong tree or not. The response back, "You couldn't help," is a sure sign the child has a problem and will, in time, probably talk about it. Even when the child says, "There's nothing wrong," you can usually tell he is really saying, "I wonder if you're *really* interested?" or "It's too painful to talk about now." Don't give up. Just keep the conversation going, and after a long enough time—or enough separate conversations—the child will usually talk about what's bothering him. Usually when he insists that "nothing's wrong" it only means that it's *really* bothering him—so badly that he's ashamed or afraid to talk about it.

For instance, Jennie, a seventeen-year-old, was often caught lying—or at least fudging with the truth or evading questions. "Nothing's wrong," she said—but after long persistence her parents finally won her confidence well enough for her to tell them what was bothering her most. She had been a middle child, always pleasant and well-behaved. She had never been very demanding, and because of that her older brothers and sisters and the younger ones had got more attention than she. In this very busy family, where both parents worked and were active socially, she had simply become "lost between the cracks".

She had no sense of loyalty or deep caring for anybody, and she didn't think anybody felt those things for her. Even her friendships outside the family were casual and transient. Lying, for her, was merely a way of avoiding complete rejection or of getting what she wanted without the trouble of explaining her real reasons.

For Jennie, the solution of her problem was not to give her long lectures on the evils of lying—that kind of rejection would have simply driven her further away and destroyed what weak bonds of affection there were. What she really needed was to have a strong emotional bond established with her parents, so that she didn't want to break trust with them. Once she knew that they really cared about her, loved her, and trusted her, she lied less and less. She no longer regarded her parents as obstacles she had to "get around" and began to think of them as wonderful people she wouldn't want to hurt or disappoint.

Another example is Jimmy, who at age ten was found to be involved in frequent lying—not to mention stealing candy and gum and other small items out of local supermarkets and department stores. His lies were usually to cover the thefts or to explain where he got all his candy. "Another kid gave them to me." "I traded my *Star Wars* laser pistol for it."

In this case, the parents found that Jimmy was spending a lot of his time with a twelve-year-old who had a lot of charisma—and a lot of influence over Jimmy. The older boy came from a disturbed home and had a history of troublemaking, petty theft, and vandalism going back to his earliest school years. A good share of what Jimmy was doing was related to his companionship with this other boy—Jimmy was picking up his swagger, his insolent way of talking, and, obviously, his contempt for the property rights of others.

The parents quickly, graciously, but firmly terminated Jimmy's association with the older boy. They candidly explained why, pointing out to Jimmy the ways that his own behavior had changed and the serious consequences if he did any more of it. At first Jimmy protested, but not nearly so much as his parents had expected, and in a short while both the stealing and the lying diminished and in time almost entirely ceased. Jimmy simply did not want to embarrass himself in front of this boy, but was just as happy to get away from a situation where he always had to do what the older boy wanted to do.

Parent-induced Lying

The hardest kind of lying for parents to deal with is the lying they cause themselves. "I don't make him lie! He does it on his own," parents will say, but there are patterns set up by parents which their children, with less fully formed personalities, cannot resist.

For instance, sometimes parents refuse to hear the truth. "I hate the baby," a four-year-old says. "I wish he hadn't been born." Some parents react as if the older child were a monster. "What do you mean, you hate the baby! That sweet, helpless little creature hasn't done you a bit of harm! How dare you say such a thing!"

Well, the child can't help it. He really *does* feel negative emotions toward the baby. But to win his parents' approval, he'll start lying about it. "I *love* the baby," he'll say, hugging the little one when the parents are watching and hitting him or yelling at him or neglecting him when the parents are out of sight. And the habit of lying is thus firmly established—the child learns that he can't tell his parents what he really feels.

How should you deal with a child's negative emotions? You have to recognize that emotions are not something that your child *decides* to feel. No child says, "Today I think I'll hate the baby." Instead, he sees the newborn being coddled and cared for, and suddenly Mommy and Daddy don't play with him nearly as much as before—and they're constantly saying how cute the baby is and they never think *he's* cute these days. Of course he's going to feel angry and hurt and afraid that he isn't loved anymore. Why shouldn't he?

When your child says he hates the baby, don't answer with, "Don't be ridiculous; you *love* the baby." You shouldn't deny his true feelings. Accept them, the way you want your family to accept *your* true feelings.

"Why do you feel that way?" you ask.

"You don't play with me anymore. You just keep playing with her and you always tell me you're busy."

"Well, you know that when you were little like that, we spent a lot of time taking care of you. But now you're bigger, you can do a lot of things on your own. After all, the baby can't even talk to me, and you and I talk all the time. Just because we have to spend a lot of time taking care of the baby doesn't mean we don't love you. You're really important to us." And prove it to him, with a special trip the next weekend, for you and him alone.

This way the parent acknowledges the child's negative feelings without making the child feel guilty about having those feelings. The parent explains that they are not being unfair—the older child had his turn to be a baby once, too. And the parent assures the child that he is not forgotten, reminds him of the special advantages he has. Thus, instead of forcing the child to hide his true feelings, the parents encourage him to be honest about them—and solve the problem by actually taking steps to remove the *reasons* for those negative feelings.

Another way parents induce lying in their children is by asking questions that invite lies. Too often, parents try to handle problems by humiliating their child. What is the child likely to do if he's playing in the back yard with two of his friends and his mother comes out and says, angrily, "I'm going to give you a spanking you won't forget if you're the one who broke the hinge on the cupboard!" Of course he's going to lie in order to avoid the total humiliation of being spanked or yelled at in front of his friends.

Parents who set traps for their children ("Have you been smoking?" "No." "Then why is this tobacco in your shirt pocket?" "I carried a pack of ciragettes for Frank.") are begging for lies. Parents who back their children into a corner ("If you stole this I'm personally going to turn you over to the police.") have no chance of hearing the truth. Interrogations designed to reduce the child to tears or accusations couched in terms that make the of-fense seem more serious than it is are bound to produce evasions.

Our ultimate goal as parents is not to punish—that is merely a means to an end. The power to punish is only *one* of the tools parents use in pursuit of the real goal, which is to help the children be responsible, "winner" adults. And it gets less and less powerful as the children get older and the parents' punishments mean less and less. A far more powerful tool is the strong, lov-ing, open relationship between parent and child. If the child loves and trusts his parent and has their respect, he will go to great lengths to avoid damag-ing that relationship. The parents should do the same. That strong relation-ship will help parents and children over the worst crises.

Of course, that doesn't mean that you use that loving relationship as a *weapon*, a means to punish. You never say or imply, "If you do that again, I won't love you anymore." What it does mean is that you can approach your child as a friend, not an enemy. You get nowhere if you seem to be trying to trap the child or prove that he's a criminal or make him feel humiliated in front of his friends or in front of you. You accomplish a great deal if you sit down with your child and discuss the problem rationally, as a loving parent who won't tolerate certain negative actions the child is performing but who cares for the child all the same.

This doesn't mean that you can never get angry. Sometimes Lois and I have found that anger is therapeutic, but you must be careful *how* you show your wrath. You shouldn't show it physically—hitting your children in anger is a one-way ticket to child abuse—nor should you show anger by verbally attacking your children. "You're nothing but a thief! You make me sick! You make me angry! I'm ashamed to be your father!" Such statements are destructive.

If you're usually very calm about discipline and discussion of problems, they'll sit up and take notice on those rare occasions when you *do* get tears in your eyes, when your voice *does* shake, when you *do* look stern or speak with real anger in your voice. It's a way of saying, "I love you, I care. I care so much that I'm willing to risk our relationship by showing you how strongly I feel against what you've been doing. I'm angry at you because I love you, and what you're doing could ultimately destroy you if you persist in it."

The kids get the message loud and clear, even though there may be a temporary rupture, momentary pain. After all, if you never showed intense emotion, no matter how serious the problems were, you would be acting exactly the way you would *if you didn't care.* Your child is never your enemy—you never attack him—but when someone that important to you hurts you or frightens you or angers you greatly, you are doing him no favor to keep it a secret.

What to Do about the Occasional Lie

If your child usually tells the truth and suddenly you catch him in a lie, it may be a good idea not to get too upset about it. A single lie is not a serious offense by itself unless it endangered someone or something important, and if a child who normally tells the truth suddenly lies, it is because of unusual stress, an unusual problem. The lie should be treated as a symptom, not a disease.

"John, I haven't known you to tell a lie since you were a little boy, but today I found out that you didn't really hit a home run in the baseball game yesterday. I ran into the coach at the drug store and told him how proud we were of your home run, and he looked really embarrassed and told me that you didn't hit one. Now, you don't have to worry—we assured him it must have been a misunderstanding and he's not going to think you're a liar."

In such a situation, it's better to get right past the lie as quickly as possible. Don't ask, "Were you telling us the truth when you told us about those home runs yesterday?" That's an invitation to back up that one lie with another. If you have the facts, let him know. Lay it on the line, and then don't make a big deal about it—because this child is not a habitual liar. If he lies there's something important going on besides the lie.

Keep Your Expectations Reasonable

Another way to prevent lying is to make sure you aren't expecting too much of your children. Unreasonable expectations can be a long-term problem. One father, a college professor, knew that his son's IQ put him in the genius range. He felt keenly his responsibility as the parent of a child with such a great potential. Unfortunately, he expressed that concern by making constant demands: if his son's grades slipped below a standard that was very near perfection, he became upset and lectured his son at great length on the importance of education and how it was a criminal waste of the boy's great intellect if he didn't do better work in school.

What he was forgetting was that his own standards were not necessarily shared by his son. The boy, this potential genius, was often bored by school. His father's lectures did nothing to make school more interesting. Furthermore, he had trouble getting along with his friends when he got exceptional grades; he found that average grades made him more friends, and he vented his quick wit by becoming something of a class clown, which did no good for his grades. His father became more and more demanding as his grades got worse and worse, and the boy began lying to evade the lectures about "wasted potential".

"Sure, I don't have any homework."

"I'm doing fine in English this quarter."

"Yeah, I'm going to get As."

"No, I don't want any help on my homework. I'm doing fine."

Every grade report, of course, came as a cruel surprise to the father, who confronted his son: "I thought you told me you were doing fine, and here you are with a C in English. And a D in algebra. You can do better than that! Why did you lie to me?" And so on. But at least this way it only happened at report card time instead of throughout the school year.

Finally the father caught on to what was happening. He simply stopped talking about grades at all. No miracle occurred—his son's grades did not suddenly shoot up to Bs and As. But gradually, over time, the lying stopped. His son was able to talk frankly about his mediocre schoolwork. He didn't evade his father's company; their relationship, after years of terrible strain, healed.

Eventually, the son found a field of work in college that was interesting to him, and with the maturity that had, quite naturally, increased over the years, he tackled the work, made up for lost time, and suddenly got grade report after grade report with straight As. Wisely, his father didn't say, "I told you so."

There are many other ways parents can pressure their children into lying because of their expectations. The mother who expects her daughter to have a wonderful social life may find herself being regaled with imaginary tales of how wonderful a particular date was, when actually her daughter loathes dating and particularly loathes the boy she just went out with—but the girl knows that if she tells the truth, her mother will be terribly disappointed at how her daughter is a "wallflower" and a "boy-hater" and will never get married.

A father who expects all his sons to be macho is likely to hear a lot of lies from a son who simply isn't interested in he-man athletics and sports.

The secret is simply to avoid deciding what your children ought to be, beyond a simple moral code and the goal of having them be self-confident, competent individuals. Much of parenting is discovery rather than shaping. Your children will decide for themselves what they want to be and do. Your job is to help them have the confidence to go out and do it well; to help them be the kind of moral, honest people who will be an asset to whatever field of work and whatever part of society they choose to enter.

The Lie to Impress Others

If you learn that your child is habitually lying in order to give the impression that he is wealthier or more popular or more talented than he really is, you are obviously dealing with a self-esteem problem. The lies will take care of themselves when the child no longer feels the need to pretend to be something other than what he is in order to get people to like him. This is one case where it would be wise not to mention the lying at all, at least at first. The child already doubtless feels a terrible tension between what others think he is and what he really is. If you then confront him with the fact that he's a liar as well, he's only going to feel worse—and lie more.

The answer here is to help him experiment with a variety of activities that you know he can master relatively easily and enjoy doing, so that he has some real and interesting exploits to talk about with his friends—or with you. At the same time his achievements should be praised, and you should make a point of letting him overhear you being proud of him for things he has really done. Of course, you must be honest—he'll quickly detect the falsehood if your praise is greater than his achievement deserves. But it doesn't hurt for a child to hear his father tell his mother, "Oh, and did you see the work Terry did on the garden? I wouldn't want to be a weed when he has a hoe in his hand." Or for a child to hear her mother tell her father, "I hope LeeAnne has time to make cookies tomorrow. I'm in the mood for chocolate chip cookies for the party tomorrow night, and she makes them better than I do."

The same kind of praise should also be given to the child directly, to build up his self-esteem—but knowing that other people even praise him behind his back does things direct praise often can't do. "Your father told me you carried most of the rocks yourself. I had no idea you were so strong." It carries a lot of weight.

Vindictive Lying

When a child is habitually lying in order to get others into trouble, the best solution is to avoid the payoff. Don't let him see you get upset, or punish the other child he was trying to hurt. But if the lying persists, one draconian approach might be to declare, "It's now a rule in this family that if one person says that another one did something wrong and it turns out not to be the truth, the person who told the lie will get the punishment he wanted the *other* child to get."

Sometimes the vindictiveness may be a form of revenge. The child who is lying may be suffering some real hurt—or even imagined hurt—at the hands of the child he is lying about. If that's the case, the parents need to find out all the details by discussing it calmly with each child *separately* and then take steps to remove the source of contention between them.

If the source of the vindictiveness is competition between the children, fostered by the parents' tendency to compare, there's a great deal the parents can do to solve the problem; it's explained thoroughly in the chapter on sibling rivalry.

When the Lie Is a Weapon in a War

If the child is lying as a deliberately hostile act in a struggle with his parents, attacking the lie is just continuing the war. The relationship is already in serious trouble, and chances are the parents don't have enough of a relationship to have the leverage to stop the lying. It's the parents' responsibility to try to heal the wounded relationship, to build bridges with the child. Often the first step is to remove some pressure that is causing contention, to start expressing positive feelings toward a child who believes his parents don't love him or like him or respect him. Sometimes, if the parent-child ties have broken down too far or if the parents are unable to see what they need to change in their own behavior to help heal the rift, it is wise to seek professional help. Remember that when a child feels a great deal of hostility toward his parents, it is almost always because he believes, either correctly or incorrectly, that they have strong negative feelings (or no feelings at all) toward him.

Very rarely is lying the problem in itself. Usually it is merely a symptom of a deeper problem, a strategy the child is using to cope with stress. The way to end the lying habit is to discover first the *reason* for the lies, then set to work solving the underlying problems.

12

Problems in School

FOR SEVERAL DECADES NOW, parents have brought me their children because of school problems. Their concerns seem to come under one or more of the following six categories:

1. The slow learner: "Jack is having a very difficult time learning the material they give him at school. His grades are way down. Nothing we or the teachers do seems to help. I think we are all about ready to throw in the towel." Or, "Shirley seems to us to be reasonably bright, but reading is almost impossible for her. She just can't learn the meaning of printed symbols."

2. Skipping or repeating a grade: "Sylvia is extremely bright for her age. Why put her in a kindergarten when she could easily do first-grade work?" Or,"Will it be better for Freddy to go through second grade again or go on to third where he'll be hopelessly behind?"

3. School phobias: "Julie absolutely refuses to go to school. Her stomach hurts all over, she says, and she's been crying all morning about how she hates school. I just don't have the heart to force her to go when she hates it—feeling so bad."

4. Poor social adjustment and peer acceptance: "Sally just doesn't get along with the other children in her class. She often comes home crying. They treat her terribly."

5. Teacher-student incompatibility: "Charlie and his teacher just don't get along. She must hate all boys, or maybe it's just Charlie."

6. Child behavior problems: "The principal called and said they're going to kick Terry out of school if he makes even one more problem for them."

The Slow Learner

There are four reasons why children may be slow learners.

First, they may inherit this tendency from their parents. This occurs in the random throw of genetic dice at conception. Bright parents tend to produce bright, superior children, and nonintellectual parents tend to produce children who don't do well in school, even though there will still be a considerable range of talent among any group of brothers and sisters.

Second, there can be some kind of brain damage from a lack of oxygen at birth, a disease like encephalitis, severe head injuries from an auto accident, or undersecretion of the thyroid gland, which retards both physical growth and/or mental development in a basically normal body.

Third, there can be special inborn conditions, such as dyslexia, which make it difficult for the child to comprehend or remember oral or written language. Learning to read is exceptionally difficult for these children.

Fourth, there are emotional problems and stressful circumstances which can greatly reduce or depress motivation, interest, or the desire or drive to learn in children who are *mentally* quite capable of doing better.

If your child appears to have been born with average or slightly low intelligence, is there anything you can do to help him do better? Perhaps there is; I go into detail in the chapter called "How to Raise Your Child's IQ". Research at the University of California at Berkeley has suggested that when laboratory animals have been raised in a rich, stimulating environment, it increases their brain growth and weight over those animals not given such stimulation. We can't do this research on human beings for obvious ethical reasons—it would hardly be fair to the understimulated group—but the suggestion is that you can increase your child's competence, knowledge, and general ability if you provide him with a stimulating environment.

Another thing to keep in mind is that children who mature more slowly may later change significantly as their brain develops further, or their natural drive forces their mental efficiency to increase. You have doubtless heard stories like this:

Henry was only an average, $C+$ student who had to work long hours just to stay in school at UCLA. He had always dreamed of being a doctor. He would probably never make it, but he did have guts, drive, and persistence, and through sheer diligence and a remarkable self-discipline, he gradually inched his grade point average up, semester by semester. He applied to twenty different medical schools. They all turned him down. He stayed around another year, raising his average a little more. That year he applied to nearly thirty medical schools, an expensive process. Again, a total turndown. Yet he wouldn't give up. He stayed around another year, raising his GPA still more. I'm not sure whether he applied to every medical school in the country that year or not, but he came close. And then, a miracle. He was accepted by a small medical school in the South. Henry is now a successful orthopedist, practicing in the Southwest, and I understand his income is about $150,000 a year.

High motivation and persistence in a child have won many victories—just as lack of motivation can make low achievers out of brighter kids.

The Brain-damaged Child   Remarkable things can happen with some brain-damaged children. If a thyroid deficiency is diagnosed early enough, medication can almost entirely remedy the problem and prevent or limit damage to the child's mind. If it's a head injury in early childhood or even later, the brain can often organize new circuits. This may take considerable physical and mental training, but it's amazing how adaptable the central nervous system is. Of course, each person's situation is unique, with the potential for recovery being determined by the site and amount of damage.

The Dyslexic Child Congenital problems like dyslexia ("reading difficulty") in otherwise bright or average children can be caused by what is called a developmental lag. For example, a delayed integration of their visual focusing mechanism may prevent them from learning to read at age six, but when they can focus and concentrate at age eight, they catch up easily. In other instances, auditory processing of language may be delayed. Sometimes time alone may take care of this kind of problem, yet the child is still labeled a slow learner. Often you can sense the intelligence and brightness in your child, but somehow doing school assignments is a struggle for him and a puzzle to you. Be patient and stimulate the child intellectually while supporting him emotionally during this hard time—as long as you believe in him, he will have a better chance of believing in himself.

But don't try to diagnose dyslexia yourself. Get an expert evaluation—perhaps at a university reading clinic—to see what kind of remedial training will be the best for the child. Don't accept the school system's first diagnosis as absolute truth; sometimes the tests are administered by counselors or teachers who are not really trained to interpret the data. (See Chapter 4 for a further discussion of dyslexia.)

Emotional Problems If a child is a slow learner because of emotional problems, the quickest, most efficient route to assisting him is to visit a guidance clinic or use a qualified counselor.

State Social Services one day requested that I do a psychometric evaluation on Jimmy, a second-grade boy who was considered severely retarded. They were considering institutionalizing him. He would show up at school and appear totally unable to function, despite good hearing and vision. He could talk some, but he appeared more often to be in a listless daydream or fog. They needed an intellectual evaluation before they could put him away.

I got the boy into a room where we could be alone. I then attempted to gently converse with him and develop some rapport. It's a kind of warming-up technique most psychologists use to guarantee more realistic and valid kinds of test results. When I had finally completed the evaluation, it turned out that his IQ was 113, considerably above average.

We immediately looked deeper into his situation and discovered there were acute marital problems at home. The father almost daily threatened suicide, and the mother screamingly denounced him and threatened to run away. These violent confrontations usually occurred at breakfast. Jimmy was caught right in the middle of a tug-of-war between the parents he loved. We recommended crisis-intervention-type marriage counseling for the parents instead of institutionalizing Jimmy. Within a year Jimmy was taking part in school activities, doing homework successfully, and actively participating in class.

Skipping or Repeating a Grade

Some parents are rightfully proud of a very bright child. "If six-year-old Cindy is doing third-grade work, why put her in the first grade?" they ask. "She'll be bored. It will ruin her mind." They may even dream of her entering college at fifteen—with a scholarship. If the psychologist says she has an IQ of 140, placing her in the upper one percent of the population in intelligence, why keep her behind with ordinary children her own age?

In my experience there are very real risks in pushing a child ahead in school. He may be with children near his *mental* age, but they will always be several years older than he is emotionally, socially, and physically. And the crunch will really hit him in his early teens, when all his friends are reaching puberty and he is still painfully, obviously a little kid. It is no easier for young girls with stick-straight figures when all their girl friends are developing physically, menstruating, and growing taller.

If your child's birthday is in the late summer or early fall, it may not hurt to advance him slightly by starting him early in first grade. He will be one of the youngest in the class, but by no more than a few months. And if he is very bright and socially advanced, he can still be a star among peers and not a midget freak in a class where his schoolmates are all a head taller than he.

If you have a child of average ability and social skills, and his birthday is in summer or fall, you may choose to enroll him on schedule. However with a socially or mentally slow-developing child you may want to delay his starting kindergarten until a year later. That way he enters school with children who are slightly younger but more nearly his social and mental peers; it also gives him an advantage in athletics, a fair compensation for his scholastic disadvantage.

The point is that even such minor adjustments should be made if possible when the child first starts school, so he is accepted naturally by the other kids and avoids the social stigma of dropping back or skipping ahead later. And all such adjustments should be made only after a realistic appraisal of the child's real ability, not just to satisfy his parents' irrational fears or unrealistic expectations.

If you sense your four-year-old boy is lagging in his general maturation, I'd precede kindergarten with a year of nursery school for him. This should not be an "orange juice and sandbox" type of baby-sitting experience; it should be the kind of nursery school that exposes him to all kinds of learning experiences in a low-key, enjoyable, noncompetitive way.

Delaying a slow maturer's entry into school is one way parents can powerfully manipulate a child's environment and make a winner out of him even if he's only average or a little below. You will also reduce the chances of his unsympathetic classmates calling him "dumbo" or "retardo". Being a year older, bigger than the other kids, with that additional time to overcome his "developmental lag", he won't get fixed with a "loser" self-image. If you are going to err in a question of grade placement, it's usually better to do it in the safe direction—holding back, not pushing ahead.

School Phobias

Sometimes a child is very panicky and fearful about going to school, and he doesn't know why. To avoid school he will cry heart-rendingly, have vague stomach aches, vomit or retch violently, or dawdle and "forget" things so he is late or can return home with an "excuse". This condition tends to occur most frequently in the lower grades of elementary school.

You should first check to see if the child is truly sick or if he has a fever. Consult with a pediatrician if necessary. Once you have determined that there is nothing medically wrong, tell him: "The doctor says you are all okay now. Tomorrow you *will* go back to school. If it'll make you feel any better I'll be happy to drive you there and pick you up afterward for a few days."

The child may cry piteously, have more vague pains, and offer many other reasons why it's impossible to go. The root cause, of course, is a vague but intense fear or phobia which has been accidentally learned by the child. It's critically important that the parent *insist* that the child return to school as soon as possible to face the fear—no matter what! If you don't do this, then each day that you let the child remain home encourages the condition to get worse. In addition, the child gets further behind in his school work, so he will also be more embarrassed about facing his teacher and classmates when he does return. Usually it takes about three days of the forced returning to school, escorted if necessary, for the fear to dissipate.

Ask the people at school to cooperate with you. They've been through this many times before and will give you a hand in keeping the child there. If things get too tough for the youngster in the classroom, he could go to the front office or the first-aid room and sit it out for awhile. But it is critically important that he stay in school a full day, with no exceptions.

Sometimes it isn't school itself the child fears. Perhaps it is the fearsome barking dog he must pass on the way to school. It may be anxiety caused by separation from the home and mother. It may involve fear of having to recite or speak in class. It may be a bully who victimizes him at recess. Often the child will not be able to pinpoint or verbalize the exact cause of this fear, but while you are working on finding that cause, make sure the child keeps going to school. It's like the youngster who swallowed a little water or had some other frightening experience in a pool. If you get him right back in the water with all the encouragement and support he needs, he'll be all right. But the longer he stays away the more frightening the thought of returning becomes.

Poor Social Adjustment and Peer Acceptance

As with all school problems it is critical that the parents evaluate *why* the child has poor social adjustment—why he's not accepted by other children. Does he wear out-of-date or unacceptable clothing? Is it a low self-image problem? Is there a lack of social skills? Does he look funny or different in any way? Is he a minority group member living in an area with prejudice? Is the child too young for his class? Does he antagonize others by his language or behavior? Is he a middle-class kid going to a lower-class school with a value and culture conflict? Is he so super-sensitive that he can't handle normal give-and-take, the rough-and-tumble common to his age group?

The answers to these and other questions will determine your counter-strategies. A number of the other chapters will help you deal with most of these problems, but let me suggest here a few general things that you can do.

Be sure that your child wears clothes and hair styles that are "in". You don't have to spend a fortune to accomplish it, but this you *can* do for your kids, make them look sharp by the standards in vogue in their age group and area.

Next, have your youngster invite one or more of his classmates to your home for an overnight party or on some family outing, and have plenty of good food. When Brigham Young was founding settlements in the heart of Indian country, he sagely observed, "It's better to feed the Indians than to fight them."

If your son or daughter takes a shine to a classmate, tactfully cultivate a cooperative relationship with the youngster's parents. Every child needs a best friend. The two give each other protection and social reinforcement. While it is not possible to create a special chemistry that doesn't occur naturally between two children, you can certainly encourage your child to look around for a friend, and help along such a friendship when it comes—though you must avoid getting so involved that you start taking sides in their quarrels!

When friends of your sons and daughters visit your home, give them a warm reception. Some homes have negative vibrations. People feel uncomfortable there and don't want to return. Make sure hospitality is a permanent, important aspect of your home. Cultivate the reputation of being the neatest and nicest Mom and Dad on the block, not because you act like another kid, but because kids can act like themselves and have a good time around you.

Make sure your children have some competence in sports so everybody wants your child on the team. He doesn't have to be a star player, but he should be competent and play hard and be a good sport. Then other kids will want him to play. Even if he is uncoordinated and clumsy at first, with your help and encouragement he can get better—a lot better. You shouldn't insist on Olympics-level performance, but you should insist on normal competence for the sake of his social life—and acceptance by his peers.

Teacher-Student Incompatibility

This does happen once in a while, and it's often nobody's fault. It's just like two pieces of a jigsaw puzzle that don't fit. Which piece do you blame?

If the conflict or incompatibility isn't too great, and it's in one of the upper grades where the boy or girl will have three to seven teachers, sometimes it's best just to stick it out. After all, school is a preparation for life, for the adult world. Wherever you live and work there are always a few people you won't particularly care for or click with. They rub you the wrong way, and you rub them the wrong way. You try to be congenial and friendly, but somehow it works out wrong or they take it wrong, but that's life. You have to handle it as best you can. You live with it. And if your child learns this in high school, so much the better.

However, if this problem occurs in an earlier grade, where the child will spend the entire year with just one teacher, you might want to consider having your child moved to a different class—but only if it's absolutely necessary. Your child shouldn't get the idea that he doesn't have to put up with a teacher he doesn't like because *you* will always pull strings. And make sure it's a genuine personality conflict. After all, your child may dislike a teacher for a while for precisely the reasons that make that teacher the right one for your child!

Most teachers—and I am one—approach their work professionally. They attempt to be responsible and fair and to do a competent job in teaching your child. Since teachers are also human, they are occasionally irritated or antagonized by a child who might just happen to be your son or daughter. Rarely will that affect how the teacher treats the child. Teachers don't like job hassles any more than you do.

However, it is also true that teachers can have stress in their lives and become neurotic, mentally ill, unbalanced, or poor in judgment, and every once in a while a teacher will indeed act inappropriately. This is usually handled by the principal or superintendent after careful deliberation and consultation and a review of the facts. The teacher may be given some counseling, sometimes sick leave, maybe even a leave of absence; sometimes the teacher is even switched to another school if the behavior is too out of line. And in several cases I know of, an early retirement was recommended and the teacher left the profession entirely.

If you have concerns, you should approach either the teacher or the principal. You should never come in anger or to "get" the teacher, but rather to find a helpful solution to the problem. Chances are good that after you are through listening to your child's point-of-view, you still don't have all the facts. Even if your child is scrupulously honest, there may be things he simply forgot or didn't understand. If you come to the school with an open attitude, just trying to get the facts and resolve the problem, you will find cooperation and a fair settlement most of the time. But if you come with an emotional, vindictive attitude, you will probably get nothing but resentment and defensiveness—certainly you will get nothing good for your child, and *you* will be regarded as an over-frantic, trouble-making parent.

Consider also that your child still may have several grades to go in that particular school, and there may be younger brothers or sisters still to come along. It's to your advantage to maintain good relations with all of the school personnel. You might on occasion win a battle by being nasty, but you could lose the war as far as your relations with the school are concerned. However, if there is a serious compatibility problem between your child and the teacher—whose ultimate effect is clearly destructive and reasonable negotiations don't change things—*get your child out of the situation anyway you have to!*

Child Behavior Problems

One of the hardest things about solving children's chronic misbehavior problems is that parents often refuse to admit there *is* a problem. If Junior behaves reasonably well at home (or, as is more common, simply isn't much noticed at home), his parents may find it hard to believe that he could possibly be disruptive or provocative at school. Worse still, some parents regard it as a deep personal offense if a teacher or principal reports to them that their child is misbehaving seriously in school. "What do you mean Junior's impossible to control! What kind of parent do you think I am? I don't raise children like that! You're making it up!" That kind of reaction guarantees that there will be no solution to the problem.

The first thing to recognize is that your child's misbehavior at school is not necessarily a reflection on you as a parent—but if you do nothing about the problem when you finally learn about it, it certainly won't help! When a teacher sends a note home or calls, or when a principal notifies you about your child's wrongdoing or disobedience, you should take the matter seriously. Believe me, teachers usually try to avoid involving parents in school problems—they wouldn't be contacting you if they weren't worried and didn't need your help.

Find out exactly what kind of misbehavior your child is displaying. Is he fighting with other children? Setting fires? Smoking pot in the restrooms?

Talking back to teachers or openly disobeying them? Horsing around in class? Cracking jokes? Playing practical jokes? The kind of action you take depends completely on what the child is doing—and why he's doing it.

Unfortunately, this advice is largely wasted. The children with real problems are usually the very ones with parents who don't care much and certainly aren't going to be very understanding and helpful in solving the problem. But the fact that you're reading this book shows that you're a parent who cares what kind of person your child becomes. That is the best news your child could have, though he doesn't know it. You can go a long way toward helping him get along better in school—and probably in his entire adult life as well.

It's best, of course, to catch the problem in the first four years of school. If the problem is serious enough to call for professional guidance counseling, that's the age when the counseling is most helpful; if you don't get chronic misbehavior under control at that age, it's almost too late when the child is in high school. Not only are habits of misbehavior deeply ingrained by then, but also the child is bigger than you and in better physical shape. He knows that there's a limit to how much control you can actually exert over him and is quite likely to thumb his nose at you. There are some things you can do, but their effectiveness is limited.

Most, though not all, trouble-making children are boys, which hints that many of these misbehaviors are either biological in origin or are part of our subtle, covert teaching of sex roles. If the problem is hyperactivity, of course, there are medication and diet therapies covered thoroughly elsewhere in this book. The misbehavior can also arise because your child is seriously disturbed, mentally or emotionally, and you should seek excellent professional guidance.

Misbehavior in school is often caused by a disturbed home life. You may not even be aware of the problem at home—things may seem fine, or at least tolerable, to you. The only symptom you may have to force you to notice the problem is your child's misbehavior or hostility in school.

Take a long hard look at your family patterns. If there's something openly wrong such as child abuse, alcoholism, abandonment, sexual molestation, or damaging quarrels between parents, the fact of your child's misbehavior should prompt one or both of you to seek the professional help you need. But sometimes you will have to probe more deeply to understand what's going wrong. Are you or your spouse constantly away from home, ignoring the children or always putting them off? Then their misbehavior at school might be a plea for love and attention. Do you and your spouse have a quiet game of one-upsmanship going on, so that while you never openly fight, you are constantly competing or struggling for supremacy? Children sense such things unconsciously and react to them. Do you or your spouse constantly criticize that particular child, so that all he hears all day is what a bad or incompetent person he is? He may simply be acting out your role expectation at school.

Have you unconsciously taught him that part of being a "real man" is being the toughest kid around, never letting anybody push him around, always solving problems with his fists? Then his pulverizing of other children is nothing more than trying to measure up to what you have taught him to be.

If, after an honest evaluation of your family life, you conclude that your family really isn't plagued with any serious problems, there are alternative causes. Your child may simply have a lot of energy; he may be brighter than other kids and bored silly with class; he may be worried about getting other kids to like him and so he wins their approval by publicly "bucking the system" and acting up in class; he may simply have wondered what would happen if he lit the weeds back of the school on fire—and now he knows!

In other words, your child may be a perfectly normal child who has chosen an unacceptable strategy to deal with the normal frustrations and insecurities of childhood. Your task is then to help him find better and safer outlets for his energy, more helpful strategies for easing his anxieties. Is he bored with class? Make sure he has plenty of exciting stimulation at home, and encourage his teacher to give him unusual, interesting extra assignments. Does he have too much energy? Get him a trampoline, a bicycle, an obstacle course, take him jogging, or get him involved in some other regular physical activity to use up some of that fidgety tension.

Is he trying to win class approval by bucking the system? Help him improve in sports, in his physical appearance, in his social skills so that he doesn't need to become the class clown in order to have approval. Was his misbehavior a one-shot "experiment" in window-breaking or fire-setting? Make sure he feels the serious consequences of such experiments by insisting that he personally make restitution for any damage—and if the misbehavior borders on the criminal, make sure he gets a good close look at what happens to kids who keep pushing the limits of the law. At the same time, increase the amount of interesting experiences he's getting so that his curiosity is constantly getting satisfied.

What if your misbehaving child is a teenager? Is the problem hopeless? If his misbehavior has been going on for years and you have done nothing to stop it earlier, the answer may be yes. But if his misbehavior has only begun in his teen years, there is probably a lot you can do. In many cases you can't get rid of misbehavior simply by punishing or lecturing. Most older teenagers are too independent, too strong, too self-willed to put up with that for long.

What you must do is strike at the cause. If it's boredom, the best solution is to find him a job. Not working for Dad or Uncle Jim, though—you may think it's a good idea to have him where you can keep an eye on him, but what *he* needs is the exact opposite. He needs to feel that he's making it on his own, coping in the adult world of employment, meeting the standards of a tough boss and earning his own way. This is especially effective if you also cut off the money supply to him—including the gasoline credit card and free use of the car. If he has to pay for his own "wheels" and his own clothes and his own records, he'll start to feel a lot more responsible about his job. And when he finds out how relatively little unskilled labor pays, he might even begin to take school more seriously.

If the cause of his misbehavior is a group of delinquent or near-delinquent school friends, the solutions may have to be more drastic. Chances are he has a lot of his ego invested in that group—what they think of him is what he thinks of himself. He doesn't dare quit doing what they're doing; they'll think he's chicken or faggy or whatever other taunts will hurt him most. Sometimes the only way you can get him away from such friends without destroying your family in the process is to let him live with a distant relative—or to move your family. It sounds drastic, but it comes down to a question of your priorities. If you really can't send him away or move your family, the best you can do is keep the lines of communication open, make sure he knows you still love him and hope he doesn't do anything too terrible before he matures enough not to need those friends or gets scared enough not to care what they think of him. I have known parents, however, who have either moved their kid or even uprooted their families, changed jobs, and moved to a completely different state with a high school and a neighborhood that simply doesn't have that kind of kid in good supply. And they have felt that it was well worth the cost; it helped their child turn his life around. It is an extreme solution, and there are many things to try first, but that alternative is still an outside possibility.

13

Teasing

IT IS 5:20 P.M. Mother is quietly preparing dinner. Suddenly a shattering scream comes from the front room, chilling Mother to the marrow. She drops a half-peeled potato and rushes to the other room, her heart pounding.

Six-year-old Melanie points accusingly at Rick. "Mama, he made a face at me," she says. Twelve-year-old Rick, lying on the floor, has a grin on his face. He intently looks at a book and pretends to be studying.

Mother then notices a triumphant smile go quickly across Melanie's countenance. No words are said. It's hopeless with these two. She returns to her potato.

Another family. It is afternoon. Mother hears quiet sobs. Someone has just entered the front door. A few steps bring her to the hallway, where she sees her son Jimmy, with a tear-stained face, shaking all over.

A few words tell it all. Once again, he has been intercepted on the way home from school by the neighborhood bully. Nothing too serious—just taunts, shoves, and jeers. But Jimmy is totally demolished. He draws bullies the way flowers draw bees. It was no different in the last two places they lived. If there's a bully within two miles, he'll always smell Jimmy out.

Mother feels frustrated and helpless to assist her son, a very loving, sensitive boy. Tears well up in her eyes as she goes to give him comfort and solace.

Why do children tease each other? All it does is create bad feelings. In some families it's like a nasty infection that won't heal. You can preach, scold, and punish, but the next day the kids are right back at it again. Why can't they ever learn?

I've found that teasing can vary from mild kidding and horseplay to vicious, destructive cruelty. Normal teasing occurs as a result of the fact that all children are in some ways rivals as they grow up together. It's normal for them to be jealous when another child is honored or praised or even thanked. And no matter how fair a parent you are, at times some of your children will get more of your attention than others. Low-level teasing and kidding can be a healthy way for the "slighted" child to get his concern off his chest. Permit it. Respond with humor. This is healthy and necessary, but you do have to draw the line if the teasing becomes deeply hurtful and destructive.

If a child is truly vicious in his treatment of other children, take him aside and privately deal with the problem. Real cruelty is not healthy for *either* child and should never be permitted. Take firm action. Do whatever you have to do to stop it. If it persists, some kind of professional counseling may be required to help this sort of youngster; he may have a serious emotional illness or personality problem. But do not let this destructive behavior continue. Your children have the right to live in your home without being chronically and seriously abused. Child abuse is child abuse, even if another child is doing it.

What some parents don't realize is that *normal* teasing is often their children's favorite indoor sport. It's a form of recreation. It's their answer to boredom, too much TV, or too little work to do. It puts a little excitement in the day. It's also a way of getting rid of pent-up meanness.

Teasing often takes the form of a game called "goat"—and mother is usually assigned the role of the goat. A charade that's extremely popular in almost every home in the country, it starts out with one of the children mildly provoking or harassing another. The initiator is usually the younger, weaker, or more helpless-looking child. (Remember—the victim of this mildly aggressive game often originally provokes it. The game works better that way, children have found.) After a brief series of escalating exchanges between the two children, there occurs the "howl for help". This is usually a penetrating scream or shouted words, and it occurs when, on the last exchange, the older or stronger youngster pinches too hard, makes too ugly a face, or is otherwise too obnoxious and provocative.

Mother, hearing the noise, does an imitation of the cavalry, flying to the rescue with flags and bugles. She spends a half hour trying to track down the real culprit, amid vigorous denials and accusations on both sides. It's full of drama, suspense, and emotion, like any good play. The kids get some of Mom's time, partake of her concern, and have a great emotional purging. Mother is drained, exhausted, and confused. She is not sure what really happened, but unwittingly she has made sure that this great dramatic production will later be played again. Tomorrow at eight, the curtain will go up and she will once again play the role assigned to her. Get your tickets now for "The Goat"—starring Mother in the title role!

What can Mother do to get out of this vicious circle? "It's your problem, not mine," she sings out merrily from the kitchen when the screams reach her ears. After a while, when the screamer runs into the kitchen, she smiles sweetly to the would-be goat-getters and says, "If you want to fight and hurt yourselves, that's your problem." If the younger one doesn't want to be offended by the older one, then he should avoid him. "Just walk away. Go to another room." It's no fun to tease if you don't get a reaction.

When the kids persist in tormenting each other, Mother should just go to the bathroom, lock the door, and start reading a pile of *Reader's Digests*. She must refuse to be their goat. If the noise out in the other room still bothers her, she can take a walk or go grocery shopping. When she returns the home will be quiet. Without the audience the show does *not* go on, and if when Mom returns they wish to tattle or give her a long tale of woe, she tells them, "Later." In a few minutes they forget.

If ignoring the teasing doesn't make it go away, or if you fear it might really be dangerous, you can also try the "time-out room." When the kids squabble or fuss, disturbing your peace, separate them. Put each in a "time-out room" (bedroom or bathroom) by himself for five or ten minutes. Absolutely refuse to discuss blame. You are uninterested in that issue at this time. When they've served their time, *no longer* than ten minutes, let them out on the condition that they refrain from further combat. But if it starts up again they should know that they will be separated and isolated again. The main point, if this is to work for you, is to avoid discussions of blame. If it's ever to be discussed it should be at another time, when they can look at it calmly and with a reasonable perspective. Your discussion should be with each child alone.

Most of the time, chronic bickering between children in a family is a reflection of the way parents handle discipline. Unknowingly, Dad and Mom may encourage teasing. While most teasing arises out of mild sibling rivalry or boredom, there may be other causes too.

For example, Father may be passive and uninvolved while Mother is neurotic, complaining, and attacking. The kids never do anything right, according to her. She keeps them on edge and irritable. This mother creates an emotional tone that is contagious. Like infection, it spreads to the children and disturbs their relationships with each other. The solution? This fault-finding parent needs some help in interaction skills—some communication workshops or classes that will teach patience and self-control.

Or, in a disturbed marriage, Father and Mother fill the air with venom. Critical and degrading remarks constantly fly back and forth between them. Through sheer imitation the kids repeat this style of interaction with each other. Insults, sarcasms, and put-downs become as commonplace as eating, yawning, and sleeping. The solution? Solve the marital problems first; you can't cure the kids of "hereditary" quarrelsomeness.

Or, in still another setting, the parents are afraid of their children. They hesitate to discipline or say *no*. The family lacks effective leadership and therefore lacks unity. The children feel uncomfortable and uneasy; in time, they become selfish, grab what they want, refuse to share. In the absence of parental initiative and direction the children have to fend for themselves. It's a jungle. There is no ultimate authority to appeal to. This can lead to longlasting bitterness and feuding because usually one of the children, or maybe two, through the sheer power of his personality or his ability to manipulate, grabs most of goodies. Resentment and bickering follow in relationships among the children, and the wounds can be deep. The solution? If you can't set family rules and make them stick with good discipline, then get some professional help so you can be more effective in your parenting role. Set goals, then develop your psychological skills and tools to accomplish them.

The Perpetual Victim

What about the child who is repeatedly teased by a schoolmate or neighborhood bully? I have often found these children to have a peculiar way of playing the victim role. It's almost as if they actively seek rejection or attacks from others, sending out nonverbal cues to others as to their vulnerability. But while some therapists argue that these children are neurotic and actively seek rejection, I don't think just saying that helps solve their problem.

Personally, I do what any parent could learn to do: I teach the youngster assertiveness skills. If the bully is physically aggressive, I teach the victim how to pop him on the nose or in the solar plexus. We don't aim to injure, but we do need to teach the bully that this "soft touch" can sting. The child must get the bully's respect in a very concrete and physical way. I tell the victim, "You've got one good unexpected blow that you can deliver. Make it count. You may get pummeled back, but you can still sting him a good one." And I teach him some pointers on self-defense, so he can do enough "damage" to send the bully looking for easier victims.

If it's a verbal battle between the bully and my kid, I role-play typical responses my child might retort with. I pretend I am the bully and prepare him with lines of pungent, effective dialogue. We rehearse these again and again. He becomes primed. He develops confidence in his ability to say the right thing when pushed or threatened by the bully. For homework, I actually send him out looking for the bully, to walk in places where he might encounter him. Now *he* is the one that actively seeks out the bully to demonstrate his new-found coping skill.

Example: Dad: "Hey retardo—wanna fight? Ya know what? You're the biggest chicken dum dum on the block."

Son: (he freezes—can't say anything)

Dad: "OK, Charlie—what'll you say to that bully when he comes up and yells that in your face? Why don't *you* play the role of the bully? You say it and I'll be the little kid. We'll figure out a good way to handle that guy. Go ahead."

Surprisingly, most young people who have this problem, especially boys, can learn to be assertive and stand up for their rights. In many cases the transformation in their self-image and self-confidence is remarkable.

Rules for Handling the Teasing Problem

1. Permit it at a low level. This form of interaction among brothers and sisters is a normal, healthy way for them to get rid of pent-up tensions, rivalries, and irritations. Use large quantities of humor.

2. It may occur as a form of recreation and game-playing by high-energy children who are bored, overly saturated with TV, or don't have enough fulfilling work to do. Keep them busy. Teenagers in particular should have money-producing employment, especially in the summer. Fill their lives with activities suited to their interests and temperament. Most communities have a great variety of activities and jobs for young people. Search these out. You might even conspire to hire your neighbor's youngster—if he'll hire yours.

3. If the teasing involves the game "goat" as a way of involving Mother and stirring up some excitement, disengage. Without you as a frustrated audience, the game quickly ceases to be fun.

4. If the teasing is truly mean and vicious, it may suggest personality or emotional disorders in the child. Stop it any way you can. Seek out competent professional help, if necessary.

5. Your child may be teased by someone outside your home, such as a neighborhood bully. If so, teach your child assertiveness skills to match the bully's.

6. Since parents themselves sometimes unconsciously encourage teasing among their children, carefully examine your particular style of discipline, your relationship with your spouse, your role in the family.

7. Sometimes parents tease. This can be destructive and brutal, and the child can be physically or emotionally injured by it. And sometimes the child returns this treatment by teasing, or taking it out on the younger children. So be cautious about your own teasing with the children. At a moderate or low level this can be friendly and enjoyable, but with some sensitive children it can be destructive. Children are not fools—they know as well as you do that what you say in jest is often quite sincere. Just because you laugh does not mean it will not sting.

8. Parents should be careful to avoid comparisons between their children. Do not indicate that one child is doing a job much better than another. That only sets him up as a target for hatred by the other child. It can lead to teasing between the two—and various other kinds of rivalry.

9. Be sure that you fill each child's life with love. See that they get personal attention, that their emotional and social needs are being met, and that deep underneath they know that they are wanted and cared for. This will produce a secure child, one who will not in a neurotic and defensive way have to lash out and hurt his brothers and sisters because he feels angry and jealous.

14

Stealing

IN THE CAR returning from the supermarket Mother noticed five-year-old Jimmy chewing gum. She was a little puzzled because gum had been a "no-no" in their house ever since their family dentist had warned them against it.

"Jimmy, is that gum you're chewing?"

Guilty look and silence.

"Jimmy, where did you get that gum?"

Long pause.

"I don't know—I found it."

"Where?"

"I'm not sure."

"Was it at the supermarket?"

"Maybe."

"Would you take that package of gum out of your pocket?"

He does. Mother turns left at the next intersection and returns to the market. Jimmy is quickly escorted into the store where he very reluctantly returns the remaining gum to the manager and pays him a dime for what he has consumed.

"Mother!" a daughter shouts angrily. "Someone has taken my earrings again out of my jewel box, and I have to leave in five minutes! We've got a thief in the house! Aren't you going to do something about it?"

A quick investigation reveals that the culprit is sister Carla, who protests, "But I just borrowed them, Mother, and besides, somebody's taken mine. What else could I do?"

The neighbors arrange an informal conference. Three homes in a two-block area have been robbed and vandalized in the last four days, when the occupants had been at work or out for the evening. A strong suspicion points to two boys in the next block, brothers, whose alcoholic father abuses them physically. Their mother is emotionally unstable and ill most of the time. The boys have been involved in a long series of scrapes with the law including assault and battery, car theft, breaking thirty windows once over at the school, and spray-painting obscenities on the neighbors' walks. Even though arrested several times, they have never served time in the detention home or state reform school. They have only been put on probation.

Why have these children stolen? Will they do it again? Can they be taught not to or be "rehabilitated"? For that matter, is stealing really wrong? Doesn't everybody steal on occasion? Isn't it just a matter of culturally determined property rights, something that varies from society to society?

Only in some of the more primitive cultures do social norms permit "borrowing" from your neighbor without his permission or knowledge. And then *everybody* does it. These are usually sparsely populated, remote regions of the world where there is an abundance of fish from the sea, tropical fruit aplenty, and pigs and chickens running loose through the villages. Life is relaxed and low-key. What's yours is mine, and what's mine is yours—that's the cultural norm.

But these people have few wants, just a bare minimum of simple clothing, a shelter to keep the rain off, and sufficient food to keep from starving. For the rest of us, in the technologically advanced societies, that doesn't work. We have, to be candid, enormous appetites for consumer goods—a nice home with two or more bathrooms, air conditioning, a summer cabin, a boat, a camper, a host of appliances, as many televisions as we have rooms, a wardrobe full of stylish clothes, and several cars.

In order to have all this, or any part of it, we need a lot of rules, codes, and customs with regard to property. We must have reasonable confidence that what we acquire we can keep. Without this, chaos would result.

How do you handle a child of yours who steals? If he is under eight years of age, in most cases it is a problem of immaturity. He has a poor concept of ownership, and nearly all children in these early years will on occasion take a toy belonging to another child. This is normal, and it provides you with a vital teaching moment. As in many other areas of behavior, children learn to do things the right way by doing them the wrong way first. If such a young child steals, accompany him to give back the article that has been taken. Explain the notion of property rights. Tell him that it is sometimes possible to borrow what he wants, but first he has to ask permission from the owner. You may even want to make it possible for the child to earn money so that he can buy these things for himself, learning that in our society goods are acquired through valuable labor.

You need to avoid tempting your child beyond his ability to resist. You should not leave valuables lying around the house—money or expensive jewelry or anything else that might be a temptation for him. With a younger-age child you should treat stealing as you would treat picking his nose in public, eating with his fingers, or going outside with no clothes on. It's not the end of the world if he does it, and you don't make a federal case out of it or hang him from the yardarm or stop loving him. But you do show and teach, again and again and again, that stealing is unacceptable behavior; you let him know that if stealing does occur there will be an accounting or reckoning with one of his parents, and there will always be that long uncomfortable trip back to return what he took.

It's critically important that children be repeatedly taught this lesson when they are young. If you see a child ransacking your purse, never look the other way or pretend you didn't notice it or think that it is cute. The child should be immediately confronted and rebuked and taught, and the issue dealt with at that time.

With our large family I've found that a different code has evolved over "borrowing" things that belong to a brother or sister as opposed to stealing something that belongs to someone outside the home. Technically it's the same crime, but the children see it differently. To them, temporarily taking something that belongs to a brother or sister without permission is poor form and will get them criticized, but it's still not "stealing". This is especially true in an emergency. Your daughter has a date, her last pair of nylons has a big run in them, and so she takes a pair out of her sister's drawer. Her sister isn't home so she can't ask her, but she has to take them anyway. They both know that someday the situation may be reversed, and within a family, while there is still a sense of "yours" and "mine", there should also be a feeling of community, the assumption that help will be given at need.

What about a teenager who steals? This youngster knows that it is wrong. He also knows that if he's caught there will usually be a penalty. He may be kicked out of school, may appear before a judge, certainly will face stern parental disapproval—yet still he steals. The masculine gender here is appropriate because males steal more frequently than females, though teenage girls sometimes *shoplift*.

The following nine reasons, alone or in combination, cover most cases of children stealing.

1. "Everybody's doing it." Involved with a delinquent gang or rowdy peer culture, the child feels that to be accepted "you gotta steal." If you remove him from the gang or the buddies who influence him to steal, you will probably cut down on and eventually eliminate his stealing.

2. "I really wanted it." The strength of the temptation overcomes conscience, prudence, and good judgment. He knows it's wrong and feels guilty afterward, but "the devil made me do it." This can occur in many normal children, when temptation exceeds inner restraints and good judgment. It happens to adults, too!

3. "I showed *you!*" Full of venom, this youngster rejects most traditional values and steals to rebel or retaliate or show anger. He is antagonistic in most aspects of his life. He usually comes from a very disturbed and damaged family. He's really hurting inside and takes it out on others.

4. "Who cares?" Some children lack conscience. They know it's wrong to steal, but they don't care about any consequences (See Chapter 3). They lack any sense of guilt or remorse. Their attitude is, "If she was stupid enough not to lock her bike up, then she deserved to have it stolen."

5. "I don't know why I did it." Sometimes a mentally ill youngster steals as just one of a whole mosaic of strange and irrational deeds. His other behaviors and verbal utterances will clearly indicate the underlying illness.

6. "Maybe now you'll notice I'm around." This youngster steals in order to get people to pay attention to him.

7. "If you love me, you'll catch me and stop me." Sometimes stealing is a substitute way of getting love and affection. Kleptomania is stealing material things as an unconscious way of compensating for lack of love and affection. Pleasure is gained by possessing something belonging to someone else.

8. "I got away with it!" It's exciting to take a risk, and a thrill-seeking adolescent often steals as an act of validating his courage and masculinity. The very fact that stealing is forbidden and, if caught, punishable makes it worth doing.

9. "I thought it was OK!" Unfortunately, some children are taught by their parents that stealing is just fine under certain circumstances. Dad brags how he ripped off his employer. Of course, Dad always justifies it: "They don't pay me what I'm worth" or "A big company like that won't miss it." The message comes through loud and clear: "It's OK to steal if you have good reason." Since stealing is attractive in and of itself, children learn such lessons remarkably fast.

Naturally, the strategies you would use to cope with a youngster's stealing have to match the underlying causes. If the youngster is psychotic and steals, you treat the underlying illness or psychosis.

If stealing is a substitute for love or a way of getting attention, you may need professional help to break the cycle. Simply giving him more love and attention (which he really needs) may only serve now to reinforce his bad behavior, unless other changes are instituted. He may unconsciously conclude, "When I'm bad, I get loved," and this may stimulate still more stealing.

With the boy who's a risk-taker and thrill-seeker, you attempt to substitute socially acceptable excitement—competitive sports of all kinds, outdoor wilderness adventures, interesting job experiences, travel, or joining voluntary search and rescue units.

With children who are occasionally immature and succumb to temptation, you change their environment a little so they are not placed in a vulnerable, high-risk situation. You also strengthen conscience and judgment through continued teaching, both formally and informally. You may also need to restrict his privileges.

If the child comes out of a badly damaged home situation which has made him mean and rebellious, he may need to be moved into another setting and receive professional help. The same goes for the child who is totally without conscience.

One thing Lois and I have found with our nine children is that even within a single family the children can vary greatly in their strength of conscience. Some have an almost intuitive inner sense of right and wrong, and comfortably live within certain boundaries. Others know clearly what the limits are but choose to make up their own minds about which rules they will abide by and which they will not. They don't have the same inner hurt that some of the other children have when they break a rule.

We have found that this doesn't necessarily reflect a tendency to do evil or be rebellious; rather it suggests a certain independence of thought and action that is part of their core personality, and it takes mature and emotionally secure parents to live with that kind of child during his middle and late adolescence. With this kind of youngster your best strategy is not to continually butt heads with him, but to establish as good a relationship with him as you can. Then, in your own personal life, model responsible ethical behavior. If he likes you, he will eventually want to become like you.

I've seen some super families with a teenager who occasionally goes on a wild rampage, acts up, or steals things. His irregular behavior is never extremely serious, but it is bad enough to cause his parents a lot of worry and grief. In nearly every instance that I know of, as the young person approaches nineteen or twenty, or sometimes a little later, he matures out of it. He finds himself and settles down.

What occurred was that he was struggling with an identity crisis during middle or late adolescence. He was unsure who he was, what his values were, where he was going; sometimes it was hell living with him. Fortunately, it wasn't permanent. It was like slow labor; everybody was glad when it was over, including him! Most of those young people have gone on to live productive lives and work out their destinies as responsible members of the community. Stealing merely represents one closed chapter in their earlier life; it is good when family and community alike forgive and forget.

However, it can be just as harmful for a child to have his parents say, "Oh, he's just going through a phase"—when in fact the problem is more serious—as it is to have his parents overreact and bring the full weight of the law down on him when he was merely going through a phase! Parents need to think carefully before they take any action. Often the first response is the wrong one—being too quick to forgive and being too quick to punish severely can be equally harmful, if a parent is merely responding by reflex. It's one of the hardest parts of parenting, to restrain your own emotions in order to make sure you're really acting in your child's best interests. In persistent cases of stealing where all your strategies just don't seem to work, I'd recommend securing professional counseling—don't wait till they're seventeen or eighteen to get this kind of help.

15

The Lazy, Unmotivated Child

KIDS ARE LAZY because parents permit it. Whenever I see a child who "can't" or won't do his homework, chores around the house, or errands for his parents, it usually boils down to being a parent problem.

"George, what in the world are we going to do with Billy? You asked him to clean out the garage two weeks ago, and it's still a mess. He's a month late in his biology homework and his English teacher says he has yet to turn in a book report in her class. And he only did part of the dishes last night. He said he got too tired to finish them. He's your son. Why can't you do something about it?"

"I'm sorry, honey, but I'm catching a flight out tonight. Remember that seminar I told you about in Atlanta? See you in a week. Do the best you can. I'll try to help out when I get back."

Before using some simple but effective behavior modification tactics, you need to check several things out.

1. Does the child have any problems seeing or hearing? A bright child with a modest hearing defect can appear awfully dumb or inattentive, and sometimes obstinate. Very often the hearing defect goes unnoticed. He may not be doing what you asked because he never heard you ask it.

2. Does he have any problems intellectually? Does he have the capacity to learn? Can he read? Some fairly bright children are dyslexic and have a very difficult time learning to read. School and learning can be a major turn-off for them. They feel so frustrated in their inability to make sense out of printed word symbols that they often just plain give up. Their motto is, "If you don't try you can't fail." So their pattern is not to try. The same can occur with slow learners. They tend to give up easily and not compete. It's just less painful that way.

3. Does he have low thyroid or a problem with a low basal metabolic rate which would slow down his body? He might have a problem of very low energy and appear quite listless, dragging around all day. While he can do the work and certainly produce some things at the request of his parents, his overall output will be considerably below that of the other children in the family. This might be the case if the child does not refuse to do the work but rather is very slow in doing it, complaining about being tired all the time. Sometimes thyroid medication can rev up their engine. A problem with low blood sugar, hypoglycemia, or anemia can produce the same result. Check it out. Consult a good pediatrician for help.

If the child's health, hearing, visual acuity, intelligence, and energy level are all within or above the normal range what then? What makes the pokey kid so slow?

That's easy. In ninety percent of the cases, it's because parents don't follow through. They ask David to do something, but he knows that if he stalls long enough Mother will eventually do it for him. Sure, he gets a lecture, but she still does his work. Fair exchange, as far as he is concerned.

David could have six jim-dandy, sure-fire excuses that always get him off the hook. For example: "I've got homework to do tonight" or "I'm really not feeling good; I've got this terrible pain in my head; or is it in my chest?" or "Mom, the minister called and asked if I could make the youth council meeting tonight" or (yelling) "That's all you ever have me do around here is work, work, work! What do you think I am, your slave?" or "Hey, Mom, you're really neat. You're the greatest. Incidently, I hate to ask you this, but, ah, do you think that you could do me one big favor?" or "Mom, I've been feeling really depressed lately. Sometimes I feel life just isn't worth living. Have you noticed in the paper all those teenage suicides lately?"

As the years roll by, David proceeds to do only what he wants, and that's about a quarter of what's asked. School performance is usually spotty from this kind of child. Sometimes he's bright enough to bluff his way through many classes and exams with minimal study. Occasionally Dad will promise ten dollars for every A or a trip to Disneyland or a pair of skis if he gets a B+ grade average this semester. Like shrewd bankers dealing with a timid applicant for a loan, David wheels and deals to increase the price of his work to as much as the traffic will bear. Then, for a few furious weeks, he does whatever is necessary to get the required grade average and the money, trip, or skis.

In a family like this, the monkeys are running the zoo. How do you put the frustrated, bedraggled zookeepers back in charge and the monkeys back in the cage?

First, train them when they are young to assume responsibility. The longer you wait and the older they get, the more difficult it will be to secure their cooperation and teach them good work habits. But start small. Don't try to change everything at once.

What particular job, chore, or behavior do you want to work on first? Putting dirty clothes in the hamper? Doing school assignments? After the parents have decided, have a conference with the child and indicate that you need his help, along with the other children, in keeping up the house. How would he feel about being responsible for his room and doing the dishes twice a week? Negotiate a commitment from him. Be reasonable and flexible. In most cases he will agree, knowing that he can probably still manipulate you and get out of it, but before concluding make it clear that if the work isn't done, there will be some consequences.

Now carefully choose consequences that are important to the child. For example, with some children it will work to permit no TV or going out and playing until the work's done and up to a standard that you will check. On occasion, I have suggested that the child be given no more food until his agreed-upon work is completed. I've never felt guilty about this. I know that occasional fasting is very good for him. It cleans out all the poisons in his system. Besides, nobody has ever missed more than one meal at our house!

You must stand firm and resolute. That's the key to success in motivating your lazy child.

"But I'll be late for school."

"Well, I'll write you out an excuse, just for this morning, but tomorrow you'll have to get up earlier. The work *still* needs to be done."

"Yes, but the problem is that I have a lot more work to do than Nancy, and that's not fair."

"Okay, next week we may switch jobs. I want to be fair to everybody. Your point is well taken, and I appreciate your suggestion, but you should still go ahead with your present job and have it finished by dinner. I would sure hate to see you go hungry again."

At a special agreed-upon time each day, monitor and check the children's work. If it's not done, then the privilege is taken away or the penalty exacted. There should *never* be exceptions. Weep with them if it means missing a party, not being able to see their favorite TV show, or missing dessert at dinner, but don't relent. Remember, they'll test you to the very limits of your will and intelligence.

Consider what you are doing as an act of love and caring. You are not unreasonable. Their boss in their adult employment will be just as unrelenting in expecting them to work. Remember that they agreed to it in a peaceful negotiation; if they are to learn responsibility, better a little pain now than a big pain after marriage or in a critical job situation. Being a parent isn't a popularity contest.

With younger children, incentives like stars pasted up by their name on a chart in the kitchen or bedroom can be very useful. These are reinforcers; you can also use other kinds of things, such as small treats or verbal praise.

Sometimes you can prime the pump of a slow child by working along with him. Plan on doing the job together for awhile—until he gets the habit. This has a lot of pluses. It allows you to talk with him and enjoy his company—and you can teach him exactly how a bathroom should be cleaned. The work goes faster and is more fun with the two of you working on it together, so the child learns to associate work with pleasure. Soon he will be able and willing to handle the job by himself.

It's important to teach children the joy of work. You tell and show them how nice it feels to do something well, like doing a great job on mopping the kitchen floor. Point out how it shines. Won't the other members of the family be pleased? Your contagious enthusiasm can make even cleaning toilet bowls a nice experience. When he has done well, give him sincere and abundant recognition. Show Dad when he gets home how well the job was done. Help the child have a sense of pride in doing a job—any job—well. And remember, without everyday monitoring and negative consequences for failure, some of your children will take the path of least resistance and do little or nothing. The lazy child needs an involved Mother and Father who are willing to follow through.

Some parents wonder if it is wise to pay children to do chores around the house and home. Shouldn't they do it without pay because they are members of the family? I have found parents who do it successfully in a variety of ways. In our home we do have certain tasks, such as keeping up one's bedroom, which they do because they are members of the family and that is a basic responsibility which they should take care of without pay. But other jobs are paid for. We do not give an allowance, but we do give them money for certain jobs, which they can choose to do. This gives them some say in determining what work they will do.

When they get into their teens, we find that it is sometimes better if they work for other people. They tend to be more responsible that way. When they work for us, they are always dealing with people who love them despite their flaws. An outside employer tends to judge them solely by their work.

Another type of "lazy" child is the dependent one. Usually there is a solicitous, over-protecting parent who consciously or unconsciously infantalizes the child. From an early age the parent does everything for the youngster. Sometimes this begins because the child has had several severe illnesses or sometimes just because the child looks helpless and frail. The youngster soon learns that if he shows much initiative or independence, his over-protecting parent disapproves. "You're pushing yourself too hard!"

By playing the dependent and inadequate role he gets a lot more emotional support, love, and goodies. He becomes helpless, and the parent then feels wonderful because she is obviously needed. In some cases such a parent is an unloved wife, enduring an unfulfilling and sterile marriage.

Often as these children mature into adolescence they start biting the hand that feeds them by making outrageous demands on the parents. They are angry about their weakness and dependence, correctly blaming their parents, but they are hooked on the freebies and the handouts and all the love and emotional support. They can be very obnoxious as teenagers, and the parents of these children take considerable abuse.

In adult years, the male is often unable to hold a job or wife for long. He spends long hours figuring out how to collect more unemployment insurance or how to put the bite on Dad for still more handouts. The female goes into marriage hopelessly unprepared. She can't make decisions or the bed. She's on the phone hourly to her mother asking what to do now. "How do I boil water?" "What should I get for dinner tonight?"

I have actually seen mothers who take a married daughter grocery shopping or come over and tell her how to arrange her bedroom furniture. The wife complains to her mother because her husband doesn't spend enough time with her or give her enough sympathy, or because he has insufficient income to provide her with all the things she thinks she needs. She is constantly whining and complaining, and the mother is constantly giving her comfort and emotional support, taking her side against the husband.

For such a woman, becoming pregnant is a disaster that may precipitate a variety of psychosomatic symptoms. She may literally go to bed for nine months, and in some cases may abort. This, of course, brings forth increased demands for sympathy and attention. Her countenance is frequently glum and depressed as she searches for others to come and rescue her by doing her housework or giving her cash or sympathy because her lot is so miserable and she has to endure so much.

The moral of this story for parents is that if you don't raise your children to be self-reliant, self-sufficient adults with initiative, then you will spend your retirement years raising *their* children because they will be unable to do it. To become adults, they must gradually be treated more and more like adults as they grow up. Keep treating them like children, and they will become grown-up children.

16

"Won't Eat" and Obesity

A WHOLE GENERATION OF CHILDREN in America were raised hearing these words at mealtime: "Eat your vegetables, Junior! Don't you know that children are starving in China?" or "Clean your plate! Waste not, want not." Few things cause parents more daily concern than whether their children are getting enough to eat; few things cause more worries later than a child who has clearly eaten far too much.

Actually most children, particularly young children, are the best regulators of their own eating—they will naturally eat as much as they need, and no more. But occasionally there are problems, and parents need to know when to be concerned and what to do when the problem is a serious one.

Children who are Finicky about Food

For all children, a balanced diet requires frequent servings from the following seven food categories:

1. Milk and milk products
2. Meat, poultry, or fish
3. Eggs
4. Green or yellow vegetables
5. Starchy vegetables
6. Fruit
7. Whole grain cereals or breads

Infants also need several drops of Vitamin D. Check your menus for the last three days and see how you're measuring up.

In some families the meal hour can become a battleground. Food selection and meal preparation are still a very important role for Mother in most homes, whether she is working or not. It's a gift of love from a mother to her family. If the family rejects the meal or only tolerates it, it can be very upsetting to the giver of the gift—Mom. Tears may be shed. Some children learn early that Mother is also giving them a club to beat her with, and many kids don't hesitate to use it in order to punish or control her. For the sake of a mother's own sanity, it is important that she not become emotionally upset if her children start rejecting food.

Here are some very effective, virtually foolproof tactics Mother may use with a finicky or "won't eat" child:

1. Put very small portions of each food item prepared on the child's plate. Since this will not be enough to satisfy his hunger, he will usually ask for more. If when he asks there is one food he has not eaten, ask him just to taste it before giving him a second helping of a more preferred food. This helps him develop a taste for the less preferred food without having him gag on it or throw it up, and it also eliminates a big fight over it.

2. Never demand that your young children eat every scrap on their plate. Next meal, however, give them smaller portions. If they habitually eat little at meals, eliminate all between-meal snacks. However, snacks should be permitted if the child is eating reasonably well at mealtime. Snacks should be nutritious food like milk, fruit, peanut butter, or juice. Sometimes children sneak foods that are high in empty calories—killing their appetites without giving them any nutrition. Most of this junk food contains a large amount of sugar: soda pop, candy, pastries, cookies, ice cream, and jam. These are very hard on the children's teeth as well as on their general health.

Our son Paul had a sweet tooth. We discovered this on his first visit to the dentist when he was found to have twelve cavities. His mouth was a mess. On investigation we found that he had a ten-pound bag of sugar under his bed that he frequently helped himself to! A craving for sweets is usually cultivated by the parents, who serve them frequently and often use them as rewards. I must confess we had been guilty of this practice on occasion, and we paid a price. Our dentist drives a chauffeured Cadillac.

3. Never equate the amount of food or dessert your child or husband eats with how much you love them. Some women have sent their spouses to an early grave and their kids to the fat farm with this erroneous, unconscious belief.

4. Since mealtime is one of the few occasions when most of the family will be together during the day, make it as pleasant, relaxed, and unstressful as possible. Make it a time for far-ranging discussions, sharing your values and interesting experiences. Never, never use it as a time to punish, criticize, or point out someone's past mistakes. Pick another time for that if necessary. It can kill an appetite more quickly than anything I know.

5. If one of the children becomes rowdy, disruptive, or argumentative at the dinner table, escort him from the room without comment. Take him to another area, out of sight and hearing, and quietly say, "When you feel better we would love to have you back." Don't argue or discuss his behavior at this time. He knows perfectly well why you have escorted him out of the room. Five minutes later invite him back, if he has calmed down. Let this be a pattern for your meals together: no contention, just pleasant conversation.

6. If a child dawdles excessively over his food you might give him one or two brief encouragements, but no more. At the end of the meal clear all the dishes off the table, including his, without comment. He may still be hungry, but a little fasting will not hurt him. Do not at this time permit between meal snacking. *What you do, more than what you say, will change his behavior.*

The same technique could be used if a child misses a meal after being called several times. There would obviously be exceptions—when prior arrangements have been made or when the youngster is late getting home for reasons beyond his control.

7. Don't criticize minor accidents or spills during the meal hour. You might say, helpfully, "Let me get you a larger spoon to dish that gravy out with" or "If you handle the pitcher this way it is less likely to spill or make a mess."

8. Table manners can be discussed and encouraged at the dinner table, but not in a condemning, accusing kind of way. Use some humor. They will learn something and not take it as a challenge to upset or punish you by further obnoxious behavior. Once when Paul was trying to get a rise out of us with atrocious table manners, like eating with his fingers, I calmly took his plate and placed it on the floor and said, "Paul, you can join Peanuts (our dog) for dinner." The air was instantly filled with laughing and barking sounds from our other children. Paul's table manners remarkably improved after that. If I had got angry, however, it would have been the payoff he was hoping for.

9. Remember, if a child's diet is well balanced it's better that he eat less than more. Some very important research on obesity suggests that much of adult and adolescent patterns for being overweight may be due to overfeeding in infancy and early childhood and from parents' insisting that the child eat every speck of food on his plate. Extra fat cells are built up at this time by overfeeding, and they remain there for the rest of the child's life. Then he has to engage in constant dieting to maintain weight control.

The Obese, Overweight Child

To be female, teenage, and overweight is absolutely miserable. Males suffer too, of course, but an obese male who is coordinated and strong can at least try out for a tackle position on the school football team. I believe obesity causes more distress and grief for either sex than almost any other concern that a young person can face.

Several years ago I helped conduct a health survey of students at the university where I teach. When asked if they felt they had a problem with overweight, more than ninety percent of the female students replied, "Yes." This was so regardless of their actual weight. Many were even underweight and still were convinced they had a problem with overweight. But for many the problem is real— a kind of nightmare that never ends. Most have tried countless diets. Some of these work for a while, but the majority don't work at all. Others get the yo-yo effect—thirty pounds off, thirty-six pounds on; twenty-five off, thirty on; and on and on.

Why can't they keep the weight off? Research clearly implicates family eating patterns and emotional and psychological factors as the major culprits. Of course, there are inherited factors that help determine body size and give some people a tendency to gain weight easily. On the other hand, heredity guarantees that some people will always be thin no matter how much they eat. They just don't have the fat genes.

Even if a child inherits the tendency to gain weight easily, he does not *have* to be overweight. If he never becomes obese in childhood, and if he is taught correct eating habits all his growing-up years, there is no reason, biologically, why he should ever be fat. Unfortunately, children who inherit the tendency toward overweight usually have parents with *bad* eating habits, and the children learn at an early age that the dinner table is a feeding trough where they should gorge themselves. The kitchen is the most frequently visited room in the house where there are always goodies just crying out to be eaten. Worse still is when children learn that good behavior is rewarded with candy or other sugar-rich foods. When they get older and have control of their own money, they quickly learn to "reward" themselves with food, and soon a weight problem becomes a disaster of obesity.

Good eating habits in children, then, must begin with their parents—if you don't want your kids to have a weight problem you must solve your own.

It's easy for all those researchers out there to tell you, "Don't eat so much", but for those faced with the fat problem it requires a tremendous inner dedication, a commitment, a different way of living. And you can't slip. Just three days on an eating binge, and it shows up on the scales immediately. If you are unloved, socially rejected, or come from a super-critical family, food may be a major psychological crutch. Despairing, you think, "Why even try?" Many don't try. They just balloon and bulge out and cry in private, hoping for a miracle some day.

Let's look at the psychological and emotional factors that contribute to obesity. They are real, but I also think they interact with genetic predispositions toward an easy accumulation of poundage. I work with many females who have every emotional and psychological reason to be overweight—but they are not. Some of them even go on major eating binges, but they still don't put on weight like their biologically fat-prone sisters. Consequently they never get caught up in that vicious circle: weight goes down some when they are feeling good, but during stress or disappointment the diet flies out the window and on come the pounds. Food becomes like a daily "fix", and these "foodaholics" gorge four, five, maybe six times a day.

Sometimes a child or an adult overeats because he is downright unhappy, lonely, or maladjusted. Food serves as a partial substitute for love. This can become a self-perpetuating cycle. The added weight tends to make the person even more unhappy, lonely, and maladjusted. In time this leads to more overeating and an endless repetition of self-pity and gorging.

So what do we counsel parents as well as their overweight children to do about the problem?

1. First I consider it important to resolve any complicating psychological or emotional problems that might sabotage a weight-reduction program. Cut down all the other stresses to an absolute minimum. You can't slay ten dragons at once. Isolate just the one—obesity—and go to it full speed. This may mean that you will have to wait several months—until you set your house in order, finalize the divorce, change schools, move to the new apartment, or change jobs.

2. Programs where you try to "go it alone" after reading a magazine or newspaper article about the latest "cure" for obesity usually don't work, I have found. You need a system that won't wreck your health and that has a good track record with others who have tried it. You also need one that has a number of supports to help you through the tough days. The outside program I have found to be the most successful with my patients is Weight Watchers. (I have no connection with their organization.) Their system, of course, doesn't work for everybody, but it's safer and works better than most other commercial programs I know of. A mother and daughter or two sisters or girlfriends might try it together. It can be mutually reinforcing. They can help each other during the tough days. But make sure you time your signing up for this diet program, or any other you choose, when other stresses on you aren't overwhelming.

Some crash diets can actually be dangerous to your health. These include the Zen Buddhist Macrobiotic Diet, the so-called Mayo Diet (*not* from the Mayo Clinic), Calories-Don't-Count Diet, Hindu Guru Diet, and the Air Force Diet (*not* endorsed by the Air Force). Especially with young growing children and teenagers, most crash diets should be avoided.

3. A private physician may prescribe an appetite suppressant, but it is vitally important that the child be on a protective diet and vitamins to prevent complicating health problems. Also, the medicine used should be carefully monitored by both the parents and the physician. Some of these medications have the potential for being abused. Few physicians prescribe amphetamines ("speed") for weight loss anymore—they don't work very well and can be dangerous.

4. Reasonable exercise is also recommended. First, it will burn off a modest number of calories; second, and more important, it will help fight depression. This should be the kind of exercise that will get the pulse rate up to 130 or 140 beats per minute: jogging, participation in active games, fast walking, bicycling, hiking, skiing, or swimming. It needs to be daily for at least twenty minutes or more.

5. And, finally, let me share with you a special diet program which I use with some of my clients who come to see me on a private professional basis. I've used it primarily with teenagers and have found it to be very safe, fairly permanent, and highly successful. It really works and involves just a few simple rules. All it requires is the teenager's cooperation.

I first get a health check or clearance from the family doctor to make sure there are no medical complications like diabetes or hypoglycemia. Then I check for any psychological factors or acute stresses that need to be neutralized before we start. For example, if final exams are coming up in two weeks and all hell is breaking loose in five other areas of my patient's life, we wait until that has passed. She must be able to focus all her energy on the weight problem because the program will involve some minor habit changes. We don't want a lot of earth-shaking distractions.

We start out with a three-and-a-half-day total fast. The only things she can consume are water (all she wants) and multiple vitamins. The idea here is to clean poisons out of the body and shrink the appetite. Besides, abstinence at first is easier than continence—if you can't eat at all, you can't eat too much!

Then, when she starts eating again, she follows these simple, easily remembered rules.

a. You can eat nothing with sugar in it. *No* exceptions. This includes soda pop, candy, all pastries, ice cream, pancake syrup, honey, pies, grape juice (which has lots of sugar added), flavored gelatin desserts or jello salads, and so on. *Sugar is "poison."* Think of it that way.

b. You can eat everything else—but it must be in *small* amounts. You never want to "stretch your stomach" or enlarge your appetite again. You should now feel full with smaller quantities of food. This will significantly cut your calories, but your food intake must be nutritious and balanced from the seven food groups mentioned earlier in this chapter. Go easy on fats. Avoid french fries or other deep-fat-fried food.

c. If you really feel hungry, it's all right—and even recommended—to have *small* snacks between meals. But these have to be nutritious, not junk food. Snack on fruits, vegetables, juice, cheese and crackers, peanut butter, milk, cottage cheese, or cold meat. But again, these have to be eaten in small amounts. You should never feel really hungry again with this system after the first three-and-a-half days.

d. Take some kind of multiple vitamin daily. I find that these protect you when under stress and help kill hidden hunger pangs, besides keeping you healthy.

This is not a rule, but an added caution: Be very careful about eating when watching TV. Many people turn the "eat button" on when they turn the TV on. It's very easy to over eat and over indulge if you eat while watching your favorite program.

Figure out ahead of time what you are going to do if you go to a friend's house to eat, to a wedding reception, a party, or any other social situation where food will be served. I have found it possible to eat right in social settings, but you have to plan your strategy *ahead of time* and not get caught off guard. You may whisper to your hostess that you are on a diet. She won't be shocked—everybody is at one time or another. She'll be on your side. And when people visit you, serve nutritious non-sugar snacks. Your visitors will love you for it—because they are all fighting the same problem you are!

You should take off a pound a week with this system. That means in ten weeks you will lose ten pounds, and they'll stay off. But the crucial thing is to make this very simple-to-follow diet a *habit*. It's flexible and easy; you are never miserable or starved. But remember—never eat anything with sugar in it. When you do eat, eat only small amounts—to keep your appetite very, very small. Appetite is a habit—a state of mind. If you usually eat little at a time, you will always feel full and content.

Good luck. This really works. All you have to do is do it.

17

Enuresis (Bedwetting)

AT 7:10 A.M. Charley, eyes downcast, shuffled out of his bedroom dragging a smelly, wet blanket and soaked sleepers behind him. Mother glanced at him and caught a deep breath; saying nothing, she shuddered and quickly turned away, returning to the kitchen. A few moments later she heard the familiar morning chug chug of the washing machine. Later, glancing into his bedroom, she noted that the plastic bed protector had somehow come off during the night, and there was the familiar wet spot on the mattress. There also was a circle of wetness on the carpeted floor where he had obviously slept after soaking his bed. Tears of helplessness and frustration welled up in her eyes. She stood just shaking her head, quietly sobbing to herself. Charley was in hiding, overcome with humiliation.

The average child should be dry by age three in the daytime except for the occasional stress-induced "accident". By age five the typical youngster should be dry at night seventy-five percent of the time. At age seven and one-half only seven percent of children are still occasionally wetting the bed at night, and this tapers down to two percent by age eighteen.

Boys are twice as likely as girls to have this problem. Thus it is not unusual for an occasional teenage boy to be struggling with bed wetting while in junior high or high school. Eighty percent of those who do wet, wet only at night. Fifteen percent wet both day and night, while five percent wet only in the daytime. In most cases, even if nothing at all is done about it, the child will gradually cease wetting on his own. And studies suggest that it is an isolated problem—neither related to nor suggestive of serious pathology, either in the family or individually.

The U.S. Navy at one time dealt with the problem of bedwetters—among boys inducted in their late teens—by stacking them in sleeping hammocks, one on top of each other. Then they rotated sleeping assignments each night up and down. Pity the poor fellow on the bottom hammock! They claimed that this was quite successful in reducing the incidence of nightly wetting. If this or some other method didn't work it sometimes became grounds for an "administrative discharge" from the service.

Causes

About one case in twenty, or five percent, is organic: a urinary tract infection, diabetes, or a urethral canal obstruction or malfunction reducing the flow of urine from the bladder. Epilepsy, sleep-walking, spinal tumors, mental retardation, or the presence of intestinal parasites can also contribute to bedwetting. Since these all tend to be quite rare, I mention them only in passing.

Possessing an abnormally small bladder or being a very heavy sleeper so that the child isn't awakened by the uncomfortable feeling of a full bladder are other contributing causes. But by far the most common reason for bedwetting is a mix of (a) maturational/developmental lag and (b) psychological/emotional causes including anxiety, insecurity, emotional stress, or family conflict. Maturational lag is a delayed hooking up of neural circuits going from the brain to the bladder and its sphincter and back again. This tends to be hereditary; often dad or mother will also have had a bedwetting problem as a youngster.

Whenever there is daytime wetting or a reduced flow or dribble of urine or accompanying fever or pain, these would strongly point to organic problems. This would suggest that you immediately contact your physician and have him do a careful diagnostic evaluation. Of course, sometimes the same child will wet the bed from a mix of several contributing causes such as developmental lag, deep sleep patterns, and small bladder—all at once.

What to Do about It?

Assuming organic disease has been ruled out, you may choose to do nothing, since children gradually stop wetting on their own without any treatment in ninety-eight percent of the cases. However, most parents choose to stop it sooner for aesthetic reasons and convenience—to stop the daily washings of smelly blankets and bed clothes. In addition, persistent bedwetting frequently brings jeers and taunts from brothers and sisters, or even from peers if they find out about it when the child goes on a trip or is invited to sleep overnight with a friend.

You may decide that you don't want to ignore the problem, if it has persisted too long. After your family doctor or pediatrician has ruled out any possibility of physical cause, you can begin to help the child overcome the problem.

Of our nine children we had only one wetter, and then only at night. If we had to do it over again, we would handle the situation differently. Jack was a deep sleeper and had a maturational/developmental lag. This is not related to intelligence: Jack was quite bright. He wet the bed frequently in elementary school and occasionally in his early teens. We let him take care of washing his own pajamas and blankets. Our strategy was not to hassle or humiliate him, knowing he would eventually grow out of it. He did.

We prided ourselves on not being uptight parents and not making a big fuss over his problem. But we could have and should have dried him out earlier. It would have saved him considerable embarrassment.

The strategy I would now use and recommend for helping most bedwetters involves several steps; if one fails, you can escalate to the next.

The Easy Steps

First, after the child has been checked medically and physical problems have been ruled out, stop all fluid intake from 4:00 P.M. on. This means no drinks of any kind, even at supper or bedtime. Having your child's cooperation, of course, is absolutely vital for this to work.

A second tactic, for children who are of school age or older, is to train them to stretch and increase the size of their bladder and at the same time teach them to strengthen and increase their control over the bladder's sphincter or "flow-control" muscle. Encourage the child to drink lots of fluid, especially in the morning, and when he has the urge to go to the bathroom ask him to delay urinating for at least five minutes. Next time he feels the urge have him delay urination for ten, fifteen, twenty, and up to thirty minutes. Tell him to imagine that the bladder is like a balloon partly filled with water. Delaying going to the bathroom will stretch and enlarge the balloon or bladder so that at night, when he is asleep, he will have an increased capacity.

You will have already explained to him that he has a special muscle, a sphincter, that releases and holds back the flow of urine, and like muscles in any other part of the body, if it is weak, it can be strengthened. One way he can strengthen it so it will hold back his urine is by exercise, and to exercise that sphincter muscle he just has to stop and start the flow of urine three or four times while urinating in the bathroom. Right in the middle of the flow, stop it. This becomes almost a game for the child. And if he understands that it will help him with the bedwetting, he will usually be very cooperative.

A third tactic is to examine the child's current life situation. Is he under a lot of stress? Is there a new baby on the scene, a divorce, an adopted child, a difficult family move, a continuing parent-child conflict? If you can, reduce the stress and give the child plenty of extra attention and security.

A fourth tactic is to set up a gentle behavior modification system so as to reward the child for being dry. (I would never punish him for wetting.) Make up a chart that covers the entire month and put it in his bedroom. Each night he is dry give him a star or ten points or some other recognition of his "great achievement". When he accumulates one hundred points or ten stars, he can trade them in for a movie, a date with one or both of his parents, or some other reward that means a lot to him. For younger children you can also give *daily* reinforcers or rewards right after every dry night—a stick of sugarless gum along with praise.

If one of these tactics doesn't significantly cut the incidence of bedwetting within two or three weeks, you should escalate to the next strategies while continuing to apply the foregoing.

Another Approach: Medication

Imipramine hydrochloride (available in tablets under the trade name Tofranil) is by far the most helpful drug for stopping bedwetting. It must be prescribed by the family physician or pediatrician. It apparently helps relax the bladder so that it can hold more urine at night, and it also makes the child a lighter sleeper. Another medication sometimes used is tincture of belladonna; it helps tighten the sphincter muscles of the bladder. A third medical strategy is to take a prescription stimulant, such as Dexedrine, at bedtime. It helps combat the deep sleep which often goes along with bedwetting. Right now Tofranil is the best choice, but it is probably most helpful when used along with the earlier tactics.

The "Conditioning Device"

The next remedy to try, but only if the child is cooperative and of school age or older, is the so-called "conditioning device". It works successfully with sixty to eighty percent of children it's used with. It can be bought, along with instructions, through Sears or other mail-order catalog companies for from $30 to $45, depending on the model. A special pad is put on the bed. When even one drop of water or urine touches it, an alarm bell or buzzer goes off. The noise awakens the child so he can finish urinating in the bathroom. This conditioning process quickly leads to the end of bedwetting with most children. The child soon learns to awaken and go to the bathroom when he feels a full bladder—before the sound of the bell or buzzer.

Parents sometimes report that the child who is a deep sleeper fails to awaken when the bell rings. If increasing the loudness of the bell or buzzer doesn't help, parents can give special training to help the child awaken to the alarm. When he is asleep in bed, the parents deliberately set off the alarm several times each night and then personally awaken the child while the bell is ringing. Usually after several nights of this the child will awaken on his own when the bell rings. Additionally, medication may be given to help lighten sleep so the child will be more easily aroused by the alarm. The bell device can even be placed a little way from the bed so the child will have to get out of bed in order to turn it off. The bedwetter should not share a bed with another brother or sister. If possible, he should be in a room by himself.

It should take about two weeks for a successful conditioning to occur, but you should not persist beyond four weeks if this strategy doesn't work. Where occasionally the device has failed, I have found that it is because the parents have not properly and strictly followed the instructions given them. Sometimes it is helpful to have a psychologist or someone familiar with conditioning techniques to give added counsel.

I do not advise making a big issue of bedwetting before school age. In most cases it's just a developmental lag that time will correct. However, if the condition persists well into the school years, I personally think it's better to try to speed up the child's control of his bladder functions—especially since it can be done gently and effectively in about ninety percent of the cases through the strategies already mentioned. When it persists despite all you do, it may be your child's unconscious reaction to extreme stress or his way of handling an emotional problem with a parent. Consult with a competent professional in such cases.

In the great majority of cases, however, you can help the child become dry at night without resorting to such help. Good luck!

18
Going with the Wrong Friends

AS FOURTEEN-YEAR-OLD KRISTINE left the chapel after the Sunday service, her minister shook her hand and asked to see her briefly in his study after the congregation had departed. There, in private, he expressed to her his concern about another parishioner family, a divorcee who had long since stopped coming to church and now had a reputation for wild living. "It's her daughter Deborah that I'm worried about. She still comes to church every month or so, and I think with love and friendship we can help her avoid her mother's path." The minister asked Kristine, who was about Deborah's age, to try to befriend the girl and get her involved in church activities. Kristine willingly agreed.

Deborah and Kristine quickly became good friends—what began as an assignment soon turned into an important emotional bond. But Deborah's mother was no fool. She guessed from the start why Kristine had first become interested in her daughter, and she resented the minister's attempt to "save" Deborah. She developed a counter strategy, courting Kristine's friendship herself and making her own life style seem as attractive as possible.

Within a year, instead of Deborah following Kristine into church activity, it was Kristine who was influenced—she became involved in drugs, sexual promiscuity, and alcohol abuse. In time she rejected her own family, whom she now thought of as "dull squares". Deborah's mother had beaten the minister at his own game. She had captured his pawn.

It took three-and-a-half years before Kristine finally regained her balance and reconciled with her family and church. And, with any luck, her minister learned a valuable lesson: when two people with different values become friends it isn't always the nicer set of values that wins.

Kristine's parents learned too late what was happening but were able, when they saw that it was out of hand, to begin the long slow process of bringing Kristine back out of the grip of a poisonous friendship. When kids are aware that they are flouting their parents' values, they rarely bring their obnoxious friends home. It's sometimes only by accident, or when disaster strikes, that the parents ever learn what powerful influences were working against them outside the home.

Steve was a very large and mature thirteen-year-old, bright and cooperative, and his parents didn't suspect that anything was going wrong in his life until one night, about 2:00 A.M., when his mother got up to visit the bathroom. On the way down the hall she passed Steve's bedroom and noticed the door was open. As she reached in to close it, she noticed his bed was empty. She turned on the light. His bed had been slept in, but the window was open and Steve was nowhere in the room—nowhere in the house, for that matter.

Steve's parents searched the house and the yard several times and couldn't find him anywhere. They remembered he had gone to bed at eleven o'clock complaining of feeling extra tired. It had been a quiet evening; everyone had been in good spirits. Nothing added up. Should they call the police or trust Steve to come home and get the explanation from him later? They were distraught and perplexed, and it did nothing to calm them down when Steve's mother went back to his room and found him in bed with the window closed. He was deeply asleep. It was almost impossible to waken him.

Where had he been? They confronted him the next morning, but all they could get out of him was vague denial and evasive explanations that were obviously contradictory and dishonest.

It was obvious Steve was going to tell them nothing so his parents went to work. After very skillful research that would have done any private investigator proud, they learned that he was leaving home regularly at 1:00 A.M. to meet with other teenage boys and girls in the basement of a vacant house several blocks away, where they partied and experimented with drugs. Each of the kids woke himself with a small alarm and left home stealthily—and until Steve's parents found out, quite by accident, not one parent had had any idea this was going on!

As far as Steve's parents knew, all his friends were decent, good kids; those kids' parents thought Steve was a "safe" friend, too. In fact, the kids *were* basically good. They were just curious. But the pattern they were beginning was a perilous one: deception, experimentation with dangerous and illegal drugs, separation from their families and their families' values. Once the facts were known, all the parents realized that there had been signs—if they had only looked for them or taken them seriously. Kids aren't usually *that* good at secrecy. The best camouflage they had was their parents' own trust.

Not that you shouldn't trust your kids, but while you trust them you have to remember that teenagers are not yet adults. In their immaturity they are looking for something else outside themselves to moor to. They really don't have the inner resources yet to guide them, to be truly independent. So while they think they are ready to stop leaning on *you*, they merely lean on their friends. In the process, they transfer much of their allegiance. They remain trustworthy, but it is their friends who can trust them now more than you.

If you have a close, loving relationship with your children, they will never completely reject you, though it might seem like it sometimes. But there are periods in almost every child's life when the paramount influence on him, regardless of his past relationship with you, is his friends. That's why you need to keep watching carefully. Scrutinize every friend or group of friends your child spends time with. Not in an open, prying way that will turn off your child, but discreetly and with a sincere desire to like the people your child has chosen to like. Keep your eyes open; listen when you are permitted to overhear a conversation; notice what the subject matter is or who is present when a loud conversation suddenly becomes soft; be sensitive. If you don't do these things you won't be able to tell the "good guys" from the "bad guys". The friends who will wreck your child's life are not always wearing the grubby clothing and speaking in language that would embarrass truck drivers. Sometimes the real wreckers are kids who look as neat and clean as yours, who treat you politely, who seem to be ideal.

Once you've spotted a friend or a group of friends who seem to be dangerous, what can you do? Do you have a right to interfere with your children's choice of friends? I've struggled with this question many times, but after seeing too many kids for too many years seduced into self-destruction by sick "friends", I've come to the conclusion that in some instances parents don't just have the right, they have the *duty* to discourage or break up a bad friendship. It's the same duty they had when their toddler tried to run into the street in front of cars. Sometimes parents have to act in order to save their children's future lives.

Of course, I'm assuming that these are parents who really are mature, who are reluctant to interfere but who see a danger and with genuine love for their child are acting to help him. There is another kind of parent who is immature himself, unable to allow his child any independence at all. Such parents keep their children constantly under control, making all decisions for them, and turning them into grown-up infants in the process. A good parent's objective is not to make sure his kids always make decisions the way he would; a good parent's objective is to teach his kids how to make intelligent decisions. The only reason a parent should consider interfering in his child's choice of friends is when those friends are influencing his child into activities that will severely limit his future choices or present a real danger. If your kid spends five years in jail on a felony charge, it cuts out his option to run for governor when he's forty. And if his brains get scrambled with a bad trip on angel dust, he's going to have a hard time even choosing to stand up or sit down in the mental hospital where he may spend part of his life.

Not every friend that you don't care for is going to lead your child to jail or the mental hospital or an early grave. Those are exceptional cases, and that's why I urge you, ordinarily, to be very reluctant to interfere with your child's friendships. There are many times you will worry a little—or even a lot—because your child's friends are from a different social background, a different income class, or because they dress disgustingly or use language or have attitudes that offend you. Unless you have clear evidence that your child is being drawn into clearly dangerous behavior patterns, I advise restraint on your part. Those "weird" kids your child brings home, unless they're involved in something really dangerous, may just be playing at being independent—just as your child is.

In fact, most friendships with kids who are very different from your own child's upbringing don't last very long. There isn't enough common background to bind them together, and they soon go their own ways. But for the brief time they are together, they help and feed each other in ways that often aren't visible to adults. Besides, it does your child no harm to have contact with people who are poorer or richer than you; it does him no harm to learn the different languages of the street and the drawing room reception. A good recipe for raising bigots is to keep blinders on them so that they don't associate with anyone even the slightest bit different from the "accepted group". Even though your child has the strongest likelihood of adopting your values and staying in your social group despite his teenage experimentation, it will make him a better person to have touched, however briefly, people who are different and yet who are still good people.

Interfere only reluctantly and after much thought; the cost of interference is very high. It had better be worth it.

Guidance Strategies

There are some things you can do to limit the influence of friends or to keep your child out of situations he isn't mature enough to handle, things that won't be perceived by your child as direct interference between him and his group of friends. Basically, the strategy consists of setting up impersonal, unbiased family rules that the kids know about from the time they're young. Then there are no surprises when they reach the age where the rules apply.

One rule we have is that none of our kids is allowed to date (one and one) until he is sixteen. Why sixteen? Actually, this is no great hardship on boys. They mature more slowly and don't really have much opportunity to date until they get their driver's license at sixteen or seventeen years of age; my sons have never squawked much about the rule. But my daughters have matured physically and socially at an earlier age and have sometimes resented the rule. Yet they have obeyed it, resignedly, because they knew all their lives that that was the way it was going to be, and Mom and Dad were not going to be very flexible on this one.

Group dates, where four or more boys and girls are together for the whole evening, were permitted earlier because that is not as risky as a one-to-one situation. I wouldn't allow individual dating before sixteen because I knew the hazards from my clinical experience.

I've seen too many girls who developed physically in their early teens and, because men were now interested in them, started dating at thirteen, fourteen, and fifteen. Just dating is only interesting for a few years. After a while all the dates start being pretty much the same thing, and the girl starts looking for more serious and permanent involvements. This greatly increases the possibility that she may marry very young, in her teens. Often girls who date too early marry before finishing high school or have to drop out of school to handle a pregnancy or an abortion. Almost always they marry unwisely, without the wisdom to avoid husbands with traits that lead too often to divorce. And even if they don't marry, they get seriously involved in relationships they are too young to handle, and they get bruised and become distrustful of closeness with members of the opposite sex.

They're too young, that's all. Just because their hormones make them look like women at thirteen or fourteen doesn't mean they are ready to handle all the stresses of an adult woman's life. Too many girls who plunged into the dating game too young find themselves nineteen years old with a couple of kids, married to a guy they've now outgrown, changing messy diapers, fixing meals—stuck. And all their friends who *didn't* date so young and so seriously are now going to college or working at interesting jobs. The no-dating-before-sixteen rule, however silly it might seem to your children, keeps them detached from adult type relationships until they are older and better able to choose their dating partners with wisdom while avoiding entanglements that seem glamorous to a thirteen-year-old and childish to an older teenager.

Another rule that helps avoid dangerous relationships is: no permanent friends more than one or maybe two grades older than you in school; no dating boys or girls more than two or three years older than you.

When there is a large age difference between your child and his friends, their influence over him is often much, much too strong. Where your nine-year-old might have no trouble saying, "No, that's a dumb idea" to his nine-year-old friend who suggests shoplifting, he probably won't have the courage to say it to his eleven-year-old friend. Where one friend is much older than the other the influence tends to go all one way. And why is the older child so eager to have younger friends? Usually because he is immature for his age and seeks younger friends *because* he can dominate them, *because* in their eyes he is so wise and interesting while in fact the kids his own age know that he isn't much. For this reason, the older child who hangs around with your much younger child is more likely to be showing off, doing dangerous and stupid and illegal things just to keep proving how neat he is—while your child, wide-eyed and naive, goes along with him.

The rule doesn't mean that you forbid your child to speak to older kids or associate with them at school. It just means that older kids don't go along on outings, your child doesn't go places with older kids after school, and when your child starts dating, his dating partners should not be significantly older and more experienced.

If the rule is carefully explained from your child's earliest years, he will already have the habit of looking for companionship among people his own age by the time he is old enough to date. Otherwise, older dating partners will often seem particularly attractive. They know more; they get around better, know better restaurants, know how to deal with social situations. They aren't clumsy about kissing, and they've already learned to keep their teeth clean and wear deodorant. They're simply more glamorous to your son or daughter.

Another strategy to help keep your children out of dangerous relationships is simply keeping the lines of communication open. Too many parents are reluctant to talk to their children about sex and dating and love and marriage. Perhaps they're afraid that by bringing up the topics they'll be encouraging their children to get involved in these "adult" activities earlier than otherwise. Actually, the opposite is true. With the onset of puberty children naturally get curious about these things. If they don't find out about them in a mature way from you, they'll find answers through their own experimentation. While they don't need you to tell them that kissing and caressing feel good; that being in love is wonderful and exciting; that sex and marriage are, ultimately, what dating is all about, talking to them about these things in an open, matter-of-fact way will help shape their attitudes. It will also make it possible for you to talk to them about their particular dating partners in an emotionally uncharged atmosphere. If you have never talked about sex with your daughter and then suddenly come to her one day, terribly upset, and say, "This guy you're dating, this George—he's a jerk, he's selfish and only wants to take advantage of you," chances are pretty good that your daughter will leap to his defense or try to avoid any conversation on the topic. It's just not the kind of thing she usually talks to her parents about, and your sudden interest is seen as meddling because she has never learned to share her social life with you.

It will help a great deal if you help your children keep dating in perspective. Their romances will seem like the most important things in the world to them, and certainly you should be sympathetic; rejoice when they rejoice, and shed a few tears with them when a particularly intense romance ends. But between times, help them remember that choosing a spouse is more important than buying a car or a house; they'd never make such a major decision without looking at a lot of different designs. "There's a lot that goes into choosing a husband besides how he looks in the cab of a pickup truck," you point out—after your daughter has broken up with the guy in the pickup. Even while the relationship is going on, because you and your children talk about such things, you can frankly ask, "What is it that you like about him? What does he do that makes you happy? And what does he do that irritates you? Is that important?" Teenage children have very few reliable measures of quality in people—they can only gain it if you help them awaken to the less obvious but still important traits in their friends. But, again, that is only possible if you make sure to build that kind of relationship with your kids from the outset.

This way, when your son is head-over-heels infatuated with a pretty girl who is obviously playing him for a sucker and likely to seduce him into a lifestyle that won't do him much good, you'll have the kind of relationship where you can say, "I don't know about you, but *I* wish she'd either tell you yes or no. Don't you think it's a little selfish of her to keep all her weekend options open while *you* stay so committed to her?"

"She doesn't know that I'm that committed," he says in her defense.

"Oh, don't you think so?" you ask, and he thinks about it. When the relationship ends or gets even rockier, he won't forget to look at her behavior and see if she isn't just a bit selfish, a bit too demanding and not giving enough.

The time to start building a close, talkative relationship with your kids is *not* when they start dating some dangerous, unpleasant person—by the time you can communicate they might be hopelessly in love. It's better to make sure you have that kind of relationship all along so that when the dangerous one appears, you can share your concerns early in their dating. You can sensitize your son or daughter to the potential problems early enough that nagging doubts will have time to form.

There is no guarantee, of course, that your kid won't fall in love anyway and go right ahead and marry or drop out of school or whatever other unpleasant thing might happen at the wrong age. But you will have done all you can possibly do. Your kid won't be going into the relationship with blinders on. And when problems arise you won't gloat and say, "I told you so." You'll just help your child where you can. Part of his growing up is the right to make wrong decisions; part of your love for him is that you want his happiness.

And who knows? Your kid may actually turn out to be one of that statistically small group of teenagers who make ridiculous mistakes in their love lives and still manage to turn them into happy and productive marriages!

Some things you can do to shape your children's associations so that they are less likely to fall in with a bad crowd or date unsuitable people are quite obvious—but often overlooked:

Your choice of neighborhood does a lot to shape your child's life. Before you buy a house look at more than the house plan and the price tag. Make some discreet inquiries among people you know who live there. Once I actually knocked on eight doors in a neighborhood on the pretext of doing a survey. I learned a great deal—and didn't buy a house there. Don't forget that just because the neighborhood consists of expensive homes doesn't mean that the families living there are good people. Some wealthy neighborhoods are loaded with pathology. If you are young, moving into a young neighborhood where most of the families are unformed, it isn't the children you need to evaluate—it's the young married couples who are raising them. Neighborhoods full of chronic family fighting, divorce, alcoholism, mental illness, frustration, mate-swapping, and unethical behavior are likely to produce quite a few children with problems you don't want to have your children dealing with.

It also helps to direct your child into structured group activities where he can meet plenty of interesting, active people his own age. Cub Scouts and Boy Scouts, Girl Scouts and Campfire Girls have plenty to intrigue active youngsters and are good places for them to form their friendships. Your religious affiliation may well have a program to involve young people in activities with children of other families with the same faith; there are also nondenominational groups like the YMCA and YWCA, or community activity programs and school clubs. The more time your child spends involved with people of similar values, the less time he'll have to find more harmful friends.

Your own friends, whose children are roughly the same age as yours, are a possibility for help, too. A joint summer vacation with two compatible families can form strong friendships between adults *and* children, and many warm traditions established over the years are threads that help bind your children—and theirs—to the kind of life they ought to lead. If you are lucky enough to live close to relatives and enjoy a good relationship with them, there's no reason your kids' cousins can't fill much of that role.

A lot of the attraction of destructive groups of friends is that they are better than loneliness, and the child who is hungry for love and can't find any friends at school among the "good" kids will take whatever comes along. So why not make it a point to give your child a pet that is all his own? He must be old enough, of course, to take responsibility for it. And it has to be a pet that is warm and affectionate, intelligent and yet absolutely loyal and uncritical—the ideal friend. There isn't an animal that fits those requirements a tenth as well as a dog, of course. Cats don't have the loyalty, and horses are a bit inconvenient to have around the house and don't show much affection. Fish and turtles just aren't in the running. (In choosing, choose for the child. A high-strung poodle may go with the decor in your living room, a doberman pinscher may be a great guard dog, but your kid needs a *friend*. Mutts are often marvelous and warm; loving breeds like spaniels and collies are also usually a safe choice.)

When the Danger Is Acute

Suppose that you have done all of the above—or that it's too late. Your kid is fifteen, and he hangs around with a group of juvenile delinquents who have got in trouble with the law several times. You know that he's no stranger to drugs, sex, and petty crime, that it's only a matter of time before his mind goes or he's stuck with an equally immature wife or he's put in reform school. It doesn't matter that you've tried to have a good relationship with him. It doesn't matter that your kid is basically good and sometimes a bit ashamed of the kind of things his friends do. He's with them, he's being influenced by them, and unless you do something *now* his whole future may be utterly ruined.

What can you do?

This is not the time to be democratic. If you have already pointed out the dangers of this association, and it has had no effect—or a negative effect, so that now he listens to you less and them more—it is not necessary to give him a vote. If he is young enough, simply forbid the friendship. Keep him home, drive him to and from school, and work to fill the hours now free in his life with better associations. If he is too old or the friends are in school with him, take more drastic action. Change schools. Send him to live with relatives in a different state—preferably relatives with a different lifestyle. Do you have a cousin or an uncle who owns a farm? Excellent. See if he's willing to take your son on as a farm-worker for six months or a year. Is your daughter sick of the boredom of your smalltown life? Send her to live with your sister's family near a big city where there are plenty of things to do that are neither illegal nor damaging. In short, uproot him from the situation *completely* so that it's impossible for him to see his unsavory friends and difficult for him to find similar people in his new environment.

What if there's nowhere to send him? I would be authoritarian. I would be gentle. I would lose my temper, raise a ruckus, be persuasive, be seductive, bribe the kid, punish the kid—*anything* that would possibly work to pull him out of a situation that could destroy him.

If all else fails, you might seriously consider uprooting your entire family for the sake of that threatened child. Change jobs, move to a different state or to a different kind of neighborhood, one where your kids will attend better schools or where drugs just aren't so available or where laws are better obeyed and better enforced—do whatever you have to do to save your child's life; if your two-year-old were just about to fall off a cliff, you wouldn't worry about whether you were interfering with his freedom as an individual as you grabbed him and pulled him back from the edge.

It is rare for the situation to get *that* bad. The most powerful weapon in your arsenal to combat the influence of harmful friends is your love for your children—and your children's love for you. If you are careful to keep the lines of communication open with your children all their lives, and if you provide them with dozens of warm, positive, memorable experiences shared with you during their growing-up years, your influence will be so strong you won't have to do very much at all to try to change your children's lives. They'll already subscribe to your values because they'll know that those values do provide genuine happiness. And if they do let curiosity or just plain rebelliousness pull them away from their closeness with you, they'll feel the absence of that closeness as a real emotional pain. They'll come back.

19

When Parents Remarry: The Challenge of Yours, Mine, and Ours

MANY YEARS AGO, a marriage counselor friend of mine lost his wife. He waited until his children were virtually raised before remarrying. Why? His counseling experience had convinced him that it was almost impossible to blend two families, each with its own separate identity and history, into one successful family. He wouldn't waste his time—and emotions—trying.

I know another man who lost his wife. He had six children. He remarried, and his new wife had no children of her own. They were very much in love, but after some months of marriage the children announced to their father that his new wife was unacceptable to them. She would have to leave.

She did. At the present time his wife lives in a separate apartment where he visits her frequently; his primary home is with the children, until they are grown. He has found this to be the only solution that will keep his marriage alive and his family peaceful.

Joining two separate families into one is the most difficult and challenging human experience I know of. These two families solved the problem by sidestepping it, and perhaps that is the safest course—to simply avoid trying to combine families. Yet with our soaring divorce rate it is obvious that there are increasing numbers of single-parent households every year. Is it fair to expect the divorced mother with two or three children to spend the rest of her prime adult years slaving at the office and coming home to work even harder in the incredibly difficult job of raising children without a spouse? Is it reasonable to expect a man or woman who has become used to the interdependence and companionship of a marriage—even an unworkable one—to suddenly decide that "for the sake of the children" he or she will forego that companionship for fifteen or twenty years?

Divorced and widowed parents do have a right to happiness and emotional fulfillment in a sustained love relationship with another adult. That right is at least as important as the children's right to have a secure and comfortable home. In fact, the children of a lonely, unfulfilled single parent are likely to have a good share of problems anyway. Yet the joining of a new spouse into a previously established family—particularly when the newcomer brings his own children to the home—is as tricky and risky a procedure as a surgical transplant. The possibility of rejection is high; there is a long, painful, difficult period in which the tiniest fluctuations in the family's "health" can be instantly magnified into major crises. At best the experience is difficult and challenging for everyone. At its worst, the new marriage is destroyed before it's fairly begun.

I have seen many such marriages in serious trouble. Marsha, for instance, came to me in tears. "But Ned and I loved each other so much when we married two years ago. Now he's cold and critical. He had two teenage sons from his previous marriage, and I have my three little ones. It's just hell all the time. His boys are constantly teasing my children, and it's cruel. The little ones are in tears all the time. When I tell Ned about it he won't do a thing—his boys can do no wrong, in his view. They're spoiled brats. And when I try to discipline them, they just laugh at me and say, 'Lay off it, old lady, you aren't our mother.'

"They even lie to Ned about me—and he believes *them* instead of *me*. He thinks I'm mean to his sons, unfair to them. *Unfair!* God knows I've tried. I just wish he'd try to like *my* kids. He isn't used to having small children around, I guess. They make him nervous. So my kids don't feel close to him at all."

What are the Risks in Remarriage?

The easiest remarriage to succeed with—the one with the lowest risk of failure—is the one in which no children are involved. There are still the hangups, self-doubts, and insecurities left over from the previous marital failure, but unless one of the partners is mentally disturbed, childless remarriages are usually workable if the partners are reasonably compatible and both want it to work.

The next safest remarriage prospect is when only the wife brings young children into the new family from a previous marriage. She already has a bonded relationship to the children, and since the husband usually works the wife is likely to have special time at home alone with the children when he is away. Then, when he comes home in the evening, the children aren't as likely to feel threatened when she gives *him* some attention—they are secure in her love for them.

In such families, it's best for the husband to take a "nice uncle" role with the children. Mother is the primary discipliner—the children won't have a radical change in the family rules with the remarriage. Gradually, if he wants to and does it carefully, with the full support of his wife, the stepfather can establish much closer bonds with the children until a full father-child relationship is formed. Yet even if such a bond never completely forms, the marriage can be liveable, particularly if there are new children born who have no reservations about loving both parents fully.

If both parents work, however, the risks increase. The mother has no extra time with the children. Both parents are already tired, and with the demands of children they may not have the energy and emotional resources to work through the normal post-honeymoon adjustment that all newlyweds seem to need. Also, the time the wife gives her new husband is perceived by the children as time "stolen" from them by this stranger.

An alternative that some single parents have tried is to remain unmarried while attempting to fill their emotional needs through a series of transient affairs. In my counseling experience I have found this usually to be a pretty rocky road. The single parent's emotional needs are not really met—there is no permanence, no commitment, and instead of providing emotional support in the parent's difficult and lonely life, the affairs too often involve strained role-playing, faking, deceptions, and brutal let-downs. They often drain far more from the single parent than they give. In time the parent may become very defensive, even paranoid about members of the opposite sex. These affairs, however discreet, always take a toll on the children's security, too. And for men and women in their thirties and forties, the singles world is often a heartless, cold place to roam.

Sooner or later, most single people with children look for some more permanent kind of union. Despite the risks of remarriage, it looks more attractive than remaining single. Is there something you can do, if you are contemplating remarriage, to improve your chances of success?

Stacking the Deck – in Your Favor

The younger your children are when you remarry, the easier it will be for them to form close emotional bonds with your spouse. Often when the children are too old, close bonding is simply impossible—and may not even be desirable. A fifteen-year-old girl may not want to call Mom's new husband *Dad*. In her view, he can never be her *real* Dad. But the new husband *can* become friends with the child, as long as he is careful not to step over the line into the role the child thinks of as *father*. It requires tact, persistence, imagination, and commitment.

As a new stepfather, you should know that having a good relationship with your wife's children will definitely improve the chances of the second marriage succeeding. Think of it as trying to sell a tough customer in your business. You wine and dine him. You do everything possible to create an amicable relationship. You don't demand instant affection or intimacy; you simply help the kids associate you with pleasant things. This may require the use of a golf course or, with the younger children, your local version of Disneyland. Play the role of the "good guy" and, especially in the first year of the new marriage, let the child's true parent do most of the "dirty work", like disciplining, though you must remember to give her a great deal of private emotional build-up.

It doesn't work quite so easily in reverse—when a stepmother is home with the kids while the father, the real parent, is at work. It is especially hard with older teenage children. Discipline is tossed into the stepmother's lap by default. What can she do?

As an at-home stepmother, you will initially have to downplay disciplining, except on the most vital issues. First you must become their friend. If they are obnoxious, just think of it as working in an office with a difficult co-worker. Ignore what you can, roll with the punches, and remain polite at all possible costs. Try to do nothing provocative, but there is no law that says you have to like them. If the aggravation gets too great it may be necessary for the child to visit the home of the other parent or other relatives for a while. Better this than go through another divorce again! To survive, newly-wed parents need constant close communication and daily recommitment to each other.

Pre-marriage Strategy

You should openly discuss ahead of time the fact that it will sometimes be stressful joining together your two separate families. You will have to be prepared to actively resist attempts by your children to divide and sabotage your relationship.

During the courtship period you must court your betrothed's children also. Bring them gifts, read to the young ones, go on joint outings, talk to them, take them to dinner, and in general develop an active, compatible, friendly relationship. If this is done skillfully, when you marry you will not be seen as a rival. The children will gain another parent, not have to share their true mother or father with you. Everybody wins.

If this isn't handled diplomatically, however, you could easily become the children's enemy. They will only know you as the stranger who always takes Mom or Dad away at night, the interloper who is usurping their true parent's place. The children will perceive the marriage as a disaster for them. It's like having to take a tremendous salary cut in emotional dollars, and they won't like it. It will feel like a *loss*, and I have found that most children tend to be very poor losers. They will attempt to scuttle your new marriage to get even, and kids can, if they want, make great wrecking crews.

If you wait too long to remarry, it can become increasingly difficult for the children to handle. They get used to and comfortable living with you as their only parent. It is even harder when some of the younger children are used to sleeping in Mother's bed with her. If this is a pattern of some years' duration, jealousy of the new spouse and rivalry for the real parent's affection and bed can erupt like exploding landmines in your new marriage. And that bruising parent-child stress will always affect the vital core of the marriage relationship. You will catch yourself thinking like this:

"Was I really fair to my children when I remarried?"

"The poor kids—no wonder they're acting so badly, when I've spent so little time with them lately."

"How can I get mad at them?"

"I'm having a terrible time with the kids, and their real parent isn't helping a bit!"

"He's not their *real* father—he just doesn't understand them like I do."

"What right does she have to get so angry at them? They're not her kids—she just doesn't have any patience with them because she doesn't love them."

Before you ever take the step of getting remarried, you need to face those questions, answer them, and refuse to doubt each other again. Set up some rules for each other and follow them carefully. Some good ones might be:

1. In an argument between children and the new parent, the real parent will always back up the new parent. This may seem unfair, but you must realize that any time the children argue with your new spouse, they are really testing *you*. If your commitment to the new spouse seems weak, it will work like the scent of blood on sharks. They will gnaw and nibble all the more. But if they see that you have no intention of giving ground—if they see that you intend this marriage to be permanent—they will gradually realize that they have much more to lose by fighting with your new spouse than they could possibly gain. It takes time—but it works.

2. Pity for the children should not excuse their unacceptable behavior. Don't be fooled—kids can manipulate you more easily through your pity and guilt than through any other emotion you have! Why do you think babies learn to fake crying or coughing at such an early age? They know it will bring Mommy and Daddy—on the run! Once they catch on that crying or getting nostalgic about their missing parent or talking about how "lonely" they are will make their real parent turn into Jello, they'll do it all the time, and your new marriage will flounder. Sure, you can't help feeling sorry for them—but it's like the man on trial for murdering his parents. Should the jury be moved when his lawyer pleads, "But after all, he's an orphan!" It's not the kids' fault that you were divorced or widowed in the first place—but that unfortunate circumstance doesn't mean they should be coddled all their lives. A spoiled brat with one parent isn't any more acceptable in a society than a spoiled brat with two.

3. You, as adults, know what the children need better than the children do. You don't give them candy whenever they ask for it; you don't let them drive at fourteen just because they want to; so why should you let them keep you single just because they think they don't like your choice of spouse?

4. The parents will help each other on request. In any marriage a good response to each other's needs is essential; but it is even more vital in a remarriage with children, to be each other's best ally and constant helper. If Mother is the real parent, and is spending the evening straightening out discipline problems, Father should relieve her of some of the burden of housework—cleaning up after dinner, maybe doing part of the laundry, bathing the younger children—so she is free to do what *only* she can do. And if Mother is dealing with a situation where her children are flatly disobedient and she openly asks for Father's help, he should be there—not to take over but to prove to the children that their nastiness doesn't drive Mom and Dad apart; it throws them closer together. "You're all against me," the child will cry, but pretty soon he will start finding ways to accomodate the situation.

5. Both parents will be understanding and patient with the high demands of the children. If you recognize, in advance of remarriage, that the children usually will be the greatest difficulty and challenge in the way of success, you will both be more understanding of the fact that when either parent spends extra time with the children instead of with the spouse it is really for the spouse's sake. It works both ways: when the stepfather takes his stepson out to the ball game instead of taking his new wife to a movie, she will be disappointed, of course—but she can't complain since the closer the relationship between child and stepfather, the easier it will be for the marriage to work. Of course, if either parent spends *all* his time with the children, you don't have a marriage—there has to be a balance. Thus:

6. Regardless of the children's complaints the parents will have at least one night a week out with each other, without the children. They may scream and moan and weep and be rude to the babysitter, but you still have to have a chance to talk and have fun together, or you'll soon be strangers. When the children see that it isn't *every* night and that it will always be *one* night regardless of how they complain, they will almost always accommodate you in the end.

There will be other rules, of course—and new ones will be required as the need arises—but the better your communication about the problems in *advance*, the fewer the decisions you will have to make under stress. Following the rules will take enormous self-control, but that's part of being a grown-up. You just can't let the children manipulate you into acting childishly toward them or toward your new spouse.

Choosing Your New Spouse

If your first marriage was a serious step, your remarriage should be an even more serious one. Once you've decided you *want* to remarry, you should be willing to take time before actually beginning your life together. If your new spouse refuses to wait, it speaks of immaturity and selfishness; the children need time to get used to him, and you need time to get used to the way he deals with you and the children in an extended relationship. Does he get easily annoyed with the children? Does his anger seem to have a violent edge to it? Is he afraid of the children? Is he more demanding than giving?

For remarriage to work, both spouses must be honest and open with each other, highly committed, loving to each other and the children, patient and unselfish, with a mature outlook and a need for each other beyond the sexual level.

The extended engagement is more than a testing ground for your husband- or wife-to-be. It is also a chance for the children to get used to their parent's new mate. The children should have at least two or three months to get used to the *idea* of your remarriage before it actually happens. Even if they have known your intended spouse for months before you decide to get married, they will probably not have been thinking of him or her as a permanent resident of their home. With that new element added to the relationship, there has to be time for them to get accustomed to the change.

The more opportunities for contact between the children and their new stepparent, the better—provided they are in a positive context. It isn't enough for you to keep telling the kids how wonderful he is. *Your* love for him will only make them feel more threatened if they don't have a chance to learn their own positive feelings toward him.

Talk to your children about the new spouse. Don't force them to suppress their negative feelings. If they don't like him at first, let them admit it, and be understanding about it. "He keeps trying to hold my hand," says your little girl. You shouldn't respond defensively ("He's going to be your new Daddy, so you have to let him."). Instead you should be helpful ("He just likes you a lot, but if you don't want him to, he'll stop for sure."). If you keep communication alive with your children, you can help guide the new spouse into a relationship with them that will be comfortable for all concerned.

Of course, you should also let your children know, right from the start, that there will be difficulties and changes. You do the kids no favor if you say, "Don't worry—when Daddy and Jane are married, not a single thing will change." Children aren't usually fooled—they know there'll be changes. And the fact that you're lying about it may only worry them more.

It is much better to say, "The only thing I insist on is that you must treat Jane nicely. If you don't want to talk to her, you don't have to, and if there are problems we'll have plenty of time to work them out. Just come to me and tell me what's bothering you. But in the meantime, you are going to have to treat her politely and respectfully because she's going to be my wife, and that's only fair. I treat your friends nicely; you have to treat the people *I* love nicely, too."

If your children know that you aren't going to hate them because of occasional negative feelings toward your new spouse, a lot of the anxiety will be eased. Because they can vent their fear and anger honestly with you, they won't have the same need to do it subtly and viciously with her. They should also sense that you will respond to their reasonable requests. "I don't want her there at bedtime" shouldn't be dismissed abruptly with "She's *going* to be there, so get used to it." The child is really saying, "I want to be with *just you* at bedtime." It's a plea for love and closeness. Treat it that way.

If you're the new spouse, of course, such rejections from the children can be hurtful. It can be humiliating when you feel warmly and lovingly toward a child and get repeatedly rejected. It takes great patience not to resent it for a long time when you kiss one of your stepchildren, and he loudly and publicly cries, "Yuck! Don't you kiss me!" But you can't afford to get angry or pout. You have to say, kindly, "I didn't know it would bother you. I won't do it again until you want me to." You may shed more than a few tears and need more than a little building-up from your mate after his or her children have put you down—but that's why you remarried, isn't it? To have that very comfort of knowing that someone loves you whether the kids or your business associates or anyone else is treating you nicely or not.

One thing that can help build bridges is to have a regular conference with each child every week—with *both* of you present. It should be a time when the child is encouraged to mention anything he wants to complain about—any unfairness, any grievances that he perceives from you or from another child. These conferences help the child see the unity you are building in your marriage and help sponsor openness between him and the new parent. Also, it forestalls their manipulating the two of you. Children like to play one parent off against the other in any family ("But *Dad* said I could!"), and in a new and fragile remarriage they can play the game even better. By having the grievances aired before both of you, they can't tell different stories to each parent. Most important, though, is the fact that it gives the child a firm reminder of the fact that he holds a unique place in the family which is not the least bit threatened by the new marriage. In fact, his place is even firmer now that you are married.

Hold these conferences on the same day every week, if possible, so that the child learns to count on them and feel secure with them.

Yours, Mine, and Ours

I've deliberately avoided going into detail so far on the problem of remarriage when *both* of you have children. The problems are essentially the same, squared. Instead of *one* of you being a new parent, *both* of you are. The only new problem is that at least some of your kids will have problems with at least some of his or her kids.

Everything that applies if only one spouse bring children to the marriage applies here.

However, there is one important change: Before you marry, the two of you must review all your family rules and reconcile them. Bedtimes need to be adjusted so that his twelve-year-old is not going to bed before your ten-year-old; chores need to be fairly reassigned so that the children are expected to do an equal amount of work; punishments need to be regularized so that you aren't putting a child on a week's restrictions when he would only have punished his child with fifteen minutes' confinement in a bathroom. In short, you must carefully calculate your unity right from the start so that when a child says, "You're not my mother! Dad wouldn't do it this way!" you can answer, firmly, "Your father and I agreed that this is the way the rules are in this house. We explained that to you three weeks ago, and if you ask your father he will tell you exactly the same thing." That statement *must* be true, or life together as a family will be impossible. It is a good idea, however, in regularizing family practices, to make sure no children perceive a serious loss—you should even up the bedtimes by letting the twelve-year-old go to bed *later*, not by making the ten-year-old go to bed *earlier*. The first way, you make a friend of the older child; the second way, you make an enemy of the younger. Only in the area of chores should you probably increase demands to even things up. The more personal stake children are given in the duties and routines of the household, as long as they see that no one is getting off easy, the more committed they will begin to feel to making the new alliance work.

What if some of your children don't get along with some of his or hers? Again, the only thing you should insist on is politeness. They aren't marrying each other, after all—they're only brought together because their *parents* are marrying. Encourage the kids to avoid quarrels at the time and bring the grievances to their weekly interviews with both parents. Then make sure you take some kind of action to solve the problem so they get used to the idea that solutions come from *you*, not from yelling at or beating up on their new housemates.

Don't try to force the kids together all the time on the theory that it will "make them learn to get along". In fact, it is a good idea to let each group of children have plenty of time alone with their real parent and their real brothers and sisters, to reaffirm the family ties that they have long counted on. The more secure they feel in their original family, the more easily they will learn to compromise and grow to feel affection toward the strangers who have moved in. And be scrupulous in dealing fairly with both sets of children. Don't automatically believe your child's story and doubt his child's version of events. In fact, in solving quarrels it is far better simply to separate the kids and wait until tempers have cooled before trying to "solve" the dispute. The children must learn quickly that they will be treated exactly equally, by the same rules, with no favoritism at all.

In combining families, your children will have many fears about the marriage before it happens. Be ready with answers. Will they have to move? Will they change schools? Will they have to share a room with a stranger or give up their private bedroom? Will their allowance change? What if the other kids want to watch a different TV show at the same time? Will your kids have to share their toys or bikes all the time, whether they want to or not?

Before the wedding make sure there are plenty of chances for the two groups of kids to combine, involuntarily if necessary, but in happy circumstances. They'll gladly go to the amusement park, even if they have to do it with "those other kids", and they probably won't stay home from a movie, either. Don't force them to kiss each other or even talk to each other—they're used to choosing their own friends. But do insist that they get used to having each other around so they can get a sense of what to expect and how to cope with it when they're around each other all the time. If you make reasonable demands of your children—courtesy and kindness, for instance—they'll be much more likely to come around on their own to the greater friendship and intimacy you would like to see them have. If you insist on that closeness from the start, you actually decrease the chance of their achieving it.

Successfully combining families is one of the hardest things you'll ever do. But if you go into it with the right spouse, with your eyes wide open, and with great stores of patience and a lot of mutual support between the two of you, it *is* possible to make it work. I've seen it happen. Just withhold your judgment for a year or two. The problems that seem insurmountable the first year are often gone by the second, if you deal with them properly. And if you find the challenge greater than you expected, don't hesitate to seek professional guidance. If ordinary first marriages often need outside help, how much more likely to need help are family mergers!

Remember that you didn't remarry for your immediate pleasure, but for your long-range happiness. You are going through that difficult, trying first year for the sake of the happiness you'll have five years down the line—and twenty years later, when all the kids are grown up and gone, and you and your husband or wife can sigh in relief and enjoy each other all the more because of the tremendous challenges you met successfully together.

20

Whining and Crying:
How to Turn It Off

WHINING AND CRYING are some of a child's earliest and most effective tools of communication—and manipulation. When a child is still an infant, the major problem with crying is to interpret correctly and understand what the child is crying *for* so we can respond helpfully. As the child grows older and learns to talk, crying and whining become less acceptable—and you may find yourself desperate to stop it before you go out of your mind!

What should you do about crying and whining? Let's look at the problem at each stage in your child's development.

After that first year, when your child ceases to be an infant, he begins to communicate by words and gestures. When he wants something he can usually let you know if it's a drink, a cookie, clean diapers, or a nap. Also, you know him better. You have got used to his nonverbal communication, to his unintentional messages, to the different nuances of his voice and his facial expressions. In other words, your kid doesn't have to cry anymore just to get what he wants.

That doesn't mean he should never cry again. It is one of the symptoms associated with child abuse when parents are unwilling to tolerate their children's occasional crying. After all, even adults still cry in times of stress or high emotional impact. Nothing is more infuriating to most parents than to see another parent yell at his crying child, or hit him, in order to get him to *stop* crying. "Just shut up and stop that crying," says this kind of parent, often walloping the offending child. It's quite predictable what happens then—the child cries even louder and the parent gets angrier.

This is inappropriate parenting, of course. It often happens in a public place where the parent is embarrassed, and because of his inability to relate well to his child or to handle stress maturely, he strikes out at the child in a childish manner.

You should never physically punish a small child to stop his crying. It only makes him cry more—and gradually impairs your relationship, since he learns that you are the cause of increasing his discomfort instead of easing it. If you catch yourself hitting your children or verbally abusing them for the "crime" of crying, then take a good, hard look at yourself. You may be a child abuser. If you find that you can't control your temper in such situations, either at home or in public, get help immediately—for your children's sake and for your own.

There are many perfectly legitimate reasons for your child to cry: if he fell down and skinned his knee or was stung by a bee; if he was seriously frightened by a big dog or a loud noise; if someone was mean to him; if he is in pain or ill; if he feels bad because he has just been punished for breaking a rule. The first is obvious, and he needs comfort as you treat the injury. Don't fall into the trap of demanding that your little boy not cry "because you want to be a big man like Daddy." He isn't a man. He's a little boy, and he has a right to cry when he's in pain.

If he is crying because of being frightened or startled, again your response should be comfort. It doesn't help a bit if you say, "You aren't frightened of a little old fire engine, are you? Don't be a baby." It does help if you give him a hug and say, "That fire engine was really loud, wasn't it? But it makes that noise so people will get out of its way," or, "That dog was scary, wasn't he? But most dogs are nicer than that. Barking is just their way of saying, 'I don't know you, so be careful around me.'" In other words, don't try to extinguish the crying—try to extinguish the *fear.*

If the tears are because someone has been mean to your child, your response depends on your child's age. If he is only one or two years old his social skills are just beginning to develop. He may cry when another child takes a toy away—or won't let him take the one he wants. Comfort him and explain that it's the other child's turn with the toy. (Or if the other child is being unusually selfish, insist that *he* share.) There are more complications if it is someone else's child being selfish, of course. But the main thing is to let your kid know that you love him and you understand his sadness and frustration, while you teach him the rules of getting along with other people.

With older children, however, who know better how to get along with other kids, there will still be some tears because someone else has been unkind. It may be a bully on the way home from school—the strategies for dealing with that are explained in Chapter 23. It may be simply the breaking up of a friendship or school romance; it may be a teacher's unfairness; it may be the cruel taunting of other children or rejection by an important social clique. If you try to stop your child from crying by saying, "You aren't a baby anymore. Cut it out! Stop your silly sniffling!" you'll just teach him that when he feels sad he'd better talk to somebody other than you. I doubt that's what you want to have happen. If he comes to you for comfort of his emotional wounds, by all means comfort him.

Does that mean you'll be "mollycoddling" your children? Of course not. You don't have to agree with his childish outlook. You don't have to say, "Yeah, what a rotten teacher! My poor kid, everyone treats him so bad!" All you have to do is show him that you recognize that he feels sad or hurt, and his sadness makes you sad, too. All you have to do is show him that you love him and want him to be happy. Once he has got his emotions under control, you can help him devise strategies to cope with the situation. "What were you doing right before the teacher got mad?" you might ask. Or, "Where was the bully waiting for you? Can you walk home by a different way?" Or, "What were you doing that the other children made fun of?" Or sometimes there simply is no strategy. "You and Jerry were really good friends for a long time, and it really hurts that he won't play with you anymore. That's happened to me before, too, and it's sad. But there are other friends you'll have who won't ever do that to you. Your Mom and I are friends, and part of being married is that you promise always to be friends even when you're mad at each other." Help the child cope; help the child take it in stride. But don't insist that he react to his problems in a completely adult way. It takes time to get control of such displays of emotion; even adults don't get complete control of their actual feelings, despite the learned ability to keep from showing them all in public.

If your child is crying because of illness, your response should be comfort and treatment of the illness.

Finally, it is absurd to try to stop your children from crying after they have been punished. If they have done something wrong and are losing a privilege or being confined to their room or getting a spanking, it shouldn't be surprising at all that they may resort to tears. They may cry because they feel guilty or ashamed. They may cry because of the loss of a privilege or the pain of a spanking or the embarrassment of being caught. They may also cry or whine in order to annoy you and get even a little! With all of these your best response is to ignore your child's tears and carry out the punishment. If he learns that his crying and whining will get him off the hook or ease his punishment or at least get him hugs and kisses, he'll cry every time you punish him. Likewise, if he knows that you get upset or angry when he whines and cries, he may cry all the more just to get your goat.

Oddly enough, parents sometimes get just as irritated when their children *don't* cry when they're punished. "Wipe that smile off your face," some parents say; or, "I'm going to spank you until you cry!" Sometimes tears are looked for as a sign that a punishment is working. "So a week's restriction doesn't bother you, does it? Then let's try *two* weeks!" Don't let your child's immediate show of emotion—or lack of emotion—influence your punishment. Every child is different. One might cry, but another child might have such pride that he refuses to show any tears or feelings at all. Other children react to their own shame by smiling—they are embarrassed, and they can't help the smile. Still others deliberately try to taunt you, but then your best strategy is to ignore it. When it doesn't work, that behavior will disappear.

Keep in mind that your objective when you punish your children is *to extinguish inappropriate behavior*. You aren't punishing in order to get a particular emotional response; you are punishing to help your children learn not to do certain things that will interfere with their eventual happiness. If you let their immediate emotional response sidetrack you from the punishment, you are losing the battle—and, in the long run, letting your child down. Only if your child's response to punishment is to break another rule—throws toys at you or hits his sister or swears a blue streak—should you respond, and then only if that particular behavior is becoming habitual with the child. Otherwise, recognize that your kids are normal human beings and don't like being punished.

Inappropriate Crying

Crying beyond the initial pain or problem quickly becomes inappropriate. It's stressful for all of the other family members. It needs to be dealt with and turned off. What you do depends on its cause. You do the child a favor if you help him turn the faucet off.

Fear of Abandonment In infancy, when the child is old enough to know who his mother and father are, it is perfectly natural for him sometimes to cry when his parents leave him with a babysitter. You shouldn't worry about it unless you're gone repeatedly, night after night; your occasional absences are something he simply must get used to, and usually, if the babysitter plays with the child and gets to know him, the crying ends very soon after you leave. Within a year or so your child will have a good enough memory to know that even though Mom and Dad are gone, they'll be back soon. He'll probably be absolutely delighted to see you when you come back, but your leaving won't lead to tears anymore—not for long anyway.

Sometimes, however, children *don't* adapt to their parents' absences. Occasionally I have seen a child whimper and cry every time his mother left him behind to go shopping. It can lead to quite a scene—the child clings tearfully to his mother's dress, wailing pitiably. When his mother tries to leave anyway the child tries to follow her to the car, even letting himself be physically dragged out with her. If someone restrains him he screams and struggles to get free and follow his mother; after she's gone he still cries and tries to go out the door after her.

Many times—but not all—the child who behaves this way has had a previous abandonment experience when he really was left for a long, terrifying period of time. Even without such an experience, some children have an irrational fear of being left by their parents. I believe it's inborn; more children than anybody realizes have recurring nightmares, deep fears of being abandoned by their parents. Why else do you think nightmare stories like "Hansel and Gretel" have survived for so long? I once started reading the unexpurgated version of that story to my children. I began to realize that as I recounted the children's attempts to leave a trail behind them so they could return home, my children were sitting spellbound, eyes fixed on me, completely involved in the story. They were identifying strongly with poor Hansel and Gretel, and it was terrifying to them when the birds had eaten the trail of bread and the children were stranded out in the forest alone, unloved and unwanted by their parents. To a child, abandonment is *possible*—and one of the worst things that can happen to him. (Personally, I put that story on the list of tales my children won't be told; others have the viewpoint that such stories help a child face and overcome those fears. I disagree.)

My friends, the Merryweathers, left on a three-week trip together, leaving their four children behind. Three of the youngsters were of school age, and the youngest, John, was nearly two. In the rush of the trip preparations, the Merryweathers neglected to prepare young John properly for their absence. Even worse, at the last minute there was a switch in babysitters. The replacement was an older woman, a little critical and irritable in nature, who really didn't like preschool children. Young John had never had her as a babysitter before.

Things went fairly well during the parents' absence, especially with the older children, but after their return from the trip young John had an emotional collapse, with chronic crying and whimpering that went on almost nonstop. This turned to near screaming whenever his mother left him, even to go into another room out of his sight. It was necessary to move his bed into his parents' bedroom to get him to sleep at night. It took a full year before he could return to normal.

I am convinced that parents need occasions away from their children for renewal and relaxation, as well as for building their feelings of love for each other and strengthening their marriage. But this cannot be done for too long a time period, especially when you are leaving behind children between the ages of one-and-a-half and three. If a trip away from the kids does occur, even for a single night, it has to be handled very carefully. The child needs to be with someone he knows, trusts, and loves, and he should be in a familiar setting—preferably his own home or a place he feels comfortable in. The child, no matter how young, needs to be fully informed ahead of time about the trip and the fact that Dad and Mother will be leaving, for how long, and when they will return. He should also be told who the babysitter will be.

You might also plan ahead of time to try an overnighter away from your child, placing the youngster with the chosen babysitter. This could be a kind of inoculation against stress as well as a way of determining if he is old enough to handle it.

Manipulative Whining and Crying One type of crying you shouldn't have to put up with is "manipulative" crying—when your child cries to try to get you to do what he wants. This kind of crying can appear very early in preschool children and is still a strategy used by teenagers from time to time. Basically, the problem is that the child cries or whines in order to get your sympathy or in order to irritate you into giving him what he wants so he'll be quiet. You see this kind of crying when children raise a ruckus in a church meeting or a party or when friends are visiting or at the supermarket, and their parents reward them by giving them candy or a treat or a toy. This almost guarantees that the crying will be repeated endlessly whenever the situation repeats itself.

"I'm sorry, Johnny, but we just can't afford to repair your bicycle right now. You'll have to wait a month." But Johnny won't take no for an answer. He whines, he sulks, he pouts. He cries bitterly because his parents don't love him and everybody gets to ride places except him. "*Please*, oh, *please* get it fixed, Daddy!" he whines endlessly. And so Dad uses money that should have been spent on bills to get the bike fixed—rewarding the behavior.

Or, which is much more likely, Dad gets mad. Or Mom gets upset. Emotions start running high. Everybody gets more irritable. The child doesn't get his bike fixed, but he *does* get another payoff; he is in control of the family. He is deciding what everybody else will feel, and if he can't have what he wants, at least he's going to make sure that he doesn't suffer alone.

This kind of manipulative whining and crying is only extinguishable when parents have the patience of Job. You can't give in, and you can't get too mad. However, you don't have to endure forever, either. For the first little while, of course, it's best to just ignore the child's whining. Without showing too great irritation or the slightest hint of softening your decision you simply say, "I'm sorry you can't have that, Dear, but that's just the way it has to be." And then don't answer at all. When the child complains or cries, simply get involved in a conversation with someone else, leave, or be busy so you don't have to pay any more attention to the whining.

If the child doesn't already have a habit of whining constantly, chances are that this will be enough to extinguish his behavior. If manipulative whining never gets more response than this. the habit of whining will never be formed. Often a child develops the whining habit with only one parent; when Dad says no, the child leaves him alone, but when Mom says no, the child begins to torment her with whines and cries. The reason is obvious—it doesn't work with Dad but it works every time with Mom, or at least often enough that it's worth a try. If you give in even once or twice you are letting yourself in for a lot of misery later.

What if your kid already has the whining habit, and you just can't stand it? If he has the habit your ignoring him won't stop his whining right away. After all, he knows from experience that if he just keeps it up long enough and loud enough, you'll eventually give in or get mad. I have seen this kind of behavior carrying even into adulthood. The wife is hurt or wants something, and the husband has not noticed. So she begins to sulk a little. When he still doesn't respond she ups the ante—she starts to cry alone in the living room, while he's in the bedroom. If he doesn't hear, she cries louder—and louder and louder until he finally comes in to find out what he did wrong. She has won the battle by whining, just as she did when she was four! If she has a legitimate need or grievance there are many more effective, more direct ways to deal with it to get relief.

What do you do when your habitual whiner just won't give up? He's screaming, he's throwing tantrums, he's crying so hard you think his throat will rip out, and certainly you know that in four minutes they will have to call an ambulance to take you to a mental hospital as an emergency basket case. What can you do?

First, Mom and Dad have to be united in their strategy. One of you can't keep giving in while the other is being adamant—the child will just play you off against each other. Also, the parent who isn't being subjected to the whining has to take the problem seriously. It isn't the kind of problem Dad can take care of just by saying, "You have to be firm with him the way I am, Honey!" Once the problem is there, it is serious, and both parents have to take note of it and act together.

Second, refuse to put up with inappropriate whining and crying in the room where you are. Without getting overly emotional, *remove* the child from the room. Especially with younger children, when they are deprived of their audience they lose interest in the performance. Five to ten minutes in the bathroom or bedroom usually is all it takes.

The third and most important step is to reward *non-whining* behavior. This sounds almost absurd. What do you do, walk up to the child and say, "Hey, you aren't whining! Here's a nickel!"? Well, not quite. But that's nearly it—and it works.

What you do is explain to the child at a time when he isn't whining that his whining and crying are going to have to stop. If it is a child under twelve who is causing the problem, it's a good idea to put up a chart, dividing each day into morning, afternoon, and evening. Then you tell him that for each part of the day that he goes without crying or whining you will draw a smiling face or paste a colored star. For every five or ten stars or smiles he accumulates he gets a reward—one half-hour of watching the TV program of his choice or a special treat at dinner or a nickel. If he earns no stars or smiles, he gets no reward.

Should he forget and whine, remind him once that if he doesn't stop immediately he loses his smile or star for that time. If the whining continues simply ignore it. If it becomes intolerable you unemotionally put him in the "time-out room" until he has been silent for several minutes. Through all this it's best not to lose your cool. Refuse to get angry, and don't make wild threats that put both of you in a bind later. You simply refuse to let him get pay-off for whining and crying. You stay in control. But act early! Act before it escalates out of control.

When you tally up for the day and give him rewards for the times he has gone without whining, make sure plenty of praise goes along with the rewards. Don't stress the one time he didn't get a star or a smile—stress the two times that he did so the reward seems worth the effort of breaking the habit. Above all, if he has earned no reward at all, don't be moved by his whining because he didn't get it! Be adamant. Depending on how serious the problem is, it shouldn't take too long to solve it. As soon as things are in control and the whining has stopped, stop giving rewards. They are a temporary measure only.

With older children the stars will seem silly. Find a more sophisticated reward system. Explain that the whining and crying will get no more results and that a valued privilege is now linked to his whining. If he whines one day he gets no television that night; if he does not whine he gets to watch an hour's program of his choice—or stay up a half-hour later or have an extra fifty cents on his earnings or get a treat at dinner. Make a point of writing down offenses and tallying up every night. It works as well for sixteen as for six.

The Over-sensitive Child Sometimes a child cries habitually, not because he is trying to manipulate you, but because he is so easily hurt. If you tell him no or rebuke him, however mildly, he immediately bursts into tears. Often he is ashamed of his crying and tries to hide it from you. It happens all the time—when another child at school speaks rudely to him, when he isn't chosen for a team, or when a teacher gives him a low grade on a test. He isn't trying to "get results"—the crying humiliates him—but he simply can't help it. He's just unable to control it, or he's so sensitive that seemingly mild offenses hurt him deeply.

First, look at the patterns in your family and in that child's life. Is he not getting his share of attention? Perhaps he needs more love and positive experiences with you and with his brothers and sisters. The problem may be solvable just by giving him more of your time and giving him plenty of experiences where he can be successful in meeting small challenges, building his self-image and his self-confidence. (See Chapter 2.)

If an increase of love and confidence doesn't seem to help, you might be wise to seek professional guidance from a qualified child psychologist. This doesn't mean your child is "crazy" or "mentally ill". The child psychologist will be able to help you find the cause of his unusual sensitivity or guide you in seeking solutions.

Why should you worry about it? In mild cases perhaps you shouldn't—it may just be a stage your child will soon get over. But the fact that your child is known to cry easily will make him an object of ridicule to his friends, either openly or behind his back. He will be more alienated from them, have less acceptance by them. He will get lonelier and more hurt, and the problem might become a vicious circle, feeding on itself. It's important to find the causes and solve the problem as soon as possible so he can get on with his normal social development. Otherwise, permanent damage may be done to his ability to get along normally with others.

These serious cases, however, are rare. Usually children's whining and crying are for good reason or as an occasional stab at seeing if Mom or Dad will bite at the bait. If you are warm, loving, and comforting when the crying is for good reason and simply ignore the crying when it is manipulative (it isn't hard to tell the difference!), then it will rarely become a problem you should worry about.

21

What to Do with the Bored Child

"MOM, THERE'S NOTHING TO DO."

Mother winces. It's the fifteenth time today that she's heard that complaint, and it increases by a hundred decibels every time it's repeated. Still, she patiently answers, "Why don't you go out and play ball?'"

"It's too hot, and there's nobody to play with."

"Would you like to help me with the dishes?"

"Are you kidding?"

"Well, why don't you do your term paper and get ahead on your schoolwork?"

"Oh, Mom, it's Saturday! I don't want to do that on Saturday."

"Why don't you go swimming?"

"Alone?" The word is said with such horror that Mother briefly wonders if she had accidently suggested that her child go out and play on the freeway. Now that she's thought of it, the impulse is irresistible. "Why don't you go out and play on the freeway?"

"Oh, Mom, be serious. What can I do? I'm so *bored*."

As far as I know, parents never sign a contract with their children specifying what they guarantee to provide for the young ones. If there were such a contract, one clause that I *know* would not be tolerable would be "Parent guarantees to entertain child to child's satisfaction at all times". It simply couldn't be done. At some time every child in the world is utterly, inexpressibly bored. And almost without exception the bored child lets you know about it. Every few minutes. At top volume. In tones of voice that express all the misery of the world.

The problem of boredom takes two forms. One is the occasionally bored youngster who is usually terribly active and suddenly finds himself at a loss as to what he can do next. The other problem is more serious: the young boy or girl who *always* seems to be bored. This chronically bored child, in my experience, is undergoing some pretty serious problems in his life: either he is mildly depressed or he has few friends or he has little imagination or he is excessively dependent and can't take initiative in his own life.

No matter what you suggest to the chronically bored child, he wrinkles up his mouth with distaste or shrugs as if to say, "You're no help if that's the best you can suggest." Despite your apparent failure ever to suggest anything fun for him to do, he still hounds you with that constant complaint, "Mom, I'm bored!"

What can you do for the chronically bored child? The first step I'd suggest is to turn off the television for at least ninety days. You may have to hide it to make this effective, and as I mention in the chapter on television (Chapter 22), turning off the TV cold turkey can be harder on the parents than it is on the kids. But the cause of boredom and lack of imagination often is simply too much TV viewing. I've found repeatedly that when television is eliminated the child begins to lose his habit of being passive, of taking no initiative, of expecting entertainment to come at the flick of a switch instead of coming as a result of his own active involvement in something. With the TV gone, the child almost always begins to be more resourceful, more active. Boredom, after all, begets boredom. When you're standing around being bored nothing is likely to sound interesting to you. But when you're actively interested in something, it doesn't occur to you to be bored at all, and your mind works a mile a minute. Try this strategy with your chronically bored child.

Eliminating television, however, is only a negative step. What do you put in its place? It isn't enough just to pull the plug—he'll not only be bored, he'll also be angry!

I recommend that you fill his newly freed time with activities that develop him in three different areas:

1. Building skills
2. Interacting socially
3. Stimulating the imagination

Building Skills

There has never been a better time than now for youngsters to develop skills in any area they want to. It's hard to think of any interest for which lessons and materials are not easily available. Your child might learn to type; to sew; to rebuild car transmissions; to play tennis, soccer, handball, or chess; to garden, swim, tap-dance, speak French, paint, practice first-aid, or karate. And don't automatically think your child is too young to learn some of these skills. With three-year-olds playing violin with the Suzuki method and five-year-olds able to operate simple cameras, it's hard to imagine a skill that a child can't work on at an early age. Remember, too, that some skills are best done young. The world's finest composers and poets have often done their best work in their teens. And many successful businessmen or inventors began selling or tinkering as little children. Just because your children are going to school to get an education doesn't mean they should limit their learning to what they get in class.

George Romney, former president of American Motors and governor of Michigan, began his business career as a child selling a product door-to-door that he knew every household needed—light bulbs. I know a teenager who, with some wise help from his father, started a used car business. He started small, but the business is growing quickly and could be the start of his lifetime work. Samuel R. Delany, one of today's successful writers, sold his first novel as a teenager.

Even if your child expresses little interest—or even hostility—at first, you should insist on his getting involved in learning some skills like these. Just because your child says that mountain climbing sounds dumb doesn't mean you shouldn't get out your gear and take him rappelling with you. After all, he's only ten years old. What does he know? *You're* the one who knows that bounding down a mountain on the end of a rope is one of the most exhilarating experiences in life. And so what if your kid says that he'd rather be dead than dance. *You* know that as he begins studying modern dance he'll discover that his body is a virtual stranger to him, and he'll feel a great deal of excitement as he learns to make it do exactly what he wants it to. Push a little, and in a short time he'll be glad you did.

Interacting Socially

I am personally convinced that there is nothing—absolutely nothing—more important in life than learning to get along with other people. If your child has a knack for making friends and you don't live at the north pole, he'll have friends. But if your child, because of fear or self-doubt or the plain inconvenience of having no close neighbors, has no friends that you know of, you need to find ways to help him meet other kids and make friends.

You can't usually do it with a child over six by saying, "Here's a nice friend I brought over for you." Children at that age are already beginning to form into interest groups. Friends aren't made just by Mom and Dad throwing strangers together with nothing to do.

After all, think of who *your* friends are. They probably can be grouped according to the interest that brought you together. Some are people you once worked with and especially liked; others are people you play tennis with, go to plays with, worked with in the last election campaign, golf with, or gossip with. Or all of the above. What brought you together was a *common interest*, and that's what will help your child make friends.

Do the children in your neighborhood ride bicycles? Make sure you teach your child to ride so that he can become one of the group. Does he long to be one of the athletes? Help him learn the skills he needs—with lessons if necessary—so that he can take part as a valuable member of the group. Or is he bookish and retiring? Get him into discussion groups at the library—or encourage him to take notice of other kids at school who always seem to be reading so he can start his own group. In fact, starting his own group is one of the best ways for your child to get involved socially. By creating your own group, inviting the other kids to *your* home or on *your* outings, you make sure you're at the center of a group's activities.

Of course, there may be some special problems your child needs to overcome. You need to make sure he knows how people ought to be treated so he doesn't drive potential friends away. It helps a great deal if you, as parents, treat each other and the children with the kind of courtesy and respect that you use with people you're trying to impress. If they are surrounded by generosity and kindness at home they'll quickly get the idea that that's how people ought to treat each other.

Obnoxious personal habits need to be broken so your child doesn't become the butt of ridicule. If he is overweight, dirty, or pimply, if he picks his nose or chews with his mouth open or dresses hideously, then he is setting himself up for loneliness. Insist on personal cleanliness; directly teach good taste; get him to a skin specialist for his acne; help him remember a handkerchief when he needs one.

As an added enticement you may want to do some above-board bribery to get other kids to come play with your shy and lonely child. Depending on your financial means, you can attract a lot of children to your house by having a trampoline, a gym set, or a swimming pool in your yard. And if those are not in the budget, just making sure your home is a warm and pleasant place for friends to visit will help. Cookies and milk may help smooth the way for your child to learn how to make small talk with friends and work with them and play with them comfortably.

After all, when your child hangs around saying, "What can I do? I'm bored!" he may really be saying, "I'm so lonely that I'd rather have you telling me to go play on the freeway than sit in my room alone for another minute!"

Stimulating the Imagination

The third area to promote is your child's inner mental life and his imagination. Books are a marvelous entry into the world of imagination. Television isn't. Books actively allow your child to enter dozens of worlds, to be dozens of different characters, to have fantastic, exciting adventures impossible in his home or school. While TV and movies paint all the pictures for the child, reading requires him to paint his own. The more your child reads, the more his imagination grows.

When children get hooked on books it's breath-taking to watch them ravenously feed their minds on the challenging experiences and grand adventures of others. They can read fast and slow; they can make their own "in-stant replays" by rereading anything they want, any time they want.

Most adults read very little. They watch television for enter-tainment—and even for learning. They are missing so much. Even the most rabid advocate of television news and documentaries willingly admits that television can only present a tiny portion of the things that informed people need to know about current events and the world around them. Why don't adults read more?

I suspect the problem begins in childhood. Learning to read is as hard, at first, as learning to play the piano—boring drills, struggles to make those lit-tle symbols make sense. If reading isn't rewarding from the start it often becomes associated in children's minds with many unpleasant feelings—fail-ing grades, the ridicule of classmates, impatient parents, and, worst of all, boredom. Who really cares much about Dick and Jane, anyway? While the early grade-school books are boring the children silly, television painlessly gives them exciting adventures they haven't yet got the skill to read about. They turn to books for painful struggling and to television for fun.

As parents, you need to help them overcome that tendency by making reading a positive experience from the start. It helps a lot if you read to your children often—exciting, wonderful stories ranging from fairy tales to elementary science, from biographies of great heroes and heroines of the past to stories of animals and children. They will love listening to the stories you read, and, perhaps even more important, they will see that such stories come from books.

Make sure you don't stop reading to them when they begin to struggle with their own learning to read. You can make a game out of it by letting the children take turns reading a sentence or a paragraph to the family, going around in a circle with all readers taking a turn. The youngest, who can't read at all, will still insist on taking his turn, even though you have to help him—or let him make it up! The seeds of a love of reading are sown in such circumstances. Reading will always be associated in your children's minds with good things, and even if they don't become bookworms they'll have a taste for reading and know how to turn to books when they want to.

It is much harder for dyslexic children who have a physical problem with reading. But as professional therapists work on helping the child overcome his reading disabilities, you can still provide the same kind of support so the child does not grow up hating books.

Of course, reading isn't the only way to stimulate imagination. Your children should be comfortable with pencils, crayons, chalk, and paint from an early age, with a lot of encouragement from you. If those squiggly lines look like a dog to your children, then a dog it is. As you encourage them through shapeless clay models and indescribably ugly mosaics they will begin to become confident and interested in one art or another, and boredom will never be much of a problem for them. They won't have to ask you what they can do—instead you'll have the much less troublesome problem of having to insist they stop what they're doing and come to dinner.

Occasional Boredom

What about the normal child who is a little restless occasionally and is looking for some kind of activity? Often the child who comes to you and complains of boredom is really just asking you to spend time with him. He doesn't *care* what he's doing as long as he's doing it with you. And why not? It's hard to think of many jobs that can't be left for five minutes—and often that's all it takes to satisfy that hunger for your companionship, at least for an hour or so.

The best thing to do is to start an activity with the child that you can leave—and he can continue happily alone. The fact that you shared the beginning of the activity with him and are interested in the outcome will help make the activity much more entertaining.

For children up to about two years of age you can keep some special toys on hand, things that they don't often get to play with—pots and pans, a special cuddly animal, even a stack of old magazines or the wooden mixing spoons from a drawer that is usually out of reach. Specialized toys that only do one thing are quickly boring; toys that can do anything, like balls and blocks, books and boxes, are much more entertaining for a longer period of time. And don't insist that the children play with the toys your way. If your eighteen-month-old would rather play with the blocks by putting them into his sand bucket and dumping them out, don't insist that he build towers instead!

Preschool children, from about two to five years old, will be interested in more sophisticated activities which, alas, are often noisier and messier. But a child who is never noisy and never dirty is probably missing out on some of the best parts of childhood. Sand, clay, and water are great fun (and a lot cheaper than a battery-powered robot that you can't do a thing with except watch). As for noise—they'll love to march around the house with drums and harmonicas and sticks to beat together. You may reach for the aspirin from time to time, but the sheer joy of making music and noise is a part of childhood you wouldn't want to take away from your children. Besides, if you join right in you'll find the noise isn't half so obnoxious. And the kids will also be excited to dress up in old adult clothes or increase their range or play by riding trikes. In short, if your active child complains of having nothing to do, think of something unusual that he can do with things that aren't usually thought of as toys.

And from time to time, you need to change their environment from the house that they have long since memorized. Trips to the zoo, circus, fire station, planetarium, play, rodeo, or concert don't have to wait until they're school age and go on field trips—take them now. Even two-year-olds often sit enthralled through action-packed children's plays, and five-year-olds are already old enough to tell their younger brothers and sisters the name of every animal in the zoo.

For six- to twelve-year-olds, I would always keep a good supply of indoor games on hand, like Monopoly, Score Four, checkers, jigsaw puzzles, cards. You might also keep educational toys and games, like science sets and map puzzles. You can fill up a rainy afternoon with a contest to see who can name all the states just from its missing shape in the U.S. map puzzle.

Children of this age can undertake fairly complex projects. Don't buy them puppets—give them cloth, help them draw patterns, and teach them to use the sewing machine. Don't buy them a stage for their puppets—give them heavy scissors and a large cardboard box with string, staples, brads, and old cloth to make curtains. No matter how beautiful and expensive a puppet show you buy them, it won't interest them half so much as the puppet show that from beginning to end they made themselves. With children this age—as with adults for that matter—it is the making that is most of the fun. Why else do erector sets and plastic bricks and tinker toys keep children so engrossed? It is the joy of conceiving something and making it take shape under their hands.

You probably will also need energy reducers for a child who is rattling around the house threatening to tear down the walls with his boredom. If he's trapped indoors, it would be nice to have a punching bag or a huge beanbag pillow he can pummel—instead of his brothers and sisters. There are also harmless physical games that can be played indoors—blind man's buff, hide and seek, button-button, and a thousand variations. And when they can go outdoors, it's nice to know you have a basketball hoop or a trampoline or foursquare and hopscotch marked out on the patio. Bicycles are almost a must except in the densest cities, and if you live in a city with a good, safe daytime bus system, you should teach your nine- and ten-year-olds to use it so they can get to the library or the museum alone. They will love going there much more, and it will increase their ability to be independent and make decisions and have confidence in themselves.

Of course, it is important not to go out and buy all the toys and games and equipment at once. To get the best advantage out of every new activity, it should be introduced alone. If your child gets fingerpaints, a tetherball, seven books, two dolls, an erector set, Lincoln logs, and a bicycle all at once, the odds are that one or two favorites will take all his attention. A few weeks later, when he's starting to get bored again, the ones he hasn't tried will look so familiar that they, too, will be "boring". Much better to try each new activity, one at a time, with no competing novelties to distract.

Boredom in teenagers is one factor that contributes to minor—and sometimes major—delinquency. Often mischief-making teenagers are over-indulged with money and free time and under-indulged with attention from parents and anything meaningful to do with their leisure. Teenagers should be provided with opportunities to earn their own money, so that they learn responsibility along with freedom and understand the connection between work and earning. Even at home you should have a list of eight to ten jobs that a child can opt for to earn a prearranged amount of money. Whether it's cleaning out the garage, weeding the garden, sewing some clothes, preparing a meal, or babysitting, the child with "nothing to do" can get a financial reward along with the less exciting (to him) rewards inherent in the job.

You should not overlook the value of a pet. While exotic pets may seem more interesting at first, what makes pets such valuable aids in child-rearing is the attachment formed between the child and the pet—and the fact that the pet is intelligent. Most exotic pets become quickly boring to children. Fish just swim. Turtles just sit around being turtles. Even cats are independent and measurably less intelligent than dogs. The best pet is the most popular one: a dog. Dogs are infinitely interesting to children who are old enough to love, understand, teach, and care for them. Because the dog is intelligent enough to develop a personality of its own, it also becomes a playmate that is rarely disloyal or disinterested in its young master. And the effusive love dogs develop for children can be a great boost to kids going through the normal self-doubts of adolescence.

A final word on boredom. Boredom is a contagious disease. If you shamble through *your* life rarely interested in anything besides television, your children aren't going to have much example of what a creative, imaginative person can do. Of course, the fact that you are reading this book (or any book for that matter) shows that you *do* have more interests than television. You need to make sure you communicate your interests, your discoveries, your enthusiasms to your children. If you love Persian rugs and know something about them, talk about them to your children. If there's something in the news or a problem in your community, don't hide it from your children—discuss it with them. From conversations with you they will quickly learn that part of growing up is getting in touch with the world around them. They will also learn that hobbies and special interests are not just things parents buy for their children—they are lifelong activities. Your daughter's love for dolls can easily translate into studying and collecting antique or foreign dolls, if she only is told that such a thing is possible. Your son's love of board games can easily develop into inventing his own games and joining groups that gather regularly to play—if someone only tells him that such groups exist and that games are created by people just like him.

In other words, one of the best ways to avoid having chronically bored children is to make sure *you* are an interesting, interested person.

22

Television: Make It Serve Your Family, Not Enslave It

IT WAS 7:40 SATURDAY MORNING. Russ, fourteen, was sprawled on our thick carpeted family room floor looking at a preschool-level cartoon show. His eyes were glazed and his jaw hung slack, as if in a stupor or trance. I shook my head and chuckled, thinking, "Here is a bright kid, school chess champ, high grades, mature and ahead of his years in many ways, caught up by these dumb nursery-school-level cartoons. What does he see in them?"

"Russ!" I said aloud. "I have to leave now. Please turn the TV off as soon as that program is over and be sure all your outside work and school assignments are done before noon. OK?" He nodded, never shifting his gaze from the set.

Some hours later I returned—in the early afternoon. To my shock and dismay Russ was still on the floor, still gazing blankly, almost uncomprehendingly at the tube. The same mindless drivel! Work and school assignments had not been touched. I felt both a surge of anger and alarm choke up inside me. How could this happen to my son—especially Russ? I quickly turned off the set, shaking my head but saying nothing. I didn't want an angry confrontation now. He left the room, groggy and in a mental fog.

A few months later Lois and I were talking together in the front room when I heard a piercing scream come from the family room. It had a terrible, compelling, and chilling quality to it that demanded instant response.

Within several seconds I was by my daughter Connie's side as she ruefully rubbed her neck and shoulder. Her brother Paul, standing by, ashamedly explained that they had been watching a TV show, *Kung Fu*, and that he had innocently started practicing some karate chops on her during the break for commercials and he must have struck her harder than he had intended. He had a very foolish and apologetic look on his face. He was just imitating what he had seen on the TV program.

I shook my head despairingly. I was doing research on the effects of TV violence in my university laboratory. I knew the professional literature on the subject. And here were the negative effects coming true in my own home, with children I loved.

Some months later I received a letter from a teenage girl who lived a few miles from my home. She told me how her twelve-year-old brother had fatally hanged himself in his bedroom. His death occurred as a direct result of his imitation of a TV program where a man had pretended to hang himself as a way of escaping from a sheriff's posse. He feigned death, then later cut himself down and walked away unhurt. This young boy was not as successful.

At this point Lois and I knew something had to change in our home. We reviewed the pros and cons of keeping our TV. I loved televised sports events plus an occasional good movie, as well as the late evening news and sometimes a talk show. For me TV was relaxing. It helped me unwind. But its presence was clearly interfering with the kids' homework, chores were not getting done, and there was also some contention over what to watch. Also, it was very clear that some of our kids were hooked on it—almost like drug addicts. At times it seemed that watching TV was more important to them than anything else in their lives. All it took was one weak-willed kid to turn it on—then, like a magnet, it pulled all the other children into the room where they fell into a zombie-like state of lethargy. All conversation stopped. *Everything* stopped, or so it seemed, while the set was on.

So we gathered the family together one night for a special meeting. I told them about the research that I and others had done on TV effects, and I pointed out that TV was obviously having an adverse influence on our own family. It was interfering with reading, chores, homework, family conversation, physical activity, normal outdoor play, and exercise. Beginning today there would be no more TV in our home. We were confiscating the set and "throwing it out". We were doing this, we explained, because we loved them. We also mentioned that it was going to be a sacrifice for us, too. We would also be giving up some favorite programs.

There was a long moment of stunned silence and incredulous disbelief. Then the storm broke. Lois and I were outnumbered nine to two.

"You're kidding, Dad! Is this some kind of a joke? What you're saying can't be true!"

They were like junkies being told they would have to take the cure cold turkey. There were tears, anger, cajoling, pleading and a remarkable series of persuasive arguments:

"Dad, Mom—I'll tell you what I'll do. I'll do the dishes *every* night. No fuss, no complaints.But *please* don't take the TV away!" They were frantic, almost desperate.

The storm of protest continued, but somehow we hung in there for about a week, refusing to reconsider. One thing that gave us some backbone was the very nature of their desperation. In a shocking way it opened our eyes to their addiction. They were really hurting and clearly experiencing withdrawal symptoms. That scared us. Did we really want something that potent in our home—something that could have such a bewitching effect on our children? Our answer to each other was a resounding, "No."

But at the end of that week the kids stopped harassing and pestering us. They finally accepted the fact that our decision was irreversible. Then some remarkable things happened. The kids started reading books again, doing more homework, playing games with each other, having more conversation in the evening, and spending more time in play with their friends. There was also less contention. They felt better.

For nearly two years we lived in a state of bliss. Then one day Connie approached me quite apologetically. "Dad, I know how you feel about TV, but I have a school homework assignment to review a *National Geographic* special on TV tonight. What do you think I ought to do? I've considered going over to the neighbors and asking if I can see it on their set—but I frankly don't have the nerve to do that. But maybe I should."

Then I thought: maybe we've thrown the baby out with the bath water. There were some great things on TV that our kids and we were missing. After talking it over, Lois and I decided to bring the TV back out of storage with some new, stringent rules. No TV during the week unless it was a special program and permission was given in advance. Weekend TV viewing would be permitted on the condition that all homework and chores were completed by *everybody*. Otherwise, the set stayed off.

These drastic limitations, plus our children's knowledge that any abuse of the rules could lead to "nothing" again, protected all of us from getting addicted again—unaware, Lois and I had become subtle addicts, too. Now there are so many other interesting things we want to do that the set is rarely on—except for something very special. The craving just isn't there anymore.

Also, with our preschooler, Becky, we found that by not having TV readily available she found active things to do to engage her time. She read, drew, jumped on the trampoline, played with other children, helped her mother prepare meals. Now she knows how to take the initiative, to entertain herself and others. She has learned to be active and expressive rather than passive and receptive. She has a new confidence in herself.

Sure, the temptation is great for us to use TV as a babysitter, but, like a friend of mine who found that giving a slug of whiskey to a crying baby really shut her up in a hurry, it's so easy to abuse its use. And that's *because* it works. It *does* shut kids up for awhile. The problem is the side effects.

There have been seven Congressional investigations, a national commission report, and a Surgeon General's study on television effects. These have tended to focus, in particular, on the area of TV violence because of our very high crime rate and the assassination of some of our national leaders. Their results could reasonably be applied to other areas as well: sex, ethics, social skills. The evidence, in sum, strongly indicates that TV is a powerful persuader. Businessmen don't pay billions yearly for TV advertising time without getting results.

There are many documented examples where children and adults have engaged in direct imitation of acts witnessed on TV, both bad and good, destructive and productive, criminal and prosocial, violent and non-violent. Dr. Albert Bandura, in one study, found that eighty-eight percent of three-to five-year-old children directly imitated aggressive acts seen in just one TV movie presentation. And this act or behavior could be remembered and produced again six months later, after just the one exposure to it! Studies by J.M. McLeod and his associates at the University of Wisconsin of boys and girls of junior and senior high school age found that the more the youngster watched violence, the more aggressive in real life he or she was likely to be. Other studies revealed that the amount of television violence watched by children, especially boys, at age nine influenced the degree to which they were aggressive ten years later at age nineteen.

In my own university research laboratories we measured the emotional responses of young boys from age five to age fourteen who belonged to two groups. One had been saturated with TV violence, the other had seen little or none of this kind of material for the past two years. We showed both groups an exciting and violent film while hooked up to a physiograph. This is an electronic machine which carefully measures heart, breathing, and galvanic skin (sweat) responses—all indicators of emotional arousal. The results clearly showed that the boys who had been heavily saturated with images of TV violence tended to be turned off and significantly less responsive emotionally than the more tender, non-exposed group. The over-exposed group could calmly watch scenes that should have disturbed them. Desensitization in the presence of repeated exposure to violent images clearly occurs—both in the laboratory and in real life.

This was brought even more forcefully home when I appeared on the Phil Donahue show with my daughter Julie. We repeated our university laboratory experiment for the TV audience. In this case Julie was a low-TV-violence child. Donahue's staff recruited another girl, her same age, who had been saturated with media gore. She was to be used as a comparison. Both girls were hooked up to an electronic monitor or oscilloscope which showed the TV audience what was happening to both of their hearts while they watched a violent scene excerpted from a network TV show. In addition, electrocardiograms were simultaneously recorded and examined immediately after the experiment.

As the TV audience and I carefully watched both of their heart responses, Julie was visibly shaken by what she saw. The other girl, only eleven, hardly varied from her normal heart pattern as she witnessed much mayhem. She was obviously bored by what she saw. The results confirmed our laboratory research.

After the show I discreetly asked this girl how she felt about the film she had just seen. She was quite disgusted and disappointed, saying, "That was nothing. It was boring. I like to see them *really* bleed before I enjoy that kind of stuff."

The research with television clearly indicates that the overwhelming proportion of parents do not or cannot control their children's TV viewing habits. And this includes the preschoolers. Most four-year-olds have more say over what they see than their parents, who just buy another set for themselves and retreat to the bedroom to watch their own favorite shows. Or they'll put a set in the kid's bedroom. Thus everybody can go get their "fixes," with no hassle.

Program content isn't the only reason why parents should, without guilt, exercise complete, thoughtful control over the TV set. Evidence amassed by Marie Winn in her excellent book on TV effects, *The Plug-In Drug*, published by Viking, that massive TV viewing by preschoolers may adversely effect left hemisphere brain development, no matter *what* they watch. This is the brain hemisphere specializing in language and speech. Too much TV could reduce left brain hemisphere commitment to language as a means of expression. As Winn puts it, "As the child takes in television words and images hour after hour, day after day, with little of the mental effort that forming his own thoughts and feelings and molding them into words would require, as he *relaxes* [before the TV] year after year, a pattern emphasizing nonverbal cognition becomes established."

This raises the scary possibility of "accidentally" producing children who have difficulty communicating, who don't develop much beyond the level of feelings and emotions. They operate more by "gut feelings," less by rational, reflective inner thought or spoken dialogue with others.

This is not an idle concern. Nielson Television Index surveys suggest that preschoolers living at home are exposed to in excess of fifty TV hours a week. This means that by the time they are ready to enter kindergarten they have spent more time in front of a TV set than the average college student will spend in the classroom during four years of college! In fact, they will spend more time watching TV than doing any other type of waking activity in their lives.

What this all suggests is that television is a two-edged sword. It can heal or poison. It can inspire and educate positively or it can teach an anti-social system of values. And, as I have already suggested, there is some possibility that any kind of TV, regardless of content, in too great a quantity can have negative effects on the development of mental functions, especially with very young viewers.

Additionally, two Air Force pediatricians, Drs. Richard M. Narkewicz and Stanley N. Graven, have discovered a syndrome among young children who over-use TV. These children show the following symptoms: anxiety, chronic fatigue, loss of appetite, headaches, and vomiting. When the children were kept from all TV or their viewing time was sharply restricted, the symptoms disappeared. However, more than two-thirds of the parents of the children involved were unable to stick to the doctor-prescribed restrictions on TV viewing, even though the children's symptoms reappeared as soon as the parents relented!

This suggests to me that if you have TV-addict children (as was our case), it's very difficult for most parents to control TV viewing because of the pressure from the kids, the great temptation to use TV as a way of getting children out of their hair or quieting them down—or because the parents have their own addictive needs for TV.

The only way I think you can ever really control it is to take the cure cold turkey. That is, get it totally out of your home for six months to a year. Kick the habit all the way. If you bring it back, do so with a lock on your set and strict rules emphasizing sharply reduced viewing hours so that homework, chores, and active recreation can take precedence.

If we wanted to eliminate the TV again from our home I would be tempted to just disable it in the middle of the night by pulling a tube loose and then express surprise the next day when the kids found that it wasn't working. I'd mumble, "Well someday, maybe, we will get it fixed." And that someday would be a long time coming.

But doing it the way we did, despite the initial controversy, created a great opportunity to discuss with the children the whole issue of television effects as well as our love for them, even to the point of doing something they didn't initially like. But when the children became unaddicted, they all saw the wisdom of what we did and were rather proud of us for our courage. They could clearly see the changes in themselves and our family life.

For most families today I would recommend having a TV lock switch which allows parents to have an effective way of controlling the set's use—especially when they are gone. Just turn the key to the off position, pull it out, and stick it in your pocket. I bought one at an electronics store and installed it myself with a small electric drill and screwdriver. I am fairly inept at doing this sort of thing which, translated, means that any reader who has the motor coordination to screw a light bulb into a socket can do the same thing for several dollars and in thirty minutes' time. Why put a lock on your TV set? Can't you trust your own kids? If they are addicted, the answer is *no*. The compulsion to view can be greater than conscience or promises.

Another possibility is to purchase a "Plug-Lok," which fits over the end of the TV plug that goes into the wall socket. Two of these with keys are $4.95 and can be ordered by mail from the Kenny Co., P.O. Box 9132, St. Louis, Mo. 63117.

Movies Can Be Worse

In my judgment, the biggest problem with TV is its pervasiveness and the volume of our time that it consumes, rather than just its content *per se*. As a clinical psychologist and media researcher, I have an even greater concern about the content of some commercial movies that are now being produced. Living in a free and open society we tolerate almost anything. It's pretty much a free market no matter how sick or reprehensible the product. This places a greater responsibility on parents with so much "media junk food" available. Parents have to say *no* more often; virtually no one else will.

I think parents have a tougher time being parents these days than at any other time in our recent history. Society has become extremely permissive, throwing onto parents nearly the whole job of socializing their children. Church, school, and government no longer adequately back up parents in their task of rearing children and teaching them values. The trend of the times is to weaken parental prerogatives and power in their relations with their children. As an example, some courts have ruled that girls in their early teens may obtain abortions without parental knowledge or consent. Child-rights advocates are broadening their efforts to give children the legal right to sue their parents. The trend of the times is indeed toward ever greater permissiveness in allowing children to do pretty much as they please in most areas of their personal life.

Not only is it tougher to say *no* to kids, but some parents I see professionally have stopped trying. They've thrown in the towel—with a shrug they just hope for the best. Like Neville Chamberlain at Munich, it has become peace at any price. Very few limits are set, and if the kids get nasty enough about it the parents even back down on those.

Fourteen-year-old Mary tells her mother that the parents of all her girl friends are letting them see a certain R- or X-rated movie. So why should Mom get so uptight because Mary borrowed someone's driver's license and went to see it last Wednesday night? Sure, it was a school night. And sure, she told Mom that she was over doing homework at Jill's. She really intended to do that homework over there Tuesday night, but changed her mind later. She really wasn't lying. And why did Mother have to stick her nose into the matter anyway? It's not any of her business if she wants to go to a movie. It's a free country, isn't it?

Mother then retreats silently, licking her wounds. She'll talk with George about it when he returns home from his business trip, at the end of the week.

Maybe Mother was right in avoiding a possible hassle. It *is* a free country, isn't it? And don't kids have some rights in these matters?

Not if you care about what kind of adults they'll make. Some modern movies are, in my view, clearly anti-social and far more destructive on my children's emerging ethical sensitivity than most TV shows. Several years ago I assembled a small research team and did a content analysis of every major motion picture playing in a medium-sized western U.S. city. We were interested in assessing the ethical content of messages being presented to the viewers. We found, among other things, that in fifty-nine percent of the films the heroes killed one or more individuals. Thirty-eight percent of the films presented criminal activity as something that pays off, or at least as a successful and exciting pastime with no negative consequences. Fifty-seven percent of the films presented dishonesty in a heroic light or as being justified because of the circumstances.

Only one film (of the thirty-seven analyzed) suggested normal sexual relations between a man and a woman legally married to each other! The model of sex presented was almost entirely illicit in terms of traditional mores.

We found that the great majority of our modern cinema heroes were anti-heroes who, for the most part, were unprincipled, unrestrained, or lacking in impulse control, and unconcerned with the rights or sensitivities of others. They could be best described as having character disorders or psychopathic personalities, for the most part. This included both males and females.

What we rarely see in modern cinema are people sacrificing for a greater good, overcoming temptation, disciplining their emotional psychological resources, modeling ordinary decency and kindness, and caring for others.

If you fill your children's minds accidentally or intentionally with these inadequate models of human functioning, I don't see how they can remain unaffected or untouched in their personal lives now or later, or in the decisions they will make on all kinds of vital issues.

We may believe in free expression in all of the arts. That's OK. But we don't have to feast on pathology or go out of our way to saturate our children (I'm including teenagers here) with anti-social fantasies. If parents take a stand on these issues then they are clearly making explicit what their values are. And kids need to know how Dad and Mom feel about these issues. On occasion they may sneak into an X-rated movie or junk film, but they know for certain where their folks stand on the issue.

As adults they will make up their own minds on such matters, but they still need a decent model from which to develop their own views. Confusion, uncertainty, apologies, and vacillation on these issues suggest to the child that the parents are in an ethical vacuum and don't really know what to believe.

Children need guidelines and direction. Parents should never fear to give them the best they can—their highest aspirations, goals, and dreams of what an honorable person and decent behavior are.

Psychiatrist Frederic Werthem once suggested that a child's mind is like a bank—whatever you put in you get back ten years later with interest. If parents turn their heads the other way and allow their children to saturate themselves with either TV or movie violence or any other anti-social behavior, they run the risk of desensitization setting in. This frankly can amount to a brutalization of the child. All people—and that includes children—have the potential of being desensitized and brutalized, with a resultant blunting of conscience. It almost invariably leads to a lessening of concern and empathy for the victim—any victim. It also makes it easier for the youngster, when he is angry and frustrated, to express aggression and violence to others. Examine the Department of Justice's Uniform Crime Statistics over the past twenty-five years; it is all too clear that we are an extremely violent society, more so than all of the world's other modern advanced societies. That this has been associated in the U.S. with extremes in sadistic and violent screen entertainments doesn't seem to me to be just a chance happening. England, with much lower rates of interpersonal violence, has less than half the violence on TV that we have.

In the Roman arena, citizens cheered as men were attacked and devoured by savage, hungry animals. Men fought to the death as a crowd-pleasing form of spectator sport. The victor would usually cut off his defeated opponent's head or throw a severed bloody limb up into the crowd to be grabbed by the ecstatic citizenry. Politicians vied for votes by promising ever more bloody and gory spectacles to please the appetite of the crowd.

We would never do that! But Kitty Genovese was attacked, raped, and killed in the presence of forty spectators who turned their back on her. Not a single one, even anonymously, phoned or attempted to get help as she fought for her life for more than half an hour. There was also Vietnam's My Lai massacre—those were our sons.

Of course there are many instances on the other side, of bravery shown, of helping others in the presence of great personal danger. But clearly the risk of desensitization is great in our current society. We have no Roman arena, but almost every movie house in the land frequently exhibits a blood bath of mayhem or human horror to the delighted squeals of the teen and young adult crowd as they watch fellow humans tortured and murdered.

Does this mean that TV and commercial cinema will make your child violent or turn him or her into a criminal? In most cases, no. But it can push him in the direction of being more aggressive or quarrelsome. And in some rare cases, through imitation, your child will repeat in his own life some behavior he has seen on TV or in movies—like the twelve-year-old boy who hanged himself.

Cleaning Up the Airwaves

Censorship is an odious and reprehensible thing in a free society. But parents should never feel guilt about monitoring and setting some limits on the type of TV fare their children are exposed to. For it is clear that some broadcasters keep testing the limits in telecasting gory violence, inappropriate sexual material, and even advertisements that are clearly not suitable for young children.

The television industry, in my judgment, is faced with an awesome responsibility in presenting a variety of fare that entertains and teaches but does not harm. Its power to teach values, socialize our children, and affect or manipulate the behavior of every family member is enormous. So what can a frustrated parent do if he or she sees highly inappropriate scenes or advertising presented during children's prime-time viewing? The suggestion that you just turn the set off is not that easy. There is no way a working super-busy parent can stand by the TV set and monitor every single minute of the children's viewing to determine what is or isn't appropriate. The television industry has to assume some responsibility for the quality, tastefulness, and appropriateness of what they are broadcasting. But what if they don't? What if they present highly offensive and objectionable scenes or advertisements during children's viewing hours? What do you do? How do you make your voice and opinion heard as a member of a free society?

A protesting phone call to the station is good. But a well-written, well-documented, and reasonable (not angry) letter to the station manager is five times better. Or do both. Don't just send the letter to the station manager. Get a few photocopies of your letter, and send them to the following additional people:

1. The program's sponsor. Sponsors absolutely hate to hear anybody say anything bad about their program. They've put a lot of money into it; they are hoping it will persuade you to buy their product. If the sponsor is the maker of a breakfast cereal, for example, look on the box for their home address and send your letter to the president—no one else. If it's a major corporation just call the local outlet, and they can give you the home address.

2. Send another copy to the Federal Communications Commission (FCC) at 1919 M St., Washington, DC. The FCC licenses all radio and TV stations every three years. They'll usually ask the station to respond to them about your complaint and will additionally put your letter in their file to review when the station's license next comes up for renewal.

3. Send still another copy to the president of the offending TV network at their headquarters in New York or Washington. Their addresses are:
    ABC: 1330 Avenue of the Americas, New York, NY 10019; phone (212) 581-7777
    CBS: 51 West 52 St., New York, NY 10019; phone (212) 975-4321
    PBS: 485 L'Enfant Plaza West, Washington, DC 20024; phone (202) 488-5000
    NBC: 50 Rockefeller Plaza, New York, NY 10020; phone (212) 664-4444

4. You might, for a few cents more, send copies to your local Congressman at the U.S. House of Representatives Office Building, Washington, DC, and Senators at the U.S. Senate Office Building, Washington, DC.

5. Another two copies might be sent to both the House and Senate subcommittees responsible for television:
    Chairman, House Committee on Interstate and Foreign Commerce, Subcommittee on Communication, House Office Building, Washington, DC 20515.
    Chairman, Senate Committee on Commerce, Science and Transportation, Subcommittee on Communications, Senate Office Building, Washington, DC 20510.

6. If your complaint involves unfair or misleading advertising, also add a copy for the Director of the Federal Trade Commission, Bureau of Consumer Protection, Pennsylvania Avenue at Sixth St. N.W., Washington, DC 20580.

7. A slightly altered version of your letter might also be sent to either the TV editor or "letters to the editor" column of your local newspaper.

If you want to organize or join a group interested in monitoring and improving the quality of television broadcasting, I suggest you contact:

1. *Action For Children's Television*, 46 Austin St., Newtonville, MA 02160; phone (617) 527-7870. This is a national nonprofit organization working to upgrade children's TV programs. You can join for $15 a year. It has a newsletter, research information, films, and library facilities. It is a very powerful and effective group of concerned citizens and parents.

2. *The National Association for Better Broadcasting*, P.O. Box 43640, Los Angeles, CA 90043; phone (213) 474-3283. This group has a newsletter, does research, and annually puts out a critique of all major TV programs being broadcast.

3. *Citizens Communication Center*, 1914 Sunderland Place, N.W.,Washington, DC 20036; phone (202) 296-4238. This group provides legal assistance, aid, and advice to citizens interested in taking action in the broadcast area.

4. *National Citizens Committee for Broadcasting*, 1028 Connecticut Ave. N.W., Suite 402, Washington, DC 20036; phone (202) 466-8407. This is another national group concerned with the quality of TV programming. They monitor and report on violence in TV programming and identify the commercial sponsors of such violent programs.

5. *Council on Children, Media & Merchandising*, 1346 Connecticut Ave. N.W., Washington, DC 20036; phone (202) 466-2584. Their concern leans in the direction of correcting abuses in food advertising directed toward children. For example, some cereals advertised on TV are little more than candy bars with sugar content as high as sixty-five percent and with minimum nutritional value.

You are most effective as part of a group. Historically, it has been groups such as *Action For Children's Television* that have had the most significant impact in keeping the television industry responsible. This has been through friendly persuasion, jawboning, picketing, class action suits, organizing community protests, filing petitions with government regulatory agencies, and "consciousness raising" via public lectures, newspaper articles, public forums, and workshops.

Since most people in a democracy tend to be fairly passive, a small group of sincere, dedicated people can do a great deal to effect social change—far out of proportion to their numbers. If you don't like what's happening on television, get organized. Remember—in the average home the TV is on forty-two-and-one-half hours a week. Children spend more waking hours looking at it than in any other kind of activity.

Television is a fantastic medium, but it can very easily be abused. You can be its slave, or it can serve you. The choice is yours.

23
The Over-Aggressive Child

BEING AGGRESSIVE isn't necessarily bad. It has a definite healthy side to it that can be vital for a child's survival. Such terms as *persistence, initiative, push, drive, overcoming obstacles,* and *refusing to be defeated* are all admirable qualities that suggest strength and toughness and can all be aspects of aggressiveness. This is what future winners and leaders are made of.

The negative side of the coin is the pushy, domineering individual who destructively overrides the rights and feelings of others to get what he wants. We call him *bossy, intimidating,* and *hurtful.* The typical over-aggressive child that I see clinically is a high-energy boy who is constantly stirring up excitement and trouble at home. He can't keep his hands off his brothers and sisters, pushing and shoving, pinching and hitting constantly. It's as if he enjoyed creating trouble. Peace bores him.

But many such children later turn into super-leaders when they've learned to harness and channel all their raw drive and energy.

If you have such an over-aggressive child in your family, you don't want to take his drive and spirit away from him. You *do* want to channel it into constructive outlets and protect the other children he comes in contact with, for he can be miserable to live with and sometimes even hard to love.

Jack was the only boy in a family of four children. He was very physical, a real muscle-flexer with lots of energy. He'd rather run than walk to school. Temperamentally, he was headstrong and impulsive. When he got bored, which was most of the time, he'd tease his sisters unmercifully and occasionally knock them around in squabbles—which he had started. He wasn't basically mean, but he was rough. He loved all sports, especially those involving body contact. He greatly enjoyed the crunch of bodies in tackle football and "mixing it up" in ice hockey.

His parents wondered if his sisters would survive until he matured through adolescence. When confronted by his Dad and Mom, he would politely listen to their protestations and vow to do better. But thirty minutes after such a conference the family would be in an uproar again. Finally they found the strategy which brought some semblance of peace to the family. They encouraged him to find and hold two jobs, to go all out for major sports, and to participate in several youth programs at the same time—while still completing his education in high school. They loaded him up with ego-fulfilling activities that kept him out of the house a lot and consumed most of his monstrous supply of energy.

When Special Help Is Needed

Two special kinds of children may appear over-aggressive, but they need special help. The first of these is the sadist, a child five years of age or older who appears to enjoy inflicting real torment on other children and animals. He takes significant pleasure in causing pain. He may actually torture or kill animals for kicks. This type of youngster is fortunately quite rare but should always get some form of professional care and therapy.

Preschoolers are not in this category. They may act very aggressive toward each other on occasion, flailing their arms in fits and attacking each other, but this is often just a reaction to frustrations, a form of temper tantrum which quickly comes and goes. It is very common at early ages. Of course, you should not let them use toys or solid objects to hit each other with, since this could cause injury. You might also provide a punching bag, a trampoline, clay, sand, water, or kick balls for them to play and work with as a healthy vent to their feelings and frustrations.

The second special type of youngster who will need help is the hyperactive child, usually a boy. The best evidence to date suggests that this problem is genetic, caused by a mild chemical imbalance in the brain. (See Chapter 3.) Physician-prescribed medication or even diet changes can in many cases help contain this problem. The hyperactive syndrome is not necessarily all or nothing. Some children may have only a mild case of it, but if it is present it is present from birth on.

There are four major types of symptoms which identify children who have this problem:

Overactivity The child appears restless, aggressive, fidgety, has high energy, and appears never to get tired. His motor never turns off, but his activity seems to be random and unfocused. He constantly touches things—and other children—leaving a long trail of disorder and upset behind.

Distractibility The child has a short attention span and is easily distracted, especially when engaged in an active task like housework or a spelling assignment. It's very hard for him ever to finish anything.

Impulsiveness The child interrupts, blurts things out, and does things without thinking. Thus, he may lie, take something that doesn't belong to him, do something he's been told many times not to, break something, run away, show very poor judgment again and again despite training and instructions to the contrary. In short, he does what he wants to whenever he wants to do it, without stopping to think of the consequences.

Excitability The child is very irritable, aggressive, and excitable; he cries easily, has frequent temper tantrums, is easily upset. He fights, screams, or destroys things at the slightest provocation.

Because of all this he has few or no friends. His parents often resent him, and his brothers and sisters often hate him. His underlying personality may still be that of a sweet, generous, loving child, but this is masked a good part of the time by the bio-chemical imbalance that produces his hyperactive behavior.

This kind of aggressive, impulsive child will need the ministrations of a pediatrician who can prescribe the appropriate medications and carefully regulate the dosage. However, you should distinguish between this kind of a child and one who is normally boisterous and just has a lot of energy. This is fairly easy to do. The medication used for putting the hyperactive child back in control will work the first day or two you use it. Within a week you, and his teacher at school, will notice the difference in his behavior. These medicines do not fog the child's mind or make a passive zombie out of him. What they do is help normalize his brain chemistry. So if you are not sure whether your "problem" child is hyperactive or just boisterous, a week on the medication will answer your question. If he responds to the medication then he is truly hyperactive; if it doesn't work then he probably isn't.

The Bully

Another type of aggressive child is the bully, a male or female of any age who can be intimidating, brow-beating, pressuring—often hurting other children. Underneath, most bullies are insecure, unsure, inadequate, and anxious persons. They are often unable to get accepted by other children in normal ways. Their bullying behavior is a compensation mechanism which allows them to boss and gain psychological power over others. They may not be liked, but they are respected and feared, and that's better than being a nothing.

It's a charade. They huff and puff, strut and bluster, and bring misery into the lives of a lot of children, but they are at heart made of cardboard and papier-mâche. They pick their victims carefully to insure easy victories. They avoid contests at which they might lose, and they often round up several henchmen or strays to be their satellites. At heart they are lonely, unliked youngsters who can't make it in the normal social scene.

Parents sometimes unwittingly encourage such behavior. Father may subtly let his son know that he's proud that his boy is the toughest, meanest kid on the block: "Nobody pushes us Browns around." Dad may vicariously live out his dreams of power and strength through his son's behavior.

Therapy for the bully requires warm, affectionate ties with at least one parent. The parents also have to actively discourage his tyrannical behavior. They need to point out how it keeps other children from wanting to be with him. They need to provide him with substitute ways of gaining respect and recognition from others: excellence in sports, development of a musical talent, participation in school plays, work on the school paper, or involvement in science fair projects.

Personal and Family Troubles

There is still another type of over-aggressive child more within normal limits. He is usually frustrated in some area of his life—struggling with problems of identity or concerned about the new baby or unable to measure up to a favorite sibling. He may not be doing well in school or be rejected by the social group he'd like to mix with. An older child might be suffering from a limited love-life—no dating. And so this child takes his anger and frustrations out on the rest of the family. He may feel somewhat guilty about his behavior, but as the frustrations continue he still may abuse the family. He can be pushy, demanding, irritable, and sometimes quite selfish.

In some cases an over-aggressive youngster's aggressiveness can be provoked by parents who are themselves highly irritable, sarcastic, and aggressive. One of the parents may be physically abusive, or the parents may be having chronic marital problems, constantly bickering between themselves; the child merely imitates his parents. In a sense the parents have unwittingly taught their child to be abusive. Violent, aggressive parents produce violent, aggressive children.

Another quite different situation occurs where one or both parents are mild-tempered and feel timid with their child. The parents cannot even say *no* and make it stick. Their inability to step in and take decisive action with the offending child is almost always caused by at least one parent's feeling of guilt. The father, for example, may feel that in some way he hurt the child. He carries a terrible burden of guilt and can't refuse his child anything. Or the mother may hate the child for all the trouble he has caused her while refusing to admit she feels that way; she mentally fears disciplining him for this would prove that she really was a miserable, unloving wretch of a mother. In this vacuum of family leadership the frustrated, aggressive child runs amok. Often he steadily escalates his violence as if crying out for somebody to set some limits and call him to account.

In dealing with these problems, first Dad and Mom have to get their act together. If their marital problems cause them to sabotage each other's relations with the children, they must get counseling from the best therapist in town or separate. I've seen many children almost immediately shape up when one of the parents moved out and the marital civil war ceased. The house was no longer divided. There was one clear authority, one person in charge, not all the confusion that existed before.

If the parents are united, then together they must first assess why their child is so aggressive. What triggers his overly aggressive behavior? In some cases it may really be little more than rowdy horseplay in a superactive, high-energy child, not done maliciously but mainly as a form of recreation. In that case let him tussle, wrestle, and battle it out on the back lawn where he won't damage property. Do not permit him to throw things or hold objects that might hurt his partner in play. Though to *you* their tussling may look like war, to them it's entertainment and a way of getting rid of pent-up tensions.

On occasion, even though the children are serious, their loss of temper, shouted words, slammed doors, and stomping feet can still be within fairly normal limits of behavior. Simply disengage them. Allow the youngsters to cool off, then visit with them privately in their bedrooms. Let them get rid of their remaining anger with words or tears while you actively listen. This means you don't judge, criticize, retaliate, or put them down. For a little while you should listen compassionately. Hear each child's side of the story, his grievance, his frustrations. Find out the triggers to his anger; you may be able to do something later to avoid those triggers. For example, if a younger brother has got into his things again you may want to put a key-lock on his bedroom door, so that you and he but no one else may get in. Most of all, in this private talk with each child, let him know that it's never any disgrace to have feelings, even of terrible anger. But he *is* responsible for what he does with his anger. He must not hurt, injure, or destroy; he should talk it out and later solve the problem through peaceful negotiation.

If you have two children who seem constantly to be quarreling violently, you may need to figure out ways to separate them. Change bedrooms. Take the TV out of the room where most of the problems start. If weekends are bad times get at least one child busy or away at that time with a job, chores, swimming classes, visits with relatives, being with friends, spending the day with Dad, or whatever else you can think of. If it's a high-energy kid you're dealing with, exhaust him—and keep him exhausted. (This is what one wife I know did with a husband who always complained about not getting enough sex. She took him on for three days straight. She totally wore him out. He never complained again.) Idle time for these kids is dynamite. Provide healthy channels for all of their energies: a basketball hoop above the garage door, a trampoline, access to a swimming pool or, for your younger children, a sandpile, a bike, a wading pool, friends. Also, cut down on the amount of violent, provocative movies and television they see.

Finally, while it's absolutely necessary to step in and stop serious fighting where significant harm can come to a child, most of the time you should stay out of children's quarrels. Let them learn to solve their own problems. If every time they quarrel and squabble you step in, soon you will find your life miserable. You can never know for sure who is to blame, which means that you can never be exactly fair. You will always wind up the bad guy; you will feel weary and exhausted, and the attention you always give may unwittingly reinforce their bad behavior. Stay out of it if at all possible.

Fighting between siblings almost always includes an older, larger child and a smaller one, or a boy fighting with a girl. It is tempting for parents to jump in and reprove the "stronger" child for "picking on" his sister or a smaller child. You should remember that if you consistently side with the "underdog", you are inviting the smaller child to torment his physically stronger sibling beyond the point of endurance. In this circumstance the younger child inevitably wins: if the stronger child does not hit him, he gets away with it; if the stronger child *does* hit him, you will intervene and punish the stronger child, and again the young tormenter gets away with it. The other side of the coin is that weaker children can live in terror of their older, stronger, aggressive siblings so it is wise to teach the weaker child, and insist that he use, strategies for avoiding confrontation. Then hold him equally responsible for avoiding conflict.

In summary, here are the rules for dealing with the over-aggressive child:

1. If your child is sadistic, uncommonly cruel to animals and other children, this suggests an emotional or mental problem. Consult a competent child psychotherapist.

2. If your child is hyperactive, consult a pediatrician for appropriate diagnosis and treatment.

3. If your child is a bully, make sure you are not unwittingly provoking or reinforcing his behavior. Meet his emotional needs, love him, find substitute ways for him to feel important. Finally, discuss and reason with him concerning the effects of his behavior so that he can make changes in how he relates with other children.

4. If your child has difficulty handling anger, engage in "active listening", letting him discharge aggressive tensions through words and language, then give him plenty of love and emotional support while you set limits on the acting out of aggressive behavior.

5. Cut down on the child's exposure to violent movies and TV.

6. Eliminate any brutal physical punishment on your part.

7. As much as you can, separate the aggressive child from those he abuses.

Get him a job; give him a bedroom by himself that he doesn't share with any of his victims. Encourage involvement in sports, clubs, and similar activities. Channel his energies into legitimate pursuits.

8. Find friends for him. You can do many things to help him develop socially. Get him in supervised contact with other children in low-pressure situations. For instance, you might invite to your home guests who have children his age; when their kids come along to the barbecue, your son can learn to deal with them better without the pressure of thinking he must "measure up" to some standard.

9. Recognize that some fighting and aggressiveness in childhood is normal horseplay, but insist that they scuffle on the back lawn, not next to your china cupboard.

10. As much as possible insist that the children solve their fights and squabbles themselves. Stay out of their contentions. And remember it's often the younger one that starts these things. Interfere only in dire emergencies to prevent some serious injury or harm from occurring.

11. Eliminate provocative or frustrating situations if possible. This may involve changing sleeping quarters, meal times, and work assignments.

12. Keep the over-aggressive child busy and occupied. Provide alternate ways for him to expend his energy. Idle time brings a high risk for these children.

13. Most of all, try to avoid thinking of the over-aggressive child as "bad". If you consciously or unconsciously label him that way you are likely to feel more distance between you; he and the other children will inevitably feel it, too, and the more isolated he becomes from those who should love him most, the more difficult he is likely to become.

PART III
A SUMMING UP

24

Ten Keys To Rearing Successful Children

IN THIS FINAL CHAPTER I would like to summarize the essence of my book into ten "Golden Rules" or Keys. If you are able to use only a few of these, they will still change your children for the better.

Everything in this book has been field tested through twenty-six years of clinical practice and in the rearing of my own nine children. I have learned from my failures as well as my successes, and I've had both. I've also learned that while parents do have a profound impact on their children, these children, as they get older, come to have a unique identity and personality apart from or in addition to family influences.

I've seen remarkable individuals emerge out of family dung-heaps where nearly all of the social-environmental factors have been adverse. I've also seen human disasters come from extremely favored environments and good parents. And I'm not sure why. Somehow, buried within each human psyche is a special identity that has the free will to make choices, both in the individual's own self-interest and, sometimes, even perversely and obstinately leading to self-destruction.

But *most* people, including our own children, can still be persuaded, influenced, taught, loved, and strengthened in the direction of good mental health and maturity. While we can never be fully responsible for their eventual happiness or most of their personal choices, we can still give them a host of advantages which will optimize their chances of enduring life's vicissitudes with grace and courage.

FIRST KEY: Stimulate Your Child's Intellect

In Chapter 4 I presented a variety of evidences suggesting that IQ can be powerfully affected up or down by environmental stimulation (or lack of it). The evidence is convincing that if parents give their children certain experiences, these may actually stimulate more branchings of neural networks between brain cells as well as increase the production of certain brain enzymes.

Psychologist J. McVicker Hunt estimates from his research that IQ's can be increased by as much as twenty-five to thirty points or more by proper environmental stimulation, but that it can drop by as much as fifty points in children who are reared from birth in extremely monotonous and unresponsive conditions. This amounts to a range of seventy-five to eighty IQ points—all caused by proper or lack of proper environmental activity and stimulation. In Chapter 4 you will find detailed practical information on how you can give your child an active enriched environment which will help raise his IQ.

Timing is crucial here because there appear to be certain ages in a youngster's life when the brain is most receptive to stimulation for a certain kind of skill or ability to develop. Miss that time period and it becomes much more difficult for the child to learn that skill later. Since parents do have great control over the environment and experiences their very young children will have—it means that they can play a powerful and direct role in raising their child's IQ if they know what to do and when to do it. I would advise every parent to take advantage of the detailed and specific helps given in Chapter 4.

SECOND KEY: Build Your Child's Self-Esteem

The vital core of every living human being is his self-image. This picture or image which we carry around in our heads will profoundly influence every decision we make. It will determine in great part the extent of our personal misery or happiness. It will also affect our job success, choice of spouse, the ability to have and hold friends, even our capacity to love. If a child has respect for himself he is then free to respect and love others. With good self-esteem he has the courage to risk, explore, try new things, and even occasionally fail—but in the end succeed.

Accepting and loving our children is important, vitally important—but it's not enough. It takes more than just telling our kids that we love them and that they are great to give them a good self-image. Their personal worth has to be validated by some tangible, successful accomplishments. The child has to do something, have some skills and abilities which bring genuinely earned praise and recognition. Every child has to slay a few dragons—do some tough, difficult things successfully. Parents can engineer this. Our kids also should have the ability or means to influence their environment, have power, make things happen, win some battles. They need to know that they count, that they aren't helpless, that they can change things.

So teach your child to be competent, to excel in some areas of his or her choice and interest, do something better than most of his peers. Also, every youngster needs a special friend—a good person who likes him. Parents can do much to facilitate this.

Earning money through successful work experiences also builds self-respect. In addition, give your children repeated opportunities to make decisions and assume responsibility; this is your way of letting them know they count. Read Chapter 2 for many more specifics and practical suggestions on building your child's self-image and self-esteem.

THIRD KEY: Teach Your Child Effective Social Skills

A great share of our children's future happiness and personal fulfillment will depend on their ability to relate effectively with others. What makes them truly human is how effectively they love, work with, and relate to others. Fortunately, these skills can be learned, shaped and enhanced by caring parents.

I have found six things that all contribute to a child having superior social skills: (1) being truly loved, providing the child with a deep inner sense of security; (2) Having a lot of exposure to people, all kinds of people; (3) looking reasonably attractive in appearance and grooming—not being too different, for that keeps other people at a distance; (4) repeatedly witnessing and observing the modeling of skilled social behavior by the parents, brothers, sisters, and peers (parents, invite a lot of friends over!); (5) having a reasonably good self-image to allow the child to respect himself and feel worthy of having friends (see Chapter 2); (6) having at least moderate verbal fluency, to be able to communicate and carry on a decent conversation (see Chapter 4).

Most shy children have a certain amount of social anxiety which makes them feel nervous around other people. They often fear and expect a negative evaluation of themselves. This is always learned. This leads in time to a negative bias against themselves; they think negatively about themselves. Soon it becomes self-perpetuating. They shun opportunities for social development, but this only makes them even more aloof and different. See Chapter 3; it lists over twenty specific helps to cure a child of social anxiety and help improve his interpersonal skills.

FOURTH KEY: Control the Use of Television – Unhook Addicted Kids

Television addiction can disturb both children's intellectual and social growth. The evidence keeps piling up suggesting that, like the Pied Piper or a magic sorcerer, TV can steal away days, months, and years of a child's lifetime. The latest research documents that the average child spends more waking hours in front of a TV set than in any other type of activity, including going to school.

The average preschooler living at home is exposed to in excess of fifty TV hours a week, according to the Nielson Television Index. This means that by the time the child is ready to start kindergarten he or she will have spent more time in front of a TV set than the average college student will spend in the classroom during four years of college.

Marie Winn has assembled evidence suggesting that such massive TV viewing by preschoolers may adversely affect their left hemisphere brain development. This is the brain hemisphere specializing in language and speech, thus producing children who later have difficulty communicating—who remain regressed at the level of feelings and emotions. They may operate more by "gut" feelings than by rational, reflective, inner thought or spoken dialogues with others.

In Chapter 22 we present a number of strategies for unhooking addicted children, of getting control of TV in our homes, of letting it serve us in useful ways—both as an entertainment medium and for educational purposes, but not as a seductive tyrant that takes time away from family conversations, homework, physical exercise or play, as well as necessary chores.

FIFTH KEY: Strengthen Your Child's Conscience

Dr. Charles E. Schaefer, a psychologist in Dobbs Ferry, New York, recently surveyed fifty parents who had "successfully" raised their own children to be productive adults and who from all evidences were apparently adjusting well to society. He asked the parents, "Based upon your own personal experiences with your own children, what is the best advice you could give new parents about raising children?"

One of the major pieces of advice given was the need for new parents to actively teach their children basic values: integrity, moral courage, honesty, and a desire to treat others as they themselves would like to be treated—in other words, to promote ethical values and conscience.

The research evidence suggests that developing a conscience and an ethical sense takes considerable time, requires repeated explicit teaching by parents of right from wrong, continual reinforcement of good behavior, and negative (but fair) consequences for bad behavior. It also takes parents who themselves model and repeatedly demonstrate responsible behavior.

If the kids like and admire you—they will imitate your behavior and tend to assume your values when they are adults.

However, there is evidence suggesting that a few rare children can have an impaired conscience due to inherited genetic defects—but even these children can be significantly protected by a healthy family and neighborhood during their vulnerable years. They can still learn that it is in their self-interest to behave responsibly in order to obtain positive rewards and avoid painful and negative consequences. They won't feel the tug of conscience as most normal children will, but they can still perceive and learn in a rational way the advantages of responsible behavior. These children cannot tolerate a weak or disturbed family situation or live in a high risk neighborhood.

In sum, there is a great deal parents can do to help promote conscience—especially before their children reach their teens and get on the rollercoaster of adolescent turbulence and shift their attachments and allegiance away from their parents to their peer culture. But do your homework early!

See Chapter 6 (on conscience development), Chapter 9 (on discipline), and Chapters 11 and 14 (on lying and stealing) for more specifics about what to do to help your child develop a strong ethical-moral sense.

SIXTH KEY: Teach Your Child to Show Love, Express Affection, and Develop Healthy Attitudes Toward Sexuality

Before one can truly love someone else he or she has to experience love. Your cup has to be full in order to share it with someone you care about. Easily the most powerful way for parents to produce affectionate loving children is to give the kids a lot of T.L.C. as they are growing up. And the kids need to see Dad and Mom kiss and hug affectionately as they greet or leave each other's company or on impulse at other appropriate moments and occasions.

It needs to be part of the family style.

If mother feels secure in her husband's love for her, this helps open up her faucets so she can pour it out on the kids. What I'm suggesting is that the single most effective thing a dad can do to express love to his children is to love their mother—to make sure his wife has her cup full. Then she can give to the kids out of her overflow.

I'm not suggesting that single parents can't also give great quantities of love to their children. They can and do. But it's not as easy and it's not the same as in a complete and integrated family unit. However, the single parent will do a better job single than when harrassed in a very difficult marriage being burdened with chronic conflict and divided leadership.

Regarding appropriate sex education, Chapter 5 provides many suggestions and ideas for parents. I have found in working with large numbers of couples that a healthy sex adjustment involves far more than having considerable knowledge about positions, technology and anatomy. It involves the whole mix of male-female relationships far beyond intercourse and orgasm. It involves such things as consideration, affection, good communication, and a nonexploitive relationship. It involves a commitment to the person as a person. And children need to understand this. If you *just* teach them about conception and the pregnancy cycle in a high school sex-education class—you do them a disservice. They also need to know about values and the importance of responsibility to their partner. These are things that only caring parents can give to their children. No formal class can possibly teach or give all of this.

SEVENTH KEY: Live in a Good Neighborhood

Whether you like it or not the children our youngsters choose as their friends will have an increasingly significant impact upon their lives, values and behavior—especially as they get older and move into their adolescent years. It is also very clear that neighborhoods and even communities or subsections of larger urban areas vary in their character, healthiness, and degree of pathology.

This means you should choose the neighborhood you live in at least as carefully as you choose your particular house; the neighborhood will provide the peer culture for your children as they grow up and that might make a critically important difference in their lives. A home can be repainted or remodeled, but you can't singlehandedly change the character of a neighborhood. And the relative affluence of the homes in a neighborhood isn't necessarily a good guide to whether the neighborhood is healthy for children. You have to make discreet inquiries to find out. Do your homework before buying your next home. I've seen an instance where every family on one side of a block was getting a divorce. The women talked to each other and fed each other's neuroses, paranoia, and hostility toward their husbands. This is infectious. It can spread.

Also check out the schools. They will play a vital role in your child's exposure to a healthy or sick peer culture and potential friends. There are great schools and sick schools in every community. Avoid the latter like the plague.

While you will not be able to choose exactly who your children will have as friends—you can do a great deal to increase the probability that their friends will be decent youngsters from healthy homes by carefully choosing where you live. If you live in a social-psychological sewer it will not be easy for kids to come out ten years later smelling like a rose.

There is indeed a "quality of life", a tempo, a heartbeat, a spirit of a community which reflects in difficult-to-measure but very real ways a community's conscience. It also indicates its values, its work ethic, the quality of people elected to office, and its moral climate—what it will tolerate and what it won't. This is one area where you as parents can really load the dice in your children's favor. Do your homework next time before you move.

EIGHTH KEY: Set Reasonable Work and Behavior Standards Backed by Appropriate Discipline

In a great variety of research studies cited in this book it is clear that children possessing higher self-esteem, confidence and personal competence come from homes where parents set high standards for their youngsters—expecting and requiring more rather than less—who in a sense run a "tight ship". These were families where parents took clear leadership roles, assuming that they knew better than their kids what would be helpful to them as adults. The parents had been where the kids still weren't. This didn't mean that the parents were tyrants or that the children had no input in making family decisions or that there was a lack of good communications. In fact these were emphasized. But these parents had no hang-ups or feelings of guilt in setting standards, giving directions, and using discipline appropriately and where necessary.

Chapter 7 (teaching your child to be responsible) and Chapter 9 (discipline) provide many suggestions for setting and obtaining reasonable work and behavior standards with your youngsters.

However, we must add that there is considerable evidence that different children from the same parents will vary, probably genetically, in their temperament and disposition. Some will grab at a challenge and run with it, being almost impossible to hold back. Others, also good kids from the same parents, will need an electric cattle prod just to move from one room into the other. Parents, don't fret. This is to be expected and is found in every home in the land. Just think of it as a leadership problem. Yours!

Positive reinforcement can work magic in motivating youngsters to perform and excel. In fact it works better than punishment in most cases. Read the discipline chapter carefully for dozens of ideas and applications which you can use, hopefully, with your own children.

Remember, responsible competent kids are not produced overnight! It's a step-by-step process which takes many years. This book is full of scores of techniques that work; they have all been child tested. All that is required is a consistent application by parents who hang in there and don't give up.

NINTH KEY: Teach Your Child Skills and Competencies

Research on men who were stress-proof as well as competent and effective across a broad spectrum of personal activities showed these men had early life experiences filled with successful achievement. They were doers from a very early age. This suggests that you might consider encouraging your children to try out all kinds of activities and new experiences. You, to a degree, can engineer their success. You make sure, in an enjoyable way, that they learn how to ski, skate, play ball, fish, hunt, tune a car, jog, raise a garden, earn some money working for someone else—plus a hundred other activities. You fill their lives with small challenges that lead to successful accomplishment. As they get older they'll be able to handle bigger challenges. Success becomes a pattern in their lives. They expect it. They learn not to give up. They persist until they've won their victory. They are not afraid of failure—because they know, given time, they will make it through.

Since each child's brain, like his finger prints, is unique and different—each of your children will vary in his inherited natural aptitudes. This means you should build on each child's special strengths and aptitudes, rather than attempting to make *both* of your sons into football stars or *both* of your girls into tennis champs or playwrights like their mother. Some will have a natural bent for math, art, or activities involving manual dexterity. Whatever their talents are—promote them every way you can. In fact, in a family of several children it's a good idea for each to have his own special thing unchallenged—so he is not constantly compared with another brother or sister. Thus, one might excel on the violin or piano and another on the drums or maybe in vocal music or whatever. What is crucial is to start providing these experiences early in life, to set a pattern of continuing challenge followed by success. But make it fun, a game, an enjoyable experience -not drudgery. See Chapters 1 and 4 for many specific helps here.

TENTH KEY: Foster Autonomy and Independence: Don't Do for Your Children What They Can Do for Themselves

Our ultimate goal in raising winner children is to prepare them to leave our homes and protection and make it on their own—successfully establishing their own homes and family situation. This requires that we constantly give them increasing responsibilities and challenges, for how will they ever make it on their own if they don't have a chance to try their wings—and sometimes fail—under our protective custody?

I remember when some of our less coordinated children first obtained their driver's licenses. I was sure they would never make it to the corner without knocking down a telephone pole. I was, for several months, in a state of acute nervous anxiety. And while we did get some dents in assorted fenders, at least nobody died, and they didn't run over any little kids in the neighborhood. My natural tendency was to put off their driving for another year or two, but no way would they tolerate that. I knew that sooner or later

I would have to turn their lives over to the gods and fickle fate and just hope that somehow they would survive those first three months while improving their driving skills using my car. Somehow they all survived.

In another instance a daughter opened a checking account not fully realizing how to record and keep a daily balance. In her first month she wrote forty checks—most for very small amounts such as $1.50 to pay for two malts. One day she received a letter from the bank indicating that fifteen checks had bounced—with a $5 charge for *each* occurrence. That never happened again. She had to learn the importance of keeping one's account balance current.

The way you teach kids these things is to give them responsibility early. Expect a few mistakes or goofs. Let them make as many decisions as possible as early in life as possible. Let them feel that they count, that their judgment is important, that to an increasing degree they do have some control over their lives and personal destinies. Parents are to cheer the kids on, give occasional advice, and maybe even a nudge sometimes. Let them try all kinds of things. Let them, where practical, participate in family decision making. Put them in charge of things. Let them work for other people—as early in their lives as possible—at things they can do successfully.

I promised you ten keys to help you in raising successful winner children. However, I would like to add one more, a bonus key if you wish, which I think you will find helpful.

BONUS KEY: Foster a Warm Relationship with Your Child Built on Good Communication

Effective positive communication is the royal road to a good relationship with your child—regardless of age. A father of a large family I knew once shared a secret that the "golden hours" with his teenagers were after midnight. He didn't mean this literally, but he was suggesting that the late hours are often best for letting down your hair and getting close to your youngster. This is when the little one is asleep, the TV is off, the phone has stopped ringing, and house visitors have long since left. The late-hour fatigue factor also tends to open the kids up (and you too). Their defenses are down. It's a time to share, open up your heart, and listen sympathetically. Most teenagers in our current culture are under a lot of stresses; a lot of them are hurting and bruised; they have a lot of unanswered questions, problems, and temptations. If you're there, uncritical, and their friend—not boss or first sergeant as earlier in the day—they may just open up. You might, out of your experience, give them an idea that might solve a tough problem or comfort the wounded ego of a rejected child who earlier in the day suffered a disastrous disappointment or a miserable putdown that rankled deep inside.

Occasionally, I find that a non-communicative morose youngster suddenly wants to talk. Its a rare occasion, and I let all other things go. I cancel an appointment or am late to something—because I'm needed then. Later may never come. My wife, Lois, is marvelous at this—she knows and senses when the right time to talk is. She'll stay up most of the night if needed—and is glad to. And it pays off . . . again and again.

There are a lot of books on effective communication, but the most important key, I believe, is that you care. This must somehow shine through, clear and unmistakable, as you talk with your youngster. You can say it almost any way you wish—as long as that is the message the child gets. It builds trust. It enables the child to endure your occasional discipline; they understand that you do it because you love them.

Above all, every child needs private, uninterrupted time with one or both parents—frequently! Take the child riding, or for a leisurely walk, or out for a bite to eat. Do it on a regular basis. Give the child private moments, when he or she alone is the center of your attention, and concern, and love.

References

CHAPTER 1: THE ROOTS OF SUCCESS: EARLY FAMILY LIFE

Cline, V.B. *A study of the characteristics of successful and unsuccessful men working in situations of extreme stress: A discussion of results.* A paper presented at the annual meeting of the American Psychological Association, New York City, September 8, 1954.

Cline, V.B.; Meeland, T.; Egbert, R., et al. *Task fighter: Description of tests and preliminary summary of results on personality inventories.* Privately mimeographed monograph. Monterey, Calif.: Human Research Unit No. 2, Human Resources Research Office, 1954.

Cline, V.B. A life wasted: Why did Gilmore do it?. *Deseret News,* Nov. 18, 19, 20, 1977. P.A.-1.

Eberle, N. Raising my children: What I'd do differently. *McCall's,* Aug. 1978.

Jencks, Beata. *Influence of the environment in preparing an animal to meet stress: Effects of isolation and of multiple stress.* Unpublished doctoral dissertation. (Available through University Microfilms Inc., Ann Arbor, Mich., Vol XXIV, No 1, 1963.) University of Utah, Salt Lake City, 1962.

Olson, Larry. *Outdoor survival skills.* Provo, Ut.: Brigham Young University Press, 1974.

CHAPTER 2: HOW TO BUILD YOUR CHILD'S SELF-IMAGE AND SELF-ESTEEM

Coopersmith, S. *The antecedents of self esteem.* San Francisco: W.H. Freeman Co., 1967.

Tagore, Rabin. *Collected poems and plays of Rabin Tagore.* New York: Macmillan Co., 1949.

CHAPTER 3: HOW TO TEACH YOUR CHILD EFFECTIVE SOCIAL SKILLS

Johnson, D.W. *Reaching out: Interpersonal effectiveness and self actualization.* Englewood Cliffs, N.J.: Prentice-Hall, 1972.

Jourard, S. *The transparent self.* Englewood Cliffs, N.J.: Prentice-Hall, 1964.

CHAPTER 4: HOW TO RAISE YOUR CHILD'S IQ

Beck, J. *How to raise a brighter child* (revised ed.). New York: Pocket Books, 1975.

Bloom, B.S. *Stability and change in human characteristics,* New York: John Wiley & Sons, Inc., 1964.

Bronfenbrenner, Urie. Is early intervention effective? Some studies of early education in familial and extra familial settings. In Ashley Montague (ed.), *Race and IQ.* New York: Oxford University Press, 1975.

Dennis, W. Causes of retardation among institutional children: Iran. *The Journal of Genetic Psychology, 96,* 1960, 47-59.

Dennis, W. and Sayegh, Y. The effect of supplementary experience upon the behavioral development of infants in institutions. *Child Development, 36,* Mar. 1965.

Doman, Glenn. *How to teach your baby to read.* New York: Dolphin Books, 1975.

Durkin, D. Children who learned to read at home. *Elementary School Journal, 62,* Oct. 1961.

Durkin, D. An earlier start in reading?. *Elementary School Journal, 63,* Dec. 1962.

Durkin, D. Children who read before grade 1: A second study. *Elementary School Journal, 64,* Dec. 1963.

Durkin, D. *Children who read early.* New York: Teachers College Press, 1966.

Engelmann, S. and Engelmann, T. *Give your child a superior mind.* New York: Simon & Schuster, Inc., 1966.

Fowler, W. Cognitive learning in infancy and early childhood. *Psychological Bulletin, 59,* Mar. 1962.

Fowler, W. Teaching a two-year-old to read: an experiment in early childhood learning. *Genetic Psychology Monographs, 66,* 1962.

Hess, E.H. Imprinting. *Science, 130,* July 17, 1959.

Hess, R.D. and Shipman, V. Early blocks to children's learning. *Children, 12,* 1965, 189-94.

Hess, R.D. and Shipman, V. Early experience and the socialization of cognitive modes in children. *Child Development, 36,* 1965, 869-86.

Hunt, J. McV. *Intelligence and experience.* New York: The Ronald Press Co., 1961.

Hunt, J. McV. How children develop intellectually. *Children, 11,* May-June 1964.

Hunt, J. McV. Psychological development: Early experience. *Annual Review of Psychology,* Stanford, Calif.: Annual Reviews, Inc., *30,* 1979, 103-43.

Kilmer, S. and Weinberg, R. The nature of young children and the state of early education. *Young Children, 30,* Nov. 1974.

Klaus, R.A. and Gray, S.W. The early training project for disadvantaged children: A report after five years. *Monogr. Soc. Res. in Child Development. 33* (4), 1968, No. 120.

Kohne-Ray, R. Motor-mental development of the kibbutz: Institutionalized and home infants in Israel. *Child Development, 39,* 1968, 489-504.

Montessori, Maria. *The absorbent mind* (revised ed.). New York: Holt, Rinehart & Winston, Inc., 1967.

Montessori, Maria. *The discovery of the child.* New York: Ballantine Books, 1972.

Montessori, Maria. *The secret of childhood* (revised ed.). New York: Ballantine Books, 1972.

Penfield, W. and Roberts, L. *Speech and brain-mechanisms.* Princeton, N.J.: Princeton University Press, 1959.

Piaget, J. *The language and thought of the child.* Cleveland: World Book Co., 1955.

Piaget, J. *Psychology of intelligence* (revised ed.). Patterson, N.J.: Littlefield, Adams & Co., 1963.

Pines, M. A head start in the nursery. *Psychology Today, 13,* No. 4, Sept. 1979.

Provence, S. and Lipton, R.C. *Infants in institutions.* New York: International Universities Press, 1962.

Ringholz, R.C. The Singer's under siege: Armageddon at Marion, Utah. *Utah Holiday, 8,* No. 4, Jan. 1979.

Rosenzweig, M.R.; Krech, D.; Bennet, E.; and Diamond, M.C. *Heredity, environment, learning and the brain.* Paper presented at the American Association for Advancement of Science meeting, Berkeley, Calif., December 1965.

Rosenzweig, M.R.; and Bennett, E.L. Cerebral changes in rats exposed independently to an enriched environment. *Journal of Comparative and Physiological Psychology, 80,* 1972, 304-313.

Schiavone, J. *Help your child to read better.* Chicago: Nelson-Hall, 1977.

Skeels, H.M. and Fillmore, E.A. The mental development of children from underprivileged homes. *Journal of Genetic Psychology, 50,* 1937, 47-65.

Skeels, H.M. Adult status of children with contrasting early life experiences. *Monog. Soc. Res in Child Development, 31,* 1966, iv-65.

Skodak, M. and Skeels, H.M. A final follow-up study of 100 adopted children. *Journal of Genetic*

Psychology, 75, 1949, 85-125.

Smith, Lendon H. *Improving your child's behavior chemistry.* New York: Prentice-Hall, 1976.

Van De Riet, V.; Van De Riet, H.; and Sprigle, H. The effectiveness of a new sequential learning program with culturally disadvantaged preschool children. *Journal of Psychology, 7,* 1969, 5-15.

Wellman, B. The effect of preschool attendance upon the IQ. *Journal of Experimental Education. 1,* 1932-33, 48-69.

Wellman, B. IQ changes of preschool and non preschool groups during the preschool years: A summary of the literature. *Journal of Psychology, 20,* 1945, 347-68.

White, Burton L. *The first three years of life.* New York: Avon Books, 1975.

CHAPTER 5: EFFECTIVE SEX EDUCATION: NURTURING AFFECTION AND THE CAPACITY TO LOVE

Brownmiller, Susan. *Against our will: Men, women and rape.* New York: Simon & Schuster, 1975.

Cline, V.B. *Where do you draw the line? Explorations into media violence, pornography, and censorship.* Provo, Ut.: Brigham Young University Press, 1974.

Cline, V.B. The scientists vs pornography: An untold story. *Intellect Magazine,* May-June 1976, 575-76.

Masters, W. and Johnson, V. *Human sexual response.* Boston: Little, Brown & Co., 1966.

Masters, W. and Johnson, V. *Human sexual inadequacy.* Boston: Little, Brown & Co., 1970.

Masters, W. and Johnson, V. *The pleasure bond.* Boston: Little, Brown & Co., 1974.

Russell, Diana E.H. *Pornography: A feminist perspective.* Privately printed paper. Berkeley, Calif., 1977.

Women against violence in pronography and media. Berkeley Women's Center, 2112 Channing Way, Berkeley, Calif.

CHAPTER 6: CONSCIENCE AND MORAL VALUES: KEEPING YOUR KID OUT OF JAIL

Corsin, S.A., et al. Interaction of psychopharmacologic and psychosocial therapy in behavior modification of animal models of violence and hyperkinesis. In G. Serbon (ed.), *Relevance of the psychopathological animal model to the human.* New York: Plenum Press, 1975.

Eysenck, H. *Crime and personality.* London: Paladin Press, 1970.

Franks, C.M. Conditionability and abnormal behavior. In H.J. Eysenck (ed.), *Handbook of abnormal psychology.* New York: Basic Books, 1961.

Glueck, S. and Glueck, E. *Identification of predelinquents.* New York: Intercontinental Medical Book Corp., 1972.

Glueck, S. and Glueck, E. *Unraveling juvenile delinquency.* Cambridge, Mass.: Harvard University Press, 1956.

Guze, S.B. *Criminality and psychiatric disorders.* New York: Oxford University Press, 1975.

Hare, R.D. *Psychopathy, theory, and research.* New York: John Wiley & Sons, Inc., 1970.

Hare, R.D. and Schalling, D. (eds.) *Psychopathic behavior: Approaches to research.* New York: John Wiley & Sons, Inc., 1978.

Hartshorne, H. and May, M.A. *Studies in the nature of character: Vol 1, Studies in deceit; Studies in self-control: Vol III, Studies in the organization of character.* New York: Macmillan Co. 1928-1930.

Lykken, D.T. A study of anxiety in the sociopathic personality. *Journal of Abnormal and Social Psychology, 55,* 1957, 6-10.

Mednick, S., et al. *Genetics, environment and psychopathology.* Amsterdam: N. Holland Publ. Co., 1974.

Robins, L. *Deviant children grown up.* Baltimore, Maryland: Williams & Wilkins Co., 1966.

Schulsinger, F. Psychopathy, heredity, and environment. *International Journal of Mental Health. 1,* 1970, 190-206.

Slater, E. and Cowie, V. *The genetics of mental disorders*. London: Oxford University Press, 1971.

Solomon, R.L. Punishment. *American Psychologist, 19*, 1964, 239-253.

Solomon, R.L., et al. Some effects of delay of punishment on resistance to temptation in dogs. *Journal of Personality and Social Psychology, 8*, 1968, 237-238.

Stein, K.B., et al. Adolescent morality. *Multivariate Behavioral Research*, 1967, Vol II, 199-210.

Wender, P. *Minimal brain dysfunction in children*. New York: John Wiley & Sons, Inc., 1971.

CHAPTER 8: HOW TO PROTECT YOUR CHILD'S MENTAL HEALTH

Lewin, Roger. Nutrition and brain growth. In (Roger Lewin, ed.) *Child Alive*. Garden City, N.Y.: Anchor Press/Doubleday, 1975.

CHAPTER 9: NOT MINDING: DISCIPLINE THAT WORKS

Coopersmith, S. *The antecedents of self-esteem*. San Francisco: W.H. Freeman, 1967.

Dobson, James. *Dare to discipline*. Wheaton, Ill.: Tyndale House Publishers, 1970.

Dobson, James. *The strong-willed child*. Wheaton, Ill.: Tyndale House Publishers, 1978.

Dodson, F. *How to parent*. Los Angeles: Nash Publishing Corp., 1970.

Dodson, F. *How to father*. Los Angeles: Nash Publishing Corp., 1974.

Dreikurs, R. and Grey, L. *A new approach to discipline: logical consequences*. New York: Hawthorn Books, Inc., 1968.

Ginott, Haim. *Between parent and child*. New York: Macmillan Co., 1965.

Ginott, Haim. *Between parent and teenager*. New York: Macmillan Co., 1969.

Gordon, Thomas. *P.E.T.: Parent Effectiveness Training*. New York: New American Library, 1975.

Gordon, Thomas. *P.E.T. in action*. New York: Peter H. Wyden, Inc., 1976.

Holt, John. *How children fail*. New York: Dell, 1964.

Holt, John. *Escape from childhood*. New York: E.P. Dutton, 1974.

Kohl, H. *Growing with your children*. Boston: Little, Brown & Co., 1978.

Neill, A.S. *Summerhill: A radical approach to child rearing*. New York: Hart Publishing Co., 1960.

Patterson, G.R. *Families*. Champaign, Ill,: Research Press, 1975.

Patterson, G.R.; Reid, J.B; Jones, R.R.; and Conger, R.E. *A social learning approach to family intervention: Vol I Families with aggressive children*. Eugene, Ore.: Castalia Publishing Co., 1975.

Salk, Lee. *What every child would like his parents to know*. New York: Warner Paperback Library, 1973.

Salk, Lee. *Preparing for parenthood*. New York: David McKay Co., Inc., 1974.

Spock, Benjamin. *Baby and child care* (Giant Cardinal ed.) New York: Pocket Books, 1946.

Spock, Benjamin. *Problems of parents*. New York: Houghton Mifflin, 1962.

White, Burton L. *The first three years of life*. New York: Prentice-Hall, 1975.

CHAPTER 12: PROBLEMS IN SCHOOL

Krech, D.; Rosenzweig, M.R.; and Bennett, E.L. Effects of environmental complexity and training on brain chemistry. *Journal of Comparative and Physiological Psychology, 53*, 1960, 509-519.

Krech, D.; Rosenzweig, M.R.; and Bennett, E.L. Environmental impoverishment, social isolation and changes in brain chemistry and anatomy. *Physiology and Behavior, 1*, 1966, 99-104.

Rosenzweig, M.R.; Krech, D.; Bennett, E.L.; and Diamond, M.C. Modifying brain chemistry and anatomy by enrichment or impoverishment of experience. In G. Newton and S. Levine (eds.), *Early experience and behavior*. Springfield, Ill.: Charles C. Thomas, 1968, 258-298.

Rosenzweig, M.R. and Bennett, E.L. Effects of differential environments on brain weights and enzyme activities in gerbils, rats and mice. *Developmental Psychobiology. 2*, 1969, 87-95.

Rosenzweig, M.R. and Bennett, E.L. Cerebral changes in rats exposed individually to an enriched environment. *Journal of Comparative and Physiological Psychology, 80*, 1972, 304-313.

CHAPTER 13: TEASING
Patterson, G.R. *Families*. Champaign, Ill.: Research Press, 1975.

CHAPTER 14: STEALING
Patterson, G.R. *Families*. Champaign, Ill: Research Press, 1975.
Patterson, G.R.; Reid, J.B.; Jones, R.R.; Conger, R.E. *A social learning approach to family in—tervention; Vol I Families with aggressive children*. Eugene, Ore.: Castalia Publishing Co., 1975.

CHAPTER 16: "WON'T EAT" AND OBESITY
Research of Dr. Clara Davis. Cited in Benjamin Spock, *Baby and Child Care* (Giant Cardinal ed.), New York: Pocket Books, 1946, 274-276.

CHAPTER 20: WHINING AND CRYING: HOW TO TURN IT OFF
Levine, M.I. and Seligmann, J.H. *The parents' encyclopedia of infancy, childhood & adolescence*. New York: Harper & Row (Perennial Library), 1978.
Patterson, F.R. *Families*. Champaign, Ill.: Research Press, 1975.

CHAPTER 22: TELEVISION: MAKE IT SERVE YOUR FAMILY, NOT ENSLAVE IT
Bandura, A. *Aggression: A social learning analysis*. Englewood Cliffs, N.J.: Prentice-Hall, 1973.
Cline, V.B.; Croft, R.G.; and Courrier, S. Desensitization of children to television violence. *Journal of Personality and Social Psychology, 27*, 1973, 360-65.
Cline, V.B. (ed.) *Where do you draw the line? Explorations in media violence, pornography and censorship*. Provo, Ut.: Brigham Young University Press, 1974.
Cline, V.B. TV violence: How it damages your children. *Ladies Home Journal, 2*, Feb. 1975, 75.
Comstock, G. and Fisher, M. *Television and human behavior: A guide to the pertinent scientific literature*. Santa Monica, Calif.: The Rand Corp., 1975.
Comstock, G. and Lindsey, G. *Television and human behavior: The research horizon, future and present*. Santa Monica, Calif.: The Rand Corp., 1975.
Comstock, G. *Television and human behavior: The key studies*. Santa Monica, Calif.: The Rand Corp., 1975.
Cook, R.D., et al. *"Sesame Street" revisited*. New York: The Russell Sage Foundation, 1975.
Geen, R.G. Some effects of observing violence upon the behavior of the observer. In B. Maher (ed.), *Progress in experimental personality research*, New York: Academic Press, *8*, 1978, 49-92.
Kaye, E. *The ACT guide to children's television*. Boston: Beacon Press, 1979.
New York Times, Doctors find TV makes child ill, October 27, 1964.
Report of the Royal Commission on violence in the communications industry: Volume one, Approaches, conclusions and recommendations. Toronto, Canada: Publications Center, Ministry of Government Services, 1978.
Winn, M. *The plug-in drug*. New York: The Viking Press, 1977.

CHAPTER 23: THE OVER AGGRESSIVE CHILD
Patterson, G.R.; Reid, J.B.; Jones, R.R.; and Conger, R.E. *A social learning approach to family intervention; Vol I Families with aggressive children*. Eugene, Ore.: Castalia Publishing Co., 1975.

CHAPTER 24: TEN KEYS TO REARING SUCCESSFUL CHILDREN

Pines, M. A head start in the nursery. *Psychology Today, 13*, No. 4, Sept. 1979.
Schaefer, C.E. Raising children by old-fashioned parent sense. *Children Today*, Nov.-Dec. 1978.

Index

Community: changing neighborhood, 188; choice of, 12–14, 186–87, 242
Competence: crisis of, 93; non-competents, 3, 5–6, 11; and self-esteem, 24, 26, 28, 238–39; and self-sufficiency, 9–10, 244; and social acceptance, 35; and success, 4–5, 7–8, 243–44; super-competents, 5–7, 10, 14
Conflict: in marriage, 67–68; parent-child, 74–75
Conscience: as conditioned fear response, 78–79; development of, 12, 72, 79–81, 131; and guilt, 78–79; and teaching moral values, 73, 80, 240
Coopersmith, Stanley, 23–24, 102–104
Crises, developing responses to, 90–95
Crying: fear of abandonment, 202–203; of infants, 107–108; legitimate, 200–201; manipulative, 203–206; from over-sensitivity, 206

Dating: and early marriage, 184; family rules for, 183–85
Delinquency: factors contributing to, 73–78; genetic influence behind, 77–78, 80
Dennis, Wayne, 45
Dependability, 38–39. See also Responsibility
Dependency, 11, 166–67
Dieting, 172–74
Discipline, 106, 121; parental unity in, 120–21; and permissiveness, 11–12, 99–101; as providing security, 25, 101, 103–104; techniques of, 106–121. See also Punishment
Divorce, deciding on, 17–18. See also Remarriage
Dobson, James, 103, 105
Doman, Glenn, 49
Durkin, Delores, 50–51
Dyslexia, 49–50, 144

Egbert, Robert, 3
Ego: control of, 92–93; inflated, 26–28
Engelmann, Siegfried, 46, 49
Engelmann, Therese, 46, 49
Enuresis, 175–79
Exemplary Reading Center, 8–9
Eysenck, Hans, 78

Family conferences, 31–32, 85, 196
Forgiveness, 38
Friendship: age differences in, 184–85; as bad influence, 75, 152, 180–83, 187–88; essentials for maintaining, 37–40; importance of, 210–11; parental interference in, 182–83, 188; and rejection, 41–42

Genetic inheritance: and intelligence, 45; and mental health, 88; and psychopathy, 77–78, 80, 240–241
Ginott, Haim, 99, 101, 124
Gordon, Thomas, 100, 120
Graven, Stanley N., 220
Guilt, 78–79

Harvard Preschool Project, 103
Holt, John, 100
Honesty, 132–33
Hunt, J. McVicker, 237
Hutchings, Barry, 78
Hyperactivity: as aggressive behavior, 228; and psychopathy, 80; and reading, 50

Imprinting, 47
Independence, fostering, 9–10, 30, 84, 244–45
Infants: discipline techniques for, 106-111; emotional bonding of, 91; environmental influence on, 45–47; imprinting, 47; toys for, 56-57
Inoculations, 89
Intelligence (IQ): and environment, 45–47, 50–51, 237–38; role of play in developing, 55–56, 60; and verbal skills, 47–51

Laziness, 163–67
Love. See Affection
Lying: cures for habitual, 133–37; as parent-induced, 135–36; pathological, 130; reasons for, 130–32, 139–40

Mace, David, 20, 67
Mace, Vera, 20, 67
Manners, 34; table, 170
Marriage: counselors, 19; dealing with conflict in, 67, 68; importance of stability in, 14–16, 89; as primary

commitment in family, 66;
remarriage, 189–98
Marriage Encounter, 20
McLeod, J.M., 219
Mealtime, 168–70
Mednick, Sarnoff, 78
Meeland, Tor, 3
Minnesota Couples Communication
Workshop, 19
Mischief-making, 74, 214
Montessori, Maria, 47
Morality: in movies, 222–23; search for
personal, 95; and sense of virtue, 24;
teaching of, 20–21, 73, 104. *See also*
Conscience
Movies, unethical content in, 222–23
Moving, effects of, 42–43

Narkewicz, Richard M., 220
Neill, A.S., 100
Nielson Television Index, 220, 240
Non-competents, 3, 5–6, 11
Nutrition, 168–69; and prenatal
development, 88–89

Obesity, 170; and dieting, 172–74; and
eating habits, 171; psychological and
emotional factors, 171–72

Parent Effectiveness Training, 100
Peer group: acceptance in, 7–8, 147;
and self-image, 34; structured
activities for, 37, 187
Perfectionism, 26
Permissiveness: and self-esteem, 24; in
society, 221–22; spoiling, 27–28,
104; as theory of child raising,
99–101
Pets, value of, 187, 215
Phil Donahue Show, 219
Physical attractiveness, 33–34, 36, 90,
211
Piaget, Jean, 60
Play, as learning, 55–56, 60
Pornography, 69–70
Positive reinforcement, 81, 113–15,
243; praise, 29, 32, 84–85; rewards,
114–15, 119
Preschool, importance of, 36, 51–52
Preschool age: activities for, 213–14;
discipline techniques for, 111–113;
and reading readiness, 48–49, 55;

self-acceptance at, 91–92;
sex-education of, 64–65; toys for,
57–59
Psychopathy, 77–80; symptoms of, 78,
130
Psychosis, 76–77
Punishment: and conscience, 12, 79;
and crying, 199, 201; as natural
consequence, 83, 115, 117–18;
penalties, 119; potential for child
abuse in, 106; scoldings, 113, 117;
spanking, 105, 110, 113; and threats,
117

Reading, 8–9; activities to aid, 52–55;
and imagination, 211–12; and IQ,
47–51, 54
Reid, Ethna, 8–9
Rejection, coping with, 41–42
Remarriage: choosing new spouse, 195;
joining families, 189, 197–98;
preparing children for, 192, 195–96;
risks of, 190–91; rules for parents,
193–94
Responsibility: and autonomy, 82, 245;
parental, 102–104; teaching, 30,
83–86, 243; toward others, 39;
training in, through chores, 85,
164–66. *See also* Discipline
Rewarding behavior, 114–15, 119
Robins, Lee, 78
Role model: father as, 6, 25; parents as,
73, 85, 111, 114
Russell, Diana E.H., 69–70

Sadism, 228
Salk, Lee, 101
Schaefer, Charles E., 240
School: choice of, 13; learning problems
in, 142–45; misbehavior in, 149–152;
phobias, 146; skipping or repeating
in, 145–46; social adjustment in, 147;
teacher-student incompatibility,
148–49
Scolding, 113, 117
Self-discipline, 92–93; and discipline,
121
Self-image: contributing factors,
22–24, 104; personal security and,
40–41; rules for building, 28–32
Self-motivation: fostering through
tasks, 164–67; and responsibility, 82